Techno Fashion

Techno Fashion

Bradley Quinn

Oxford • New York

First published in 2002 by
Berg
Editorial offices:
150 Cowley Road, Oxford, OX4 1JJ, UK
838 Broadway, Third Floor, New York, NY 10003-4812, USA

Paperback edition reprinted 2006

Berg is the imprint of Oxford International Publishers Ltd.

Library of Congress Cataloging-in-Publication Data
Quinn, Bradley.
Techno fashion / Bradley Quinn.
p. cm.
Includes bibliographical references and index.
ISBN 1-85973-599-1 — ISBN 1-85973-620-3
1. Costume design. 2. Fashion designers. 3. High technology. I. Title.
TT507 .Q65 2002
746.9'2—dc21

2002011077

British Library Cataloguing-in-Publication Data

A catalogue record for this book is available from the British Library.

ISBN 1 85973 599 1 (Cloth)
1 85973 620 3 (Paper)

Typeset by JS Typesetting Ltd, Porthcawl, Mid Glamorgan.
Printed in the United Kingdom by MPG Books, Cornwall.

This book is for Ana Avalon.

Contents

Acknowledgments

This book was a pleasure to research and write. Each interviewee gave generously of their time and knowledge, and this book would not have been possible without their participation. I am indebted to all of them, and to Chris Moore for allowing me to publish his catwalk photography. In particular, I would like to thank Andrew Bolton, Daniel Herman, Hussein Chalayan, Lucy Orta, Michiko Koshino, Pia Myrvold, Simon Thorogood, Tristan Webber, Walter De Brouwer and Yeohlee Teng for their inspiration and support.

My editor, Kathryn Earle, cannot be thanked enough for her enthusiasm, encouragement and practical advice. I am also grateful for the help of friends: Alison Howell for coordinating my research in Los Angeles, Birgitta Hosea for providing access to resources and materials, Bo Madestrand, Maria Friberg and Sara Goodstein for their help in New York, Hélène Armstrong for correcting my French translations, Robyn Dutra for being a source of knowledge; Brett Schaenfield, Dorita Sheriff, Markus Sterky, Vivienne Bellamy and William Timbers for commenting on the manuscript; and Valerie Steele for facilitating my research at the Fashion Institute of Technology. A special thanks to Ian Critchley and the rest of the team at Berg.

For this book and for related projects, I especially appreciated the help I received from Adam Thorpe and Joe Hunter at Vexed Generation; Annika McVeigh and Omar Nobil at Hussein Chalayan; Haruko Sekihara at Comme des Garçons, Krystyna Kolowska at Michiko Koshino; Joanna Mcleod at Dupont; Sophie Quinn at Modus Publicity; Nick Collins at Patrick Cox; Isabelle Peron at John Ribbe; Jan Hamling and Elena Perazzo at Prada; Simon Charlesworth at Nike and Michel Andenmatten at home.

Introduction

From digital dresses to remote-control couture, *Techno Fashion* exposes the revolutionary interface between contemporary fashion and technology. Wearable cameras, wireless communicators, metallic nodules and electronic embroidery may sound like the stuff of science fiction, but these devices are real enough to revolutionize the meaning and function of fashion forever. Right now, teams of chemists, physicists, fashion designers and engineers are busy creating the high-tech future of fashion. Tomorrow's garments will do more than just look good and feel great: they will have an intelligence of their own. You will know, because they will tell you.

These visionary designs are known collectively as 'techno fashion'; their technical abilities are made possible by wireless electronic devices fully integrated into fabrics and accessories. As personal electronic devices became adapted for wear as jewellery or accessories, the scope to integrate them into fabric became apparent. Mobile phones, personal stereos, laptops, digital organizers and music players are being fully integrated into items of clothing to form part of a wearable 'body area network' that can also surf the Web, monitor vital signs and even administer medication through the wearer's skin. These systems are activated by sensors that respond to voice-recognition software and body movement, and are programmed to detect and respond to other networks in the home, office or urban environments.

The potential of techno fashions may have profound implications for our experiences of body and mind, our communication abilities, health care and lifestyle. One of the obvious questions triggered by this new genre is why science tuned in to the aesthetics and sensibilities of fashion in the first place. Fashion, as an essential component of everyday life, provides the ideal means for information technologies to be constantly accessible and widely relied upon as they become indistinguishable from clothing. Fashion also allows technologies to engage with the human body in a comfortable and aestheticized form. Each new generation of technology will have multiple opportunities to market itself as the ephemeral trends of fashion bring it to the consumer with each new look.

Techno fashions will also function in an industrial context. The military is exploring how clothing can be better adapted to equip soldiers for battle and reconnaissance missions, and security companies are developing wearable surveillance systems that transmit information at high speed. Health care promises to be one of the biggest markets for techno fashion, but, ironically, the high-frequency electromagnetic waves used to operate techno systems create potential health hazards because of their proximity to the body. While industrial research into techno fashion holds the potential to turn every wearer into an urban warrior or self-diagnostic doctor, it also reveals that there are considerable risks associated with its use.

One of the most ambitious intelligent clothing projects to date was the development of the 'i-Wear' prototypes created by Starlab, a scientific research laboratory based in Brussels. With the technology of the Internet and cellular communication already changing the way most of the world works, lives, shops and even thinks, Starlab predicted that fashion was also ready to undergo significant changes, even transcending its medium. Starlab placed fashion on the cutting edge of both marginal science and advanced technology by acknowledging fashion's inherent mobility and communicative ability and used the rubric of science to amplify these. This radically altered the relationship between science, which had traditionally dismissed fashion as frivolous, and fashion, which is now heralded as a legitimate area of enquiry and critique.

The impact of technology is also breeding a generation of designers-cum-scientists who use technology to probe new territories and fresh directions. These designers are more interested in fitting clothing with personal thermostats, remote-control systems, signal transmitters and power grids than following colour trends or seasonal styles. Their designs explore the extent to which dress can detect and respond to temperature fluctuations, identify and combat bacteria, screen out ultraviolet rays, change colour and wick away moisture.[1] Their work is even changing the accepted fashion vocabulary – they describe their clothing as being engineered, constructed, processed and installed rather than sewn and manufactured. The concept of 'couture' has also been redefined and updated, moving away from the traditional salon to reference works of designers who tend to produce multiples and *prêt-a-porter* ranges.

Hussein Chalayan was one of the first of this new breed to pioneer wireless garments activated by remote control. Chalayan uses high-tech systems and materials to establish a dialogue between the wearer and the environment, while exploring the extent to which fashion, interiors and architecture can be integrated in a single design. According to Chalayan, 'This way of thinking about fashion is still quite new to the fashion world, but it's what is moving things forward.'[2] Though Alexander McQueen is best known for his unique approach to the body and the use of cutting-edge materials, he also shares Chalayan's vision: 'As for the future, technology is what will move fashion forward, the new fabrics and engineering. I cannot wait to do a seamless suit, where you just climb in and that's it.'[3]

As the boundaries between clothing and machine are reconfigured, the roles, functions and identities traditionally associated with codes of dress are also changing.

Tristan Webber claims to have identified a 'hyper-breed' of woman, who is redefining the traditional woman of fashion. 'I don't believe in the "real woman" of fashion,' he said. 'I'm not designing for a glamour goddess . . . I design for women regardless of their physical scale, women who are proud of their intellect and their potential,' he explained.[4] As the lifestyles of urban women around the globe begin to change, they look to fashion to provide for their practical concerns, welcoming the new functionality that technological innovations bring. Women are increasingly turning to sportswear for the comfort, performance and durability necessary for the fast-paced, high-tech world we now live in. Others find practical solutions in designs that can be transformed into furniture, luggage and even shelters. Designers of transformable fashions, like C P Company, Patrick Cox and Kosuke Tsumura, find that experimentation with space and construction allows them to refine and maximize the wardrobe beyond its wearable potential, as they transcend established boundaries and challenge conventions in fashion.

Both designers and consumers find that the Internet is having a marked impact on fashion and is rapidly becoming a new platform from which fashion can be shown, designed and purchased interactively. Pia Myrvold is one of the first to explore the possibilities offered by cyberspace, where she creates her innovative range of couture-inspired clothing via her website. Myrvold's departure from conventional fashion results from her mission to circulate the ideas behind her collections simultaneously with her clothes, using sounds, images, films and texts on her website to give her collections a new dimension. Cyberspace also provides a platform where fashion shows can be webcast to a global audience by downloading catwalk images or streaming live shows digitally. In fact, digital technology creates a new format for 'virtual' fashion shows that feature models, catwalks and music able to be projected in practically any venue. This enables designers like Simon Thorogood to present their collections using a computerized catwalk show with virtual models to give viewers scope to interact with the running of the show. Digital systems also lead to a wealth of possibilities for clothing construction and fabric design.

The dialogue between technology and fashion is nothing new. Looking back over the past two centuries reveals how fashion itself can be considered to be a history of technology. From the publication of Jules Verne's *From the Earth to the Moon* in 1865, the possibilities and potentials that technology held for clothing fascinated fashion and science alike. At a time when the design techniques used to create crinolines, corsets and soldier's uniforms were considered to be technical innovations, the spacesuits that Verne's fictitious characters wore would have been a nineteenth-century fashion fantasy. The principle of a spacesuit suggested that clothing could perform tasks and penetrate environments previously unthinkable, and that humans could even survive in a portable microcosm that would carry them through unexplored worlds. As the idea spread it became a topic for journals and novels, eventually creating the science fiction genre of the twentieth century. By 1929, American comic-strip character Buck Rogers was depicted travelling in space, wearing an armour-like metal suit with a glass helmet, carrying radio transmitters and oxygen tanks.

The space race developed many of the high-performance materials and design techniques for the spacesuit later used to engineer techno fashions.

Ten years later, the American designer Gilbert Rohde devised a spacesuit-like 'Solo-suit', resembling a jumpsuit worn beneath an outer shell that incorporated a wide metallic belt, Plastiglass panels and a hat equipped with transmitter antennae. Rohde was one of the nine designers American *Vogue* invited to create garments based on visions of the future, to correspond with the opening of the 1939 World's Fair in New York.[5] The fair showcased the ultra-modern 'industrial' aesthetics redefining most aspects of design, and *Vogue* succeeded in showing that fashion also had the capacity to embrace high-tech materials and new systems. It was at this point, some sixty-four years ago, that 'technologized fashions' began to emerge, and from which the term techno fashion is coined today.

Rohde's Solo-suit was not intended to predict future styles, but prophesy how life would be lived in the twenty-first century. Rohde envisaged a future of streamlined efficiency, and made the garment functional and time-saving by using a special crease-proof fabric that repelled dirt, and long zips instead of buttons. Beryllium-copper wire was woven into the material, intended to regulate body temperature and change colour. Rohde speculated that omega radio waves transmitted from a control base could heat the wiring and even change the fabric's colour. Chrome-plated chains on the suit's outer shell were meant to function as communication receivers. By relaying omega

The artist Lucy Orta uses principles of fashion to create wearable shelters and interconnecting survival sacs, made viable by high-tech fabrics that are both wind- and waterproof. Orta's work makes a strong comment about community and identity, social policy and urban alienation.

waves between the base and the communication receivers, they constituted a two-way analogue mobile telephone.

As a pioneer of industrial design rather than a fashion designer, Rohde's engagement with fashion heralded the many interdisciplinary collaborations to come later in the twentieth century. By the 1980s and 1990s, the principles of architecture, furniture design and technology were fusing together in a variety of garments ranging from sportswear to couture, collapsing many of the traditional boundaries between them. Fashion designers like Rei Kawakubo and Yeohlee Teng often work with concepts that appear to have more in common with architecture than fashion, while Lucy Orta turned her back on the fashion world to express herself as an artist, combining the principles of clothing and architecture to create housing pods and wearable shelters.

Just as the Solo-suit encased the body in sheaths more akin to machines than fashion items, the techno fashions of today integrate technology into clothing to perform a range of sophisticated functions. The textiles Rohde envisaged were so progressive that they could heat the body, transmit signals through their conductive threads, and even change colour; these characteristics are echoed in the techno textiles being developed today. High-tech textiles resulting from advances in manufacturing processes and new synthetic fibres present fashion designers with an opportunity to explore ideas previously limited by traditional materials.

Though fashion seemed ready for Rohde's innovations, the outbreak of World War II focused most designers on finding the means to survive despite the restrictions of wartime clothing rations. Understandably, technology was largely absent from fashion until the 1960s. As the space programme gained momentum in the United States, technology and clothing fused in the development of the spacesuit. The new materials and design techniques that evolved as a result have had a significant impact on the evolution of technologized clothing.

The space race presented fashion with the ultimate test: to predict how fabric surfaces, linings, coatings, plastics and metals would react in outer space. Flexible, expandable fabrics were required that would have insulating properties and the durability for continual wear over a period of days. On earth, valves in the blood vessels keep blood circulating correctly, but in space the absence of gravity means that body fluids shift upwards, expanding the waist, chest, neck and upper arms. These changes in body mass meant that sizing had to be self-adjusting. Issues of comfort, physical well-being and mobility kept designers in constant dialogue with technicians and scientists for over fifty years, as feedback from the Mercury, Gemini and Apollo missions resulted in adjustments to the suit. As they became more sophisticated, spacesuits regulated body temperature, and were equipped with transmitters to relay information about the wearer's vital signs – a system Starlab explored adapting for i-Wear.

Space exploration relied heavily upon high-performance textiles such as Gore-Tex, Teflon, Mylar and nylon. Coated with aluminium, these materials took on reflective properties that made them shiny and silvery. Silver colours and shiny metallic finishes characterize many space-age looks, but it was not easy to make them in materials that were comfortable against the skin. The US National Aeronautics and Space Administration (NASA) designers turned to materials such as vinyl, polystyrene, Lucite, acrylic and polyvinyl chloride (PVC), which were easier to craft in sleek, sharply cut, minimal shapes, and could incorporate built-in visors, plastics and metallic panels. Thermoplastics, such as polyethylene, were later produced in bright colours with textured surfaces, and widely used by fashion designers in the 1960s and 1970s.

The spacesuits completely transformed the way humans saw themselves and expressed a new mythology based on technological change that seemed to anticipate future societies. These visions of the future suggested fashion would eventually evolve away from the system that had existed for centuries towards a single, functional style of clothing. The parallel universes depicted in Stanley Kubrick's *2001: A Space Odyssey* and the classic *Star Trek* series presented a powerful vision of fashion's future, where simple tunics were fully integrated with the wireless communication devices contained within them. But the spacesuit goes to an extreme that differentiates it from fashion, giving the body over to the control of technology entirely, effectively making technology a part of the body's systems. Techno fashions are designed to bring the

Yeohlee's reverence for the wearer's role in giving function to form is visible in graphic shapes juxtaposed against the proportions of the body. She cuts the fabric to define a feminine shape in her garments, mirroring the architect's approach to integrating a building in its environment.

technology under the control of the wearer, but the extent to which the activities of the wearer will be vulnerable to being monitored by others is an open question.

The futurism associated with the space age provided a perfect antidote to the fashions of the early 1960s, which were dominated by youth culture, street style and mod fashions. Emanating from London, these styles expressed dissatisfaction with the social structure and voiced a message of resistance to convention not found in other fashion capitals. Paris, the traditional centre of the fashion world, was completely lacking in youth culture, and found it impossible to compete in this arena. French fashion designers explored futurism as a style that would appeal to young people, and 'Space Age' immediately became a metaphor for youth, charging fashion with optimism and vitality. In Paris the young clearly wanted to break away from couture; reportedly, when Chanel made a bid to dress Brigitte Bardot, the young star contemptuously replied, 'Couture is for grannies.'[6]

As French couture redefined itself within the youth revolution, a fashion race began to run parallel to the space race. Yves Saint Laurent, André Courrèges, Pierre Cardin and Paco Rabanne pioneered the space-age look, encapsulating within it the image they wanted to project into the future: avant-garde, intelligent, progressive and thoroughly modern. Space-age fashion expressed a new mythology predicated on technological change, which generated popular interest in new technology and the future. Fashion, for many, was its most tangible expression, signalling changes in lifestyle and spawning new ideas about the future evolution of the body. Taller, slimmer models appeared, their figures accentuated by sleek tunics, short skirts and high boots. Courrèges noted that the fashioned body would also change with the new age, predicting that women of the future would retain youth and vitality. 'I think women of the future, morphologically speaking, will have a young body,' said Courrèges, outlining changes he expected to see by the end of the 1960s.[7]

The space-age fashions of Paco Rabanne used alternative, experimental materials such as the aluminium used in spacesuits. Rabanne used aluminium to craft futuristic chain-mail dresses and headdresses suggestive of a female warrior. They were so exquisitely made that they resembled pieces of jewellery rather than clothing. Pierre Cardin spun off into space with boldly coloured jersey tunics, into which he carved geometric shapes. He made uniform-like suits like for men, complete with military epaulettes, and accentuated the collection with asymmetric zips, steel belts and silver buckles. These designs were later echoed in the flight uniforms of the shuttle astronauts, who orbited the earth without leaving the spacecraft.

Throughout the 1960s, American designers also explored the appeal of the space age. Betsey Johnson designed mini-dresses and short skirts using metallic fabrics riveted with metal studs, creating an utilitarian look. Her aluminium-foil tank dresses caught Andy Warhol's eye, who perceived silver clothing as part fashion, part conceptual art. In her New York boutique Paraphernalia, Johnson began to collaborate with Warhol and combined her take on the space-age look with Warhol's musings on plastics and reflective surfaces. A stint working as an assistant to the fabric editor at *Mademoiselle* had inspired Johnson to make her clothes in, 'what the industrial people used, stuff they were making car interiors out of . . . the materials with which they were insulating spaceships,' she said.[8]

With silver firmly established as the colour of the space age, plastic was heralded as the material of the future. Deana Littell used plastic materials to make a range of clothing, including incandescent evening coats. Tiger Morse, also based in New York, was credited with initiating the transition from plastic to psychedelia. In 1964, she opened the fantastic Kaleidoscope showroom, displaying dresses made from Mylar, vinyl and PVC, and electrified dresses that lit up.[9]

The new materials meant that designers had to rethink traditional production methods. Paco Rabanne's chain-mail dresses were constructed with wire and pliers, making needle and thread redundant, but increasing production costs substantially. Evaluating economics and innovation eventually led Rabanne to design dresses made of paper, which he described as, 'Very cheap, and the woman will only wear it once or twice. For me, it's the future of fashion.'[10] Pierre Cardin's vacuum-formed and moulded fabrics had not been handled by traditional garment-makers before, but today a single piece of clothing can be moulded or bonded from one length of material, or shaped by lasers. While these innovations could make weaving and sewing redundant, they also provide new possibilities to develop them further. These trends are especially prevalent in Japan, where leading Japanese designers work alongside technical experts to test and develop the potentials of new fabrics and new production technologies.

Even couture practices are being redefined by technology as scanning devices map individual sizes to produce a 'couture' garment tailored to an individual fit. DuPont's three-dimensional colour Body Scanner uses lasers to enable designers to pinpoint exactly how the body of today has changed from conventional sizing. Pia Myrvold's vision of cybercouture is premised on consumers having three-dimensional body scans available to email designers, enabling them to craft made to measure garments purely through e-commerce transactions. This is already generating a scientific analysis of shaping that can chart and predict the evolution of the human body as it transforms along with emerging fashion trends. The use of this advanced technology has helped create the type of 'Seamless' technology McQueen is anticipating.

Fashion's potential to engineer and enhance traditional materials, replace computerized devices and assume new forms entirely promises to forever disrupt the historical narrative of fashion evolution. The fact that technicians and designers are engaging in promiscuous collaborations promises that fashion will not desist – but opens a forum for debating what forms it will take. Unlike previous generations of designers who looked to the past to recycle previous eras, these designers now focus on the high-tech future to forge new directions, moving fashion drastically forward and charging it with an optimism not felt in fashion since the 1960s. With the possibilities technology offers, fashion may never look back again.

one

Fashion and the Built Environment

You see them in streets, subways, airports and highways – but surroundings like these are not the places you once thought they were. Anonymous figures conceal their faces inside hooded parkas, or gaze vacantly from behind tinted visors. Heavy, shapeless coats of reinforced fabric appear to swallow the entire body, while other clothing is so tightly padded that it gives the wearer an insectoid shell. Coloured in greys, blacks and browns, the individuals melt into the cement and brickwork of the urban landscape. Has the city been raided by riot police? No, this is just the first wave of techno fashion.

You could be right in thinking that this new look is the ultimate way to hide a bad-hair day or puffy eyes, but what the clothes really conceal are electronic devices, transformable objects and built-in thermometers that activate heat particles. This is why Andrew Bolton,[1] author of *The Supermodern Wardrobe*,[2] insists that getting hot under the collar is just another fashion experience. Bolton considers these designs to be the ultimate expression of modernity. 'In an increasingly interactive world, what could be more appealing than self-reliance?' Bolton asks. 'The clothes have the potential to respond rapidly to environmental changes, offering utopian solutions to the hassles of modern life.'[3]

In his concept of supermodern clothing Bolton identifies a dimension central to the evolution of techno fashion: its engagement with the urban environment. Part of the momentum driving techno designs is the proliferation of public areas and open spaces typical of most modern cities. The construction of zones to sustain leisure, sport, shopping and transport increases the accessibility of information, the ease of social control and the commodification of time through automated systems. Essential for commerce and communication, the flow of human traffic these zones permit also designates them as spaces where the visual exchanges of modern life are transacted. These are the transitional spaces, or 'non-places' as French sociologist Marc Augé dubs them, that create scope for a technologized fashion aesthetic, to address the contemporary issues of visibility, surveillance, noise and pollution within the built environment.

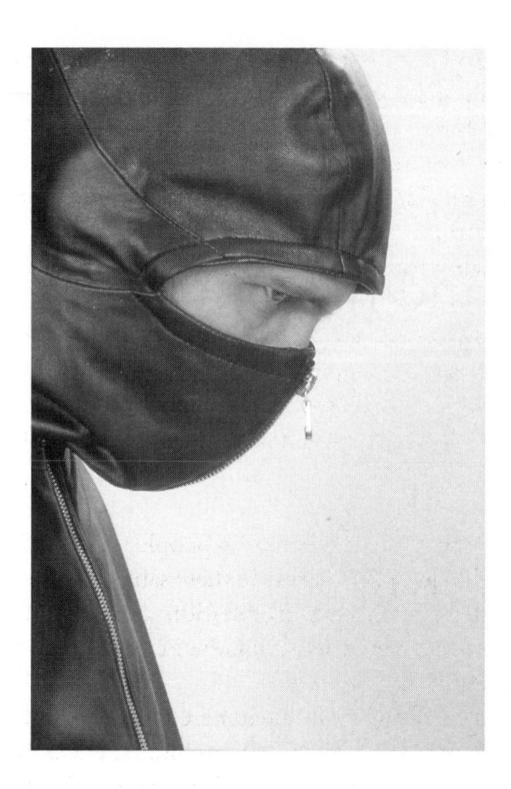

Vexed Generation imbue their collections with principles of surveillance and visibility. They interpret fashion as a form of communication and resistance that can initiate long-term changes to the social infrastructure.

'Supermodern is a term borrowed from Augé, who uses it to describe the late capitalist condition,' Bolton said. 'It's all about excessive information and urban spaces that are now within a few hours of each other.' Augé outlined the concept of 'supermodernity' to describe the *raison d'être* of these late-capitalist phenomena. Augé believes that non-places have a profound effect on consciousness – they accelerate our consumption of physical space and psychological information while simultaneously increasing our need for physical and psychological protection.[4] While most outer clothing only provides cover from the elements, technologized clothing is defined by its ability to respond directly to the environmental problems found in these urban centres. Technological innovations include tempered visors and built-in headphones to give wearers the potential to switch off from the world around them.

Fashion plays a crucial role in the construction of urban identity. Some of the most significant shifts in fashion have been the innovations that enable it to mirror the functions of urban environments. Clothes like these work with greater functionality through their technological devices, enabling them to extend the body's mobility and potential to interact with larger systems.

As garments evolve to create self-controlled environments that provide the wearer with heat, music, privacy and communication, they amplify fashion's primary function as shelter, and signal fashion's capacity to assume the functions of modern dwellings. This questions to what extent contemporary fashion can be considered a built environment in itself, or a part of a larger one, and holds the potential to redefine the boundaries between clothing and architecture.

As Marshall McLuhan wrote:

> Clothing, as an extension of the skin, can be seen as a heat-control mechanism and as a means of defining the self socially. In these respects, clothing and housing are near twins, though clothing is both nearer and elder; for housing extends the inner heat-control mechanisms of our organism, while clothing is a more direct extension of the outer surface of the body.[5]

Dwellings are fundamental to society, bringing people together for warmth, safety and protection. As clothing is equipped to provide these same functions, fashion could shape and rearrange the patterns of human association and community, dislocating and dividing individuals into their own self-contained environments rather than unifying them in a single environment.

As the margins between clothing and shelter are redefined, so too are the boundaries between the individual disciplines of fashion, architecture and even art. When fashion designers like Hussein Chalayan and Yeohlee Teng explore their ideas for a collection, they often find that they have more in common with architects than their fashion contemporaries. Neither of them likes to think of themselves as purely fashion designers: both describe themselves as an 'ideas person'. Lucy Orta has turned her back on fashion altogether, and established a track record as an artist who works amidst sculptural spaces in clothes, housing capsules and wearable pods. The work of these three innovators will be detailed in turn later in this chapter.

Mirroring Orta's work, other designers are developing ranges of multi-functional clothes for the urban environment, including parkas that convert into tents and sleeping bags (these are detailed further in Chapter 6). Problems of air pollution and noise are solved by jackets that feature anti-smog masks and detachable headphones plugged into the hood's lining. These garments are made functional by new high-tech fabrics that are both wind- and rainproof. 'The supermodern designers are almost scientists,' Bolton said. 'They expand the boundaries of fashion through their engagement with technology and use of innovative fabrics.'

Techno fashions define a niche aesthetic between occupational dress, such as uniforms, and the individualized dress of civilians, by appropriating elements of military and police uniforms to derail the power that dress has as a form of social control. From martial uniforms comes the masculine edge given to supermodern clothes. 'Most supermodern fashion is designed with principles of menswear in mind, like the functionalism inherent in sportswear,' Bolton said. Vexed Generation have used military fabrics like Kevlar to create parkas with high collars and zipped panels that conceal the face as well as the head. 'Hiding the face offers psychological as well as physical protection,' Bolton explained. 'It gives the wearer a look that is both aggressive and disturbing, heightened by the fact that the parka's hood allows only partial recognition of the wearer's identity, minimising the possibilities of casual exchanges. Interaction with a hooded individual is a one-sided relationship with someone who is not fully present.'[6]

Menswear is often an afterthought in the ready-to-wear and couture markets dominated by female customers, but techno fashions reverse this norm by originating designs with masculine features which are later streamlined into feminine versions. With military camouflage in mind, hues of brick, concrete and stonework – the colour palette of non-places – were chosen to blend the garments into the urban landscape. Lucy Orta's designs deploy bright primary colours to consciously define the wearer against the cityscape, increasing the individual's visibility.

As the body is symbolically assimilated into the larger fabric of technology, it suggests a double discourse in which the body reads as an invincible superstructure, when in reality technology only provides temporary protection against the body's innate vulnerability. 'In a sense supermodernity exploits the frailty of the organic body,' Bolton said. 'There is a paranoia driving this trend to protect the body from its fragility.' Though the rationale behind this aesthetic validates fears of the body and the obsession with personal security, its unique look makes the wearer a vehicle for self-exposure. Standing out from the crowd may suggest that the wearer has something worth hiding.

Screening out noise, filtering pollution and keeping warm make practical sense; withdrawing into a shell in a society where awareness is a survival tactic does not. Bullet-proof textiles and protective visors are grim reminders of the ever-present threat of violence in the urban environment. Fashion's new solutions to the hazards of urban life will soon be redundant unless it addresses the harsh realities that can be found in the built environment. As Augé reminds us: 'The world of supermodernity does not exactly match the one we believe we live, for we live in a world that we have not yet learned to look at.'[7]

Yeohlee Teng

A less cynical response to the demands of the urban environment manifests in the visionary designs of Yeohlee Teng. Based in New York, Yeohlee works in response to the imperfections in the world around her. Her intense analysis of modern life inspires her to experiment with new forms and fabrics to produce clothing that is both practical and beautiful, and at the very cutting edge of fashion.

'I like the nomadic nature of our lives right now,' she explained, 'and making clothes that enhance that nomadic existence is interesting.'[8] Yeohlee's *Urban Nomads* collection (autumn/winter 1997) engaged with the crazy acceleration of global travel and the aesthetics of transitional zones like Renzo Piano's Kansai International Airport in Osaka. 'I was taken with how very curvy the building is. I was looking at the interiors and noticed that the other travellers were in a mess as they traversed the space. They looked very interesting and textural, but Kansai looked so modern that it made the travellers look so dated. I did a collection around how I thought people should look in that space.'

Yeohlee's approach is not to echo lines of contemporary edifices in the cut of fabric, but to assimilate visual and intellectual principles of architecture into fashion, interpreting the two disciplines in terms of congruity of ideas. 'Fashion and architecture operate along the same principles,' Yeohlee said. 'It has to do with appreciation of material, the ability to organise information and how humans function within their environments. Where they enter, exit and congregate. Egress is therefore an essential consideration for both disciplines. Whether or not a button-fronted shirt is chosen instead of a turtleneck has to do with egress. How we get in is important to consumers because of time – our most precious commodity,' she explained.

In refining her signature mode of minimalism, Yeohlee revisited the starting point of fashion to determine its essence: 'The nature of fashion is information. I think that what we choose to wear is impacted by things around us.' But Yeohlee's minimalism is not just negation, subtraction and purity: she reduces the creative process to the basic concepts of volume, function and proportion to arrive at an architecture of the body itself. As Yeohlee relates the human shape to fabric and scale, she engineers a fluid structure around it with the same considerations an architect would have for a building project. She explained: 'For a fashion designer, there are traditional approaches, like sketching pictorial references on paper or draping muslin on a mannequin. I use geometry to plot something two-dimensionally and make a flat pattern that will have three-dimensional proportions. Knowing these measurements is like making a witch's brew: you throw numbers into the pot and come up with a formula. To determine the sweep of the garment you have to calculate the stride. Once you attribute that to the scale of humans the whole equation is demystified.'

Yeohlee exhibited a selection of garments alongside the work of architect Ken Yeang at the Aedes Gallery in Berlin, in a landmark presentation of the two genres. Yeohlee and Yeang share the desire to create environments defined by spatial awareness, working with and against the human form to create spaces whose meaning does not depend on an associated discourse or an evaluation of the natural landscape. Both believe in the conservation of energy and material, and map the boundaries of the body by creating climatic ecosystems around it. As Yeang layers his buildings in different materials for better adaptation to climate, Yeohlee's strata of clothing is determined by the use of tiers rather than conventional layering, which is a more efficient way of circulating air and body heat. The open spaces captured in the clothing's folds vary from open edges to thin vacuums, giving the garment's walls and centre spaces the same related values apparent in Yeang's architecture. Studied together, their designs suggest symbiosis of the aesthetics of fashion and architecture, although Yeohlee's simplicity makes a sharp contrast to Yeang's complex architectural designs.

'There is an aspect of clothing as portable architecture,' Yeohlee said, 'and our clothes, which are modular, are also our shelters, which is the main function of buildings. Depending how extreme you want to be, you could say that clothes are your ultimate home. There has always been a dialogue between the two disciplines. It is a constant in our lives. I think it is a very practical step for designers to explore the possibilities and potentials the two yield,' Yeohlee explained. Her expression of functionality is a far cry from the shapeless unisex garments that usually characterize functional clothing. Yeohlee's understanding of the body's contours means she cuts the fabric to define a feminine shape in her garments, mirroring the architect's approach to integrating a building into a landscape.

Yeohlee's process and methodology extend beyond the garment and the wardrobe, into the living sphere of the wearer's everyday world. She explores this vision of human life through the micro-shelter provided by a garment and the macro-shelter of architecture and technologized spaces. Intrigued by the prototype A3XX aeroplane that can transport up to six hundred people, Yeohlee considered how travelling in such a huge crush of people would impact upon the urban nomad: 'I would like to travel wearing the most efficient outfit possible. I would want my outfit to define my space, making a clear and concise statement about my relationship with my surroundings,' she said. 'Clothing is an essential tool for people to define their space. The designs are not just about clothing or spaces but also about posture and movement. Where you situate pockets affects your stance and movement. Everything is interconnected and interconnecting.'

Yeohlee's use of geometric shapes and subtle gradations of colour captured the attention of the art world. Susan Sidlauskas featured Yeohlee's designs in *Intimate Architecture: Contemporary Clothing Design* at the Massachusetts Institute of Technology's (MIT) Hayden Gallery, of which Sidlauskas wrote: 'Her geometric sheaths, on which squares or triangles float on a contrasting field of colour, challenge spatial perceptions in a manner reminiscent of a Richard Serra drawing of a black plane skewed against a white page.'[9]

Richard Martin also recognized Yeohlee's work as three-dimensional art, describing the spirituality evident in her spare approach to the essentials of form. Above all, Martin prized Yeohlee's reverence for the wearer's role in giving function to form. Noting how her soft layering created textile environments that enabled the wearer to navigate both weather patterns and climate-controlled interiors, Martin credited Yeohlee with developing a 'fifth season' of fashion. In Martin's essay 'Yeohlee: Energy and Economy, Measure and Magic', he wrote:

> While Yeohlee conforms to fashion's seasonal calendar of showings and store delivery of merchandise, her clothing . . . often surpasses the seasons, allowing wearers to function in the 'fifth season'. The year-round wardrobe offers another economy from what was

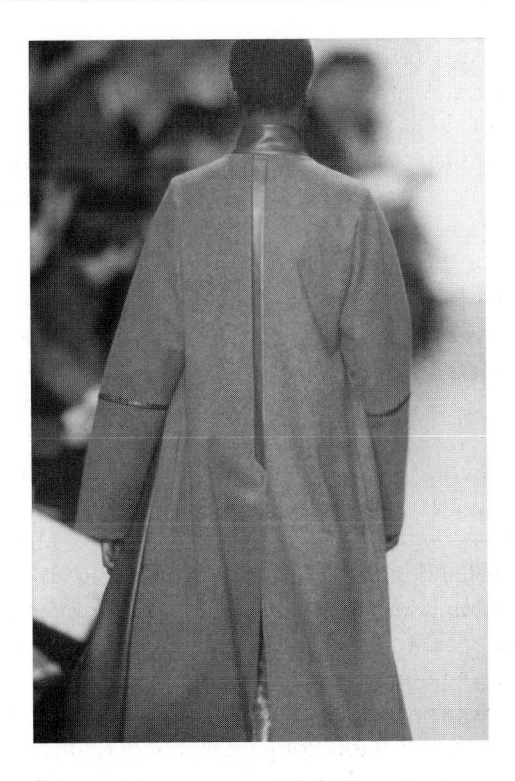

Yeohlee's vision of urban chic anticipates a future lifestyle characterized by people on the move. Yeohlee's overcoat explores principles of the micro-shelter the garment provides the body with and the macro-shelter afforded by architecture and technologized spaces.

turn-of-the-twentieth-century's apportioning of the year and closet space into four separate parts.[10]

Martin's critique identified the blueprint that had previously remained invisible in Yeohlee's work. Her minimalism scales the wardrobe down to layered, interchangeable components that facilitate individual expression. The use of high-performance fabrics, like Teflon, polyurethane, nylon and polyester, creates breathable water-repellent surfaces that empower the wearer to negotiate environmental conditions in clothes succinctly tailored to create a formal feel and still meet the needs of the everyday casual dresser. Yeohlee refines the norm of conventional cuts by conceiving unconventional shortcuts, such as combining the bust dart and side seam by contouring them into one. 'An essential part of minimalism is knowing where to stop – I think that is really important,' she said.

Critics of Yeohlee's work allege that her purism divests fashion of fantasy, an element many designers consider to be at the very epicentre of their work. Yeohlee's critical examination of the principles of clothing steers her away from ornamentation, much

Yeohlee's work is a journey through simplicity and functionality. Her spare approach to the essentials of form creates a minimalism that scales the wardrobe down to subtle geometric shapes and gentle gradations of colour.

like Alexander Rodchenko's vision of Constructivism consciously rejected decorative elements to integrate technique and organization with fashion design. Yeohlee's work echoes the space-age geometry of Paco Rabanne and André Courrèges, bringing to mind the sci-fi sets and costumes of Kubrick's *2001*. Though Yeohlee may not be inspired by fantasy *per se*, her garments anticipate a future lifestyle that is already a part of contemporary visual culture.

Yeohlee's oeuvre is a journey through simplicity as much as it is through minimalism. 'Basically I am a simple person. I like simple solutions, so the minimalism comes from that. Simplicity captures truth and elegance. So from my Chinese culture, to say that someone is a simple person is a supreme compliment meaning they have the ability to be humble, and it encompasses a lot of intellectual values,' she said. Though Yeohlee left her native Malaysia for New York several decades ago, she often references her Chinese heritage and Malaysian upbringing in her designs. 'Some of my inspiration has come from the connection between Muslim culture and clothes, and the use of shrouding,' she said. 'What people conceal and what they choose to reveal depends on

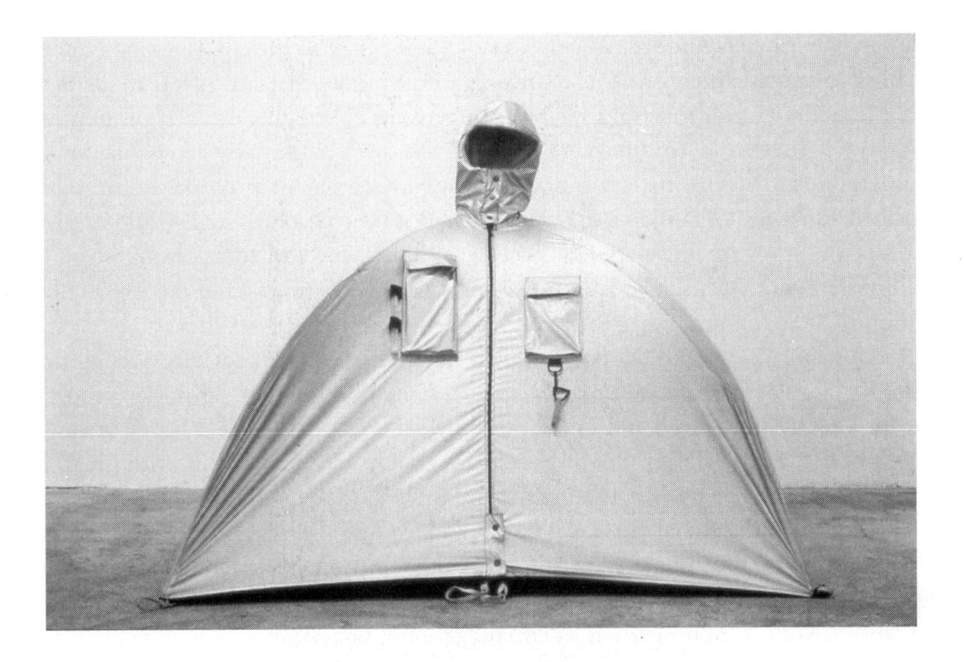

Compared with Yeohlee's understated temples, Lucy Orta's Refuge Wear *is more like a fallout shelter. But Orta also uses clothing to produce and define urban space, conceptually as well as materially.*

their culture – some Muslims will reveal the nape of the neck and ankles or emphasise the waist, others reveal only the eyes. To me this creates a sense of mystery.'

Having stripped fashion bare and simplified it to cloak the shortcomings of the aesthetic world, Yeohlee's vision of future worlds enables her to confront the problems of twenty-first-century living. By using fashion innovation to solve the dilemmas of the modern human, she fuses fashion with principles of self-sufficiency, security and interactivity, giving fashion the challenge of transcending its medium.

Lucy Orta

Lucy Orta is an artist who refuses to accept the 'superficiality' of fashion. Her work inverts the idea that clothing and built environments are separate entities. With art as her medium, her work examines the axis between buildings and garments, reclaiming both of them as sculptural, tactile and architectural expressions of society. Orta's wearable shelters critique social and political issues and provide practical solutions to the problems of transitional living.

She uses her experience as a former fashion designer to articulate social concerns and humanitarian issues, creating convertible garments that are often described as 'portable architecture', 'survival suits', or 'refuge wear'. Though Orta designs items that can be worn, they are no ordinary garments. Even she has difficulty categorizing them completely: 'They are one-off pieces that are designed to provoke some sort of conscious awareness of certain issues in society. But they work on many different levels – on a poetic level, on a metaphoric level, and on the level of social awareness.'[11]

Compared with Yeohlee's body consciousness, Orta's *Refuge Wear* is more like a combat wardrobe. Orta's point of departure from conventional fashion was her use of clothing to produce and define urban space, conceptually as well as materially. Recognizing fashion's potential to delineate degrees of separateness and individuality, Orta took this concept literally to explore and create separate spheres for temporary habitation.

Orta connects the design process to issues much wider than the individual. The inspiration behind her work is the human form, the body's need for protection against the elements and the social elements fashion addresses – but her work explores issues like homelessness, the integrity of the individual and society's awareness of its own needs. Orta designs according to clothing principles and works with a range of high-tech fabrics. Multi-functionality is a central feature in her clothing, which convert from parkas, anoraks and ponchos into tents, sleeping bags, or furniture. The garments come apart into pieces of modular textiles, designed like flexible architectural components that can be instantly transformed into individual or collective survival shelters. These structures are engineered from durable weaves and synthetic fibres and use a system of pockets and zips to disassemble and reassemble.

Lucy Orta lives in Paris and is married to the Argentinian artist Jorge Orta.[12] Orta's affinity with the homeless resulted from an installation at a Salvation Army shelter in Paris, where she determined to use her design skills to create garments that would give them a sense of security, and facilitate a renewed expression of personality and individuality. She also began a series of practical workshops and activities that focused on identity, the body and ideas of home. Orta's concern with the increasing problem of homelessness inspired her first *Refuge Wear* prototype: the 'Habitent', a portable mini-environment designed to provide the wearer with a degree of personal comfort and the efficiency to relocate easily. As well as being effective tools in the struggle against social exclusion, *Refuge Wear* is engaging fashion with disciplines ranging from architecture, art, social regeneration and ideological activism. The titles of her principal projects, which can be interpreted as both art works and fashion items, speak for themselves: *Nexus Architecture*, *Refuge Wear*, *Modular Architecture*, *Commune Communicate* and *Citizen Platform*.

Orta's designs relate the story of the tension between movement and stillness, between the visible and the invisible. Orta feels that to be homeless in today's urban society is tantamount to invisibility; that the homeless 'literally melt and disappear into the margins and framework of the city'. Homelessness often indicates a nomadic existence as authorities try and get the homeless off the street and into shelters, or simply tell them to 'move on'. Addressing the disenfranchised meant confronting social taboos and ethical issues to gauge how she could make a real difference. Paradoxically, Orta brought the invisible into sight by giving them space in which to feel secure.

Throughout the *Nexus Architecture* series Orta uses fabric as a membrane or second-skin around the body. In Orta's work, the body is composed of many 'skins': underwear, the layers of clothes themselves, the overcoat; she considers the sleeping bag to be one of these layers, then the tent as an outer layer. Orta views each outer surface of her work as a second skin – the text, symbols and images she transfers onto the fabric voice statements of identity. On the outer shell of one *Collective Wear* outfit she showed at the Venice Biennale in 1995 is the clear-cut statement: 'Me, I've got a lot to say'. Orta borrowed this expression from a participant in her first *Identity+Refuge* workshop. Each *Collective Wear* piece articulates that the wearer, whether homeless or not, is claiming their right to voice their views.

Like packaging, Orta designs clothes that convey information, covering them with text. Packaging has a dual role; its primary function is to facilitate transport, and its secondary role is to market the product. In the way that packaging attracts customers, Orta uses text to attract members of society towards problems that are continually avoided.

Many of the homeless Orta worked with expressed fears about living in housing or shelters due to the traumatic and alienating circumstances they had experienced living with other people. Acknowledging this led Orta to consider how the street could be appropriated as an extension of the household. The Habitent achieves this by equipping people with their own mini-environment, where they can live in relative comfort and safety without moving into an institution or residence. For some of the homeless, the means to survive on the street gives them an alternative to the confines of an institution, meaning that, for some, the Habitent also voiced a message of resistance and independence.

Orta began using fashion to address human suffering on a global scale as a response to the crisis of the Gulf War. Unstable political environments, famine and war resulted in growing numbers of refugees and displaced persons. Orta made a series of drawings entitled *Refuge Wear* to articulate her initial thoughts about finding a response to the homelessness many of these people now faced. Based on the drawings, Orta fabricated a series of multipurpose clothing that doubled as temporary shelters, giving them the generic term *Body Architecture*. The shelters could be comfortably worn as weatherproof clothing, then transformed into simple pod- or tent-like structures.

Each *Refuge Wear* item was designed as a personal environment that could be varied in accordance with weather conditions, social needs, necessity or urgency, and was capable of being equipped with an integrated medical supply. *Refuge Wear* is intended to give refugees some sense of agency and sanctuary as they struggle to mesh their domestic world with larger systems of political mandates. Within a camp or an emergency zone it marks a boundary between public and private domains. In practical terms the units provide the functions of shelter and protection, but the space inside is a symbolic expression of intimate dwellings. Like a house, they encircle families or individuals with walls of defence, establish points of contact with the outside world, and provide spaces that refugees can appropriate as their 'home'.

Orta also addresses the vulnerability of children. Living under extreme conditions deprives them of the security and intimacy they had while living with their families in their own homes. The idea behind *Collective Dwellings* is to create modules that can be personalized for and by children to establish their own boundaries by surrounding themselves in fabrics, textures and colours.

Orta's remit to highlight the problems of marginalized groups extended to challenge the issue of social visibility, as her focus widened to include the invisible poor and the socially disenfranchised. She continued to use *Refuge Wear* as a medium, staging *Refuge Wear* installations in urban centres. The installations attracted the attention of the art world, who dubbed them 'relational aesthetics' because of their universal message and interactive properties. Orta regarded these public shows as her first 'interventions': 'It's about taking the art outside the institutional venue and into the street. It's also about developing a team and about initiating ideas and seeing how they can develop afterwards.' Interventions often resulted in cementing social solidarity to counteract the problems of homelessness, and fostering a drive to redress the issues.

Like other conceptual designers, the ideas behind each piece remains central to the understanding of Orta's work. 'My motivation is to communicate,' she explained. 'To communicate a new art form which can involve all sorts of genres, from performance, to intervention, to object-making, to installation, to media. But at the same time to bring to the fore some social awareness, through the objects, or dialogue, or discussion.' Squatted buildings, housing estates and railway stations became the locations for subsequent interventions. Orta's interventions have added impact because they translate the narrative literally where the problems were occurring – an approach that attracts media attention and coverage on British and French television.

Following her interventions throughout 1992 and 1993, Orta expanded her protest from the plight of the socially disenfranchised to explore the larger problems of displaced communities. Orta's *Body Architecture* series developed with the protective principles of *Refuge Wear*, but advocated interdependency rather than individual or group isolation. Its high-tech fabric domes and tent-like structures suggest physical and psychological refuge within a larger protective enclosure. *Body Architecture* heralded a new direction in Orta's work; she shifted her practice away from the microcosm of the individual to the macrocosm of the community, from practical protective clothing to temporary modular shelters. Orta cites the writings of Paul Virilio, to explain why her work expanded to express collectives:

> The precarious nature of society is no longer that of the unemployed or the abandoned, but that of individuals socially alone. In the proximate vicinity our families are falling apart. Ones individual life depends on the warmth of the other. The warmth of one gives warmth to the other. The physical link weaves the social link.[13]

Nexus Architecture *seems to be the most emblematic of Orta's approach.* Nexus Architecture *forms a web of humanity that acknowledges diversity and emphasises the importance of community.*

Of all Orta's projects, *Nexus Architecture* seems to be the most emblematic of her approach. More symbolic than functional, *Nexus Architecture* takes its name from 'nexus', meaning a link or a tie, or a linked series or group. The collection is made up of individual outfits made to emulate the body suits worn by Greenpeace activists during anti-nuclear protests. Unlike the Greenpeace suits, which were made to be worn individually, Orta's suits have attachable tubes of fabric that can zip the wearers together to form a single collective garment. As the fabric tubes link participants together at the front and the back of the garments, it enables the individual suits to form one garment worn by hundreds of people. *Nexus Architecture* interventions have been staged in Europe, the United States, South Africa, Bolivia and Mexico, joining together over one hundred people in a single column. Orta describes the tubes of fabric that connect one person to another as a literal representation of a 'social link'.

Part of Orta's philosophy of collectivism is to plan events and workshops beyond the interventions, that teach a skill or bring people together to raise awareness of key issues. 'In Johannesburg I created a workshop and employed thirteen migrant labourers to come and make their own *Nexus* links,' she said. 'So it was about passing on a skill, how to make a garment, but at the same time making them aware of how they can work together as a team to create something and giving them the possibility to manifest something.' Making their own clothing also involved them in making the aesthetical and planning decisions for their suits, instilling a notion of individuality into each.

Modular Architecture combines the communal principles of *Body Architecture* with the protective function of *Refuge Wear*. *Modular Architecture* consists of temporary, portable dwellings made up of individual sections, panels or units that can be combined to make a number of different forms, or simply worn as protective clothing. Orta bases them on multiples of four, where groups of four individual units combine to become one single construction. They provide efficiency and protection for the urban homeless as well as the adventurous nature lover. For example, a group of four people could travel together, each wearing a hooded, waterproof, insulated, ski-suit-like outfit, equipped with pockets to store food and water. When they stop to rest, each unit is taken off and zipped together to make a four-person tent. Made of aluminium-coated polyamide, the tent is waterproof and windproof. It is held up by supporting posts and secured to the ground by pegs along the base. The suits are practical, but also sculptural in form, inhabitable installations with aerodynamics and wearability.

The *Life Nexus Village Fête* is an evolving architectural and social configuration that expands the collective principles behind Orta's *Modular Architecture*. Though these evolved through her experimentation of fashion, the design does not facilitate the same wearability that most of her other models do. The installation comprises aluminium-coated domes, or 'Primary Structures' as Orta calls them, interconnected by *Nexus* extensions. Each dome has space for up to three people and room for folding tables, chairs, or plinths. The Primary Structures are positioned in a hexagonal shape encircling a central space (foyer) that provides a forum for community workshops. The hexagonal layout provided the structural axis from which further Primary Structures can radiate. These constructions, together with the participants, create the feel of a traditional village festival, which Orta uses to create a dialogue among all members of a community.

The 'Connector' is a similar architectural infrastructure to create a modular social network. This infrastructure forms the basis of a mobile village, a refugee camp or a conference centre; it is an architectural axis that can grow in size according to population. Individuals can attach and detach at will to join other groups or move to different sectors of the community.

Orta's interventions have demonstrated her *Refuge Wear* and *Body Architecture* garments in a wide range of urban environments in central Paris, its suburbs, and at the 1995 Venice Biennale and the Johannesburg Biennale in 1997. One of Orta's most renowned interventions did not feature clothing or shelter, answering another of the body's needs instead. Entitled *All in One Basket: a reflection on hunger and food waste*, the intervention was held at the Forum Saint-Eustache des Halles in Paris in March 1997. The idea came to her the summer before, when she saw television news coverage of French farmers tipping trailers of fruit onto the highways to protest against European

Lucy Orta designed these wearable structures to form the basis of a mobile village or a refugee camp. It is an architectural axis that can grow in size according to population.

Community agricultural legislation. Troubled by these images, Orta realized that, in a less dramatic manner, the Paris market traders also dumped fruit and vegetables at the close of the markets. She reacted by organizing the collection of leftover food and produce in the Les Halles quarter of Paris, and asking a celebrity chef to cook it. The food was served on a buffet and passers-by were invited to eat. The people of Les Halles, whether rich or poor, participated in a demonstration of gastronomic recycling.

The *All in One Basket* project led to Orta's incorporation of food into her humanitarian projects. She created a solution to demonstrate how emergency meals could be provided in times of crisis. Titled *70 x 7, The Meal, Act III*, the work was installed at the Kunstraum gallery in Innsbruck, Austria (2000). The project was, according to Orta, 'the third act in a series of actions that bring the community together via the ritual of a meal thus creating links and engaging the lives of the broader community'.[14] The '70 x 7' formula symbolizes the infinite, taken from the biblical signification. Orta's idea was to transform the symbol into reality by organizing meals that could expand exponentially in divisions of seven to accommodate an infinite number of guests. *70 x 7, Act III* consists of an extending seventy-metre tablecloth set with 490 Limoges dinner plates manufactured specifically for the work. The Kunstraum then organized a series of meals for multiples of seven guests, using surplus produce from local farmers. Orta had a limited edition of seventy wooden cases made to hold seven plates and a forty-nine-metre printed tablecloth.

Orta's fashions and interventions make strong statements about clothing, humanity, individuality and communality. But are they fashion? Art installations? Architectural structures? Orta's work collapses such categorical denominations of media and genre one into the other. Fashion, installation art and architecture can all be considered as interventions in space. To a certain extent, fashion designers and architects struggle with the same considerations of egress, proportions, aesthetics and materials, but Orta does not create permanent dwellings in the literal sense, she merely explores the spaces traditionally allocated to buildings by deploying temporary shelters.

The common denominator linking Lucy Orta's different projects is the staging of a social bond. Orta attempts to rethink fashion as the testing ground for what social responsibility can achieve. She takes fashion as the starting point for the transformation of the individual and the society, using it to prompt social metamorphosis. The power of her temporary environments rests in the idea that the material expression of a cultural idea can have lasting effects on people long after their original construction.

Hussein Chalayan

Hussein Chalayan is one of the most influential fashion designers of our age. He draws heavily upon technology to revolutionize the form and function of clothing, often taking inspiration from the built environment and the body's relationship to it. Chalayan's clothes are minimal in look but maximal in thought; his fascination with architecture, aerodynamics, bodily form and identity leads to designs based on concepts, or renders his own interpretation of spatial dynamics. Chalayan's sense of the visual is ultimately true to his grasp of the practical and cultural needs resolved by clothing.

Chalayan rose to fashion fame soon after he received his BA degree from Central Saint Martin's School of Art in 1993. His final year collection *The Tangent Flows*, is the now-infamous series of buried garments that had been exhumed just before the show and presented with an accompanying text that explained the process. The ritual of burial and resurrection gave the garments a dimension that referenced life, death and urban decay, in a process that transported garments from the world of fashion to the world of nature and back. The work attracted the attention of the London boutique Brown's, who borrowed the collection to feature in it their window display. Since then, he has collaborated with architects, artists, textile engineers and set designers, won awards, and produced collections for other established fashion labels.[15]

What makes Chalayan's work so intriguing is his ability to explore principles that are visual and intellectual, tracing the fabric of urban structures and interiors through tangibles like clothing, architecture, aeroplanes and furniture; and through abstractions such as beauty, philosophy and feeling. Chalayan's work represents a congruity of ideas

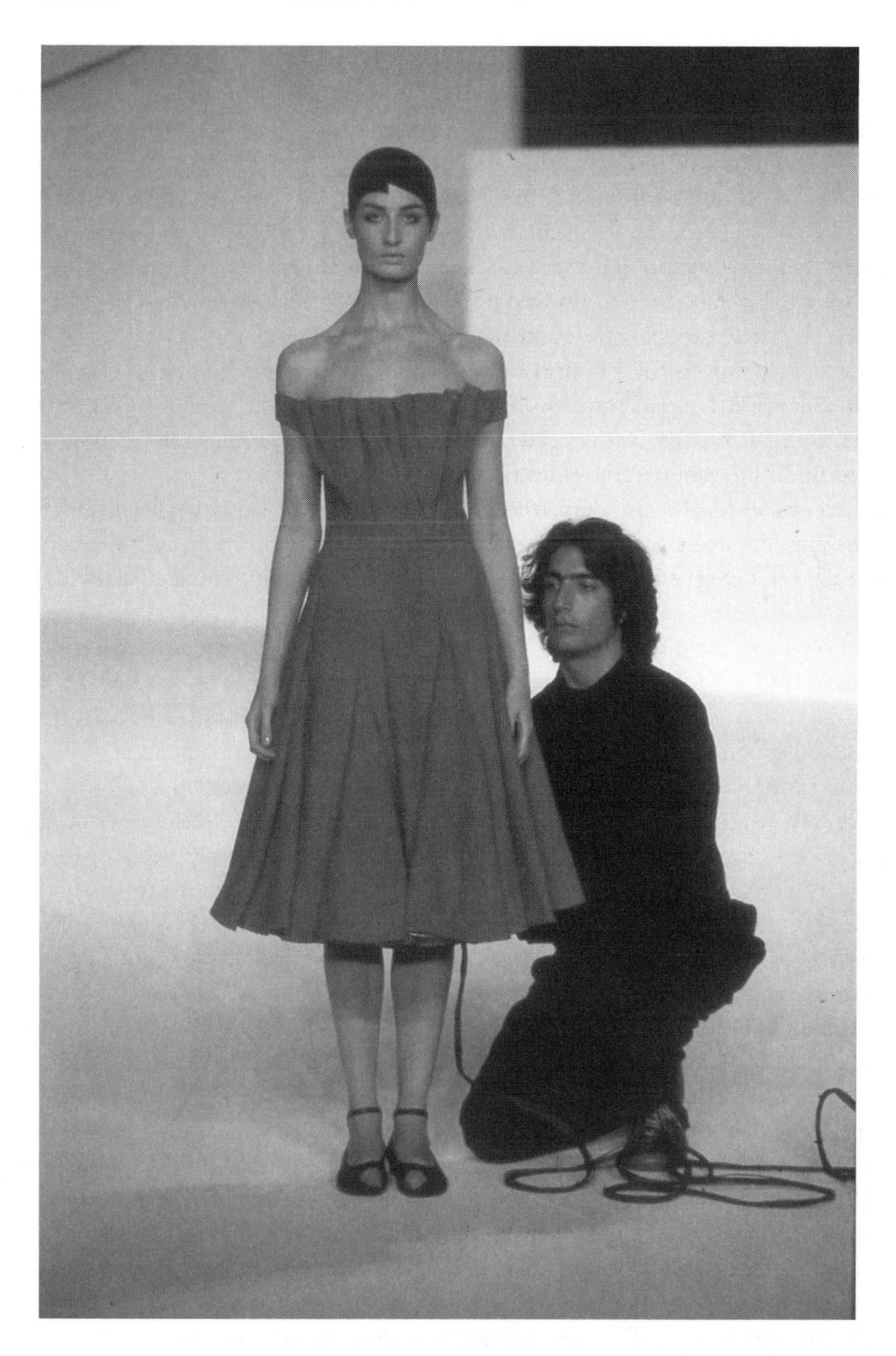

Hussein Chalayan's 'Memory Wire Dress' is constructed with electric coils that expand, opening 'like the flowers that remember how to take several forms'. The dress is controlled by the wearer but operates independently of the body, a theme Chalayan continues to explore through technical innovation.

that indicate fashion and architecture are coming closer together than ever before – far beyond the fashions of the 1920s that echoed, in the cut of dress, the architectural lines of buildings. Chalayan's strategy is to integrate clothing with its surroundings – not by merely making dresses look architectural, but by rendering a comprehensive understanding of different environments and the diverse factors that create them. He reconciles the practical reasons for clothing while interpreting them as components of a modular environmental system where garments relate to larger architectural principles. Chalayan said: 'One thing to keep in mind is that when fashion looks modular and structured, people automatically call it architectural when it isn't – it takes a lot of structuring to make a dress truly architectural. Architecture can be designed in a fluid and unstructured way that doesn't look architectural, but it is still architecture. I mean, you don't call buildings fashion just because they don't look architectural, so why call fashion architectural unless it really is?'[16]

Chalayan sees all objects, structures and architecture as externalizations of the body. His *Geotrophics* collection (spring/summer 1999) featured 'Chair Dresses' that represented the idea of a nomadic existence, and a completely transportable environment. This concept was later expanded in Chalayan's ground-breaking *After Words* (autumn/winter 2000) collection. Presented at Sadler's Wells theatre in London, the show featured a bare, white stage flanked by asymmetrical planes on three sides containing 1950s-style furniture that the models adapted as clothing in the show's finale and either carried or wore off the stage. The show was based on the idea of having to evacuate home during a time of war, hiding possessions when a raid was impending, and using the agency of clothing as the means to carry away possessions more quickly. The theme was painfully close to real life; it was an autobiographical expression of Chalayan's Turkish Cypriot roots and the political events that affected his childhood. The show's finale recalled the 1974 Turkish military intervention that divided Cyprus in half and displaced both Turkish and Greek Cypriots from their homes.

After Words expressed a political reality that articulated relationships between garments and cultural narratives, but was not intended to transform the garments into inhabited environments like the pieces made by Lucy Orta. But like Orta's work, *After Words* explored notions about expatriation and the idea of being able to transport an environment from one place to another in times of crisis. The 'Table Skirt' and the entire set from the show were later featured in the Tate Modern's *Century City* exhibition in 2001, chosen because of their expression of the evolving dynamic between the built environment and the physical transience of urban life.

Some of the garments in the collection were equipped with pockets and compartments that would hold essential belongings, or fuse with other items of clothing so that they could be put on more quickly. 'A part of the idea was camouflage, so that things could be left in an obvious place and still be there when people came home again. That was part of the concept behind the dresses, that they were something valuable disguised as chair covers that no one would take,' Chalayan explained. 'Things like that happened to my family in Cyprus. I heard stories about things that happened to them and everyone else. Somehow people would sneak back to their homes to get things that belonged to them – which they weren't allowed to do – so I was also showing how a space could be emptied little by little, almost in secret.'

The space occupied by clothing is central to Chalayan's vision: clothing defines the intimate zone around the body, architecture a much larger one. In *After Words*, Chalayan expressed how either could become a danger zone and a refuge, a means of transportation for what could be carried and a disguise for things left behind. Symbolically, the models were able to transport items from a 'threatening' environment to a safe place, re-establishing the safety and familiarity associated with them in different surroundings. It is significant that they transported the garments by bringing them into contact with the body, rescuing them as one would carry a child to safety. Again, this referenced Chalayan's family experience: 'All those things happened when I was a kid, but nobody forgets it. I was moved during the show. Of course my family was there watching the show, but at first they didn't realise what was going on. When they did, they were moved too.'

Despite his education and long-term residency in London, Chalayan is true to his identity as a Turkish Cypriot, only recently coming to terms with being labelled a British designer. 'I'm grateful that I have a bi-cultural background,' he said. 'I was exposed to more things. You have more to respond to and you question things more.' The idea of 'national' style is problematic for the fashion world, where designers of diverse nationalities show in the fashion capitals. While his work overlaps with the genre that Yeohlee also explores in New York, Chalayan seems to have more in common with Issey Miyake and Rei Kawakubo, who show in Paris, than any British designer showing in London. Fellow Turks Rifat Ozbek and Nicole Farhi are also acclaimed for their collections, but they bear no similarity to Chalayan's work at all. 'Now I would say that I see myself as a British designer, because I was educated here and have had opportunities that I couldn't have in Cyprus. So in terms of discipline, yes, I am anglicised, but as for my sensibilities, my approach looks at architecture, environments and technology which means I am not like most other designers here,' he commented.

Chalayan never harboured a deep-rooted desire to become a fashion designer. As a child, he wanted to be a pilot, and then considered training to be an architect. Both professions have influenced his career as a designer: the former in the flight-path prints he began exploring in autumn 1995, his 'Aeroplane Dresses' and his 'Kite Dresses'; the latter evident in the spatial awareness directing the relationship between his garments and the body, and his use of architectural proportions to amplify their interplay with their surroundings. 'To me there are two sides to fashion's engagement with the built environment. One is the lifestyle concept that magazines like *Wallpaper** are pushing, showing what you should wear, how you should live, what furniture, which flat – selling the lifestyle as a fashionable status thing,' Chalayan said. The commercial relationship between interior design and fashion promotes a lifestyle dimension, where mainstream designers are selling household products alongside clothing, offering consumers an overall 'look'. 'The other, and the one where I come from, is that everything around us either relates to the body or to the environment. I think of modular systems where clothes are like small parts of an interior, the interiors are part of architecture, which is then a part of an urban environment. I think of fluid space where they are all a part of each other, just in different scales and proportions,' he explained.

The series of 'Architectural Dresses' Chalayan designed for the *before minus now* collection (spring/summer 2000) evolved through his collaboration with b consultants, a London-based firm of architectural engineers, with whom he continued to explore his affinity with architecture. The dresses featured wire-frame architectural prints against static white backgrounds, generated by a computer program that allows designers to draw within a range of three-dimensional perspectives inside an architectural landscape. The images were then transferred onto silk and cotton fabrics using a mechanized fabric-printing process. 'I have always been interested in technology, and there are elements of technology in my clothes. And I work in a cross-disciplinary way with people in other fields who contribute to what I am doing. I am interested in forms generally, not just in clothing but in other things too.' In the *Echoform* collection (autumn/winter 1999) Chalayan created thought-provoking designs like leather dresses inspired by car interiors to represent 'externalising speed and putting it back on the body', and mimicked aeroplane interiors by attaching padded headrests to dresses to evoke thoughts on speed, spatiality and well-being.

The *before minus now* collection also featured the 'Remote Control Dress' (further detailed in Chapter 2), which amplified Chalayan's interest in technology and proved to be a ground-breaking triumph. The dress was based on the Aeroplane Dresses series made by means of the composite technology used to construct aircraft, and incorporated the aerodynamics of aeroplane travel into its form and aesthetic. The contours of the dress are characteristic of vehicle construction, while its hard exterior gave it shield-like properties reminiscent of snails and crustaceans. Gaston Bachelard would have regarded such objects as 'inhabited shells' that 'invite daydreams of refuge'.[17] But in Chalayan's case, it is the formation rather than the form itself that inspired him to fabricate a technologized environment directly onto the surface of the body.

Chalayan's fashion shows can be thought provoking and intense, often suggesting fine art or performance more than fashion, which Chalayan regards as coincidental. 'I am not really up to date with what is going on in the art world or the performance world,' he explained. 'I just do what is good for my work. As a designer I have lots of ideas about how clothes should be worn and creating an atmosphere around them. A lot of these ideas remain invisible until I have a show, and then I can put them across in the show.' His fashion shows are characterized by minimal sets and a mood of suspense, incorporating elements of contemporary interiors, urban architecture and geometric structures. Chalayan succeeds in taking the audience to a space governed by his concepts alone, which some critics liken to the kind of thrill associated with Diaghilev's productions early last century.

Panoramic (autumn/winter 1998) was one of Chalayan's most dramatic fashion collections. The collection culminated in the idea of infinity, which was expressed in

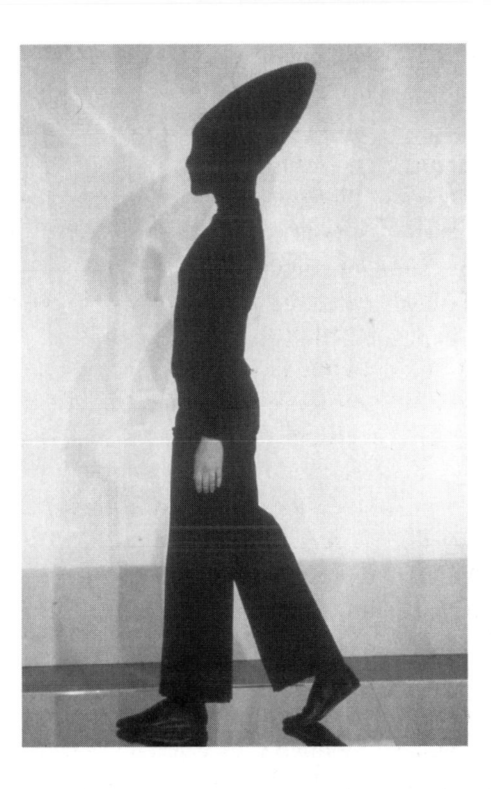

Chalayan created dramatic silhouettes to evoke a non-distinct cultural/ethnic identity, using architectural proportions to distort the models into generic shapes.

a surreal cityscape of geometric forms and distorted images. Chalayan created an environment that eradicated perimeters and built environments and blurred cultural boundaries, camouflaging the body by merging it into the surroundings or multiplying its image in mirrors placed at intersecting angles. The models were distorted into generic shapes and unified by architectural proportions; cones were fixed to the tops of their heads, while their faces and bodies were swathed in black to obscure their identities. The purpose behind these dramatic silhouettes was to create a non-distinct cultural/ethnic identity. As Chalayan explored the idea of representing nature in the collection, he broke it down into its most basic graphic representation – pixels. Body and clothing were then merged into a digital landscape, which was recreated in enlarged cube-shaped pixels carried by a column of models clad in sombre bodysuits as they processed slowly down the catwalk. The overall effect was that of experiencing spatial geometry created by bodies and cloth, interchanging the basis of fashion's relationship to the body and its surroundings.

Chalayan, Yeohlee and Orta are among the most ambitious innovators working with fashion today, and belong to the few whose work avoids commercially minded values and fashion trends. In ignoring these restrictions, they have set up a critical discourse of the principles of clothing. Even though they revert to the fundamental purpose of clothing, their work offers ground-breaking progress as they continue to imbue garments with architectural, environmental and technological principles. As they explore fashion's relationship to the built environment, they reveal the extent to which fashion, interiors and architecture can be truly integrated in design. 'This way of thinking about fashion is still quite new to the fashion world, but it's what is moving things forward. The fashion audience doesn't really know about technology or architecture,' Chalayan explained, 'But they soon will.'

two

Twenty-first-century Bodies

Not only is the technological revolution changing the world of fashion, it is transforming the fashioned body. The growing symbiosis between body and machine now extends beyond the heroes of science fiction, bringing with it a new body consciousness. As designers explore new construction processes and new thoughts about the body's capabilities, body ideals are slowly beginning to define fashion rather than be shaped by it.

The modernist body of fashion made it possible for women to reconstruct themselves by any means possible, resisting the body's nature in order to achieve a firm, toned exterior that conforms to sexual stereotypes. The ideal figure of fashion has never been the celebration of the natural, but the test of a woman's ability to resist it. As Rebecca Arnold points out: 'Fashion is rather a form of seductive and beautiful coercion into believing in the miracle of perfection that awaits those faithful to its decrees.'[1]

Historically, the desire for an ideal body has driven many women to the extremes of radical dieting and brutal corsetry; more recently, dynamic exercise and cosmetic surgery have become contemporary alternatives. The twenty-first-century body, like the bodies of the preceding centuries, is still engaged in the eternal quest for an ideal shape. While the practices of dieting, exercise and surgery are still widespread, these methods may be superseded as new body images are created through technological enhancement. In fact, the drive towards enhanced bodies is so strong that women with unmodified bodies seem to be depicted in a kind of limbo.

Beauty ideals in the twenty-first century are becoming aligned with ambitions to maximize the body's potential, making the appeal of technology more potent. As modern women gain more power socially and politically, they strive to have bodies that reflect their power and efficiency. Bodies like these were once more common to sportswear than couture, but as designers begin to identify a new 'hyper-breed' of woman and encase the body in high-tech systems or weapon-like body extensions, the fashioned body morphs into a new form. Some designers recall the 'Bionic' woman of the 1970s; others predict that cyborgs or even virtual bodies will dominate the future.

Tristan Webber designs for a new breed of woman, ready to face the twenty-first century as an individual rather than a fashion drone. His work also penetrates the body's surface, finding inspiration in the biological theatre of the body. Webber investigates principles of anatomy to reconfigure the symmetry of the body, making a statement about the technologies of medical science and the body, and the body's future evolution. Webber's tailoring can be likened to dissection; his seams are precisely cut to reshape the body underneath.

McQueen's bodies are best known for their expression of pain. He finds beauty in imperfect flesh, in juxtapositions of pleasure and agony, and in the examination of destruction and decay. In McQueen's work, the woman of fashion is always being added to, symbolically enhanced beyond the 'human' with the technical extensions of aggression. Weapon-like projections of extreme jewellery and clothing constructed from razor-sharp objects make her menacing to others, but also require a body tough enough to withstand wearing these materials. Bodies that look like they are 'being-added-to' could imply 'technophilia';[2] a fetishistic regard for the body's interface with technology in order to perfect it, but also bring to mind the image of the cyborg, one of the most established metaphors of 'being-added-to' in our cultural legends. Historically, the cyborg is said to originate from automatic dolls with clockwork parts dating back to the fifteenth century, or to much earlier examples found in China, Greece and Egypt.

This type of body also features in Chalayan's oeuvre, as the traditional woman of fashion begins to recede and take on a new technologized identity. His Aeroplane Dresses and Architectural Dresses have always incorporated technological principles, but his Remote Control Dress is constructed with technological systems integrated into its structure. Chalayan has always maintained that clothing for modern life should be a machine in itself – a dynamic interface between the body, its physical capabilities and the environment.

The work of these three designers is pulling together some of the most predictive strands of body thought in circulation. As the body continues to be recognised as a legitimate site of enquiry and research, its role as a signifier of fashion space highlights its ability to fuse nature, culture and technology within the domain of embodied experience. Body empowerment, visions of the cyborg and technical enhancements all suggest exciting new directions, but they are not necessarily mitigated by the pursuit of beauty alone. These principles hold the potential to equip the body with completely new skills and augment existing ones, and even end radical cosmetic modifications. As these body ideals unfold, with them come ground-breaking materials and different ways of using them, different shapes, new functions and new purposes for fashion in the twenty-first century.

Tristan Webber

Fashion, in the hands of Tristan Webber, may be the key to human evolution, because it holds the potential to change and shape the body of the future. Webber's fascination with medical science fuses fashion with the biological theatre of the body as he uses principles of anatomy to reconfigure traditional cuts of fabrics and the placement of seams. Often referencing muscle groups and skeletal structures, Webber's work examines the fashioned body with the forensic scrutiny of a medical autopsy.

Webber's tailoring has been described as surgical, making each collection a mastery of fabric, anatomy and construction, cut with precision to redistribute the planes and contours of the female body. His treatment of fabric has been compared to dissection and grafting techniques; his garments are moulded to fit the body without restricting its movement. Some garments are created through the combination of simple shapes, giving them a modular, almost architectural feel. As he builds a distinctive carapace for the axis of shoulders, breasts and hips, the female body takes on an insectoid look – making it predatory but ultimately vulnerable.

Webber even rethinks the symmetry of the body, radically inverting its proportions by decentring the central axis of the body. As he moves away from traditional silhouettes, the body is treated like a superstructure composed of mechanical parts. The focus of this approach highlights the machine-like properties reflected in the bodies of our age, which are exercised and toned to be powerful and efficient for modern life. Social and cultural forces construct the body so that it is as analogous to a machine as possible – efficient, productive, predictable, uniform and well-ordered.[3]

Webber's constructions also address the flaws and inefficiencies of the flesh underneath, correcting them through seams and stitching. 'That's something I want to take further,' Webber said, 'but at the same time I also want to see the potential of bare skin to communicate through the formations of marks on the surface of the body, a kind of physical Morse code that could pulse along the skin like tribal markings. This idea has affected my work, where I've put markings on fabric with communication in mind.'[4]

Webber's anatomical tailoring reflects a wider social trend to shape and control contemporary bodies. Medically and beauty-orientated, reconstructed through surgical procedures or radical exercise – bodies and body parts are loaded with cultural symbolism. The body's representations in visual culture encourage us to believe that the body is the passport to all that is valued in life; health, youth, beauty, sex and fitness are the positive attributes that can be achieved through the right body image. This creates a culture of self-surveillance, where individuals control their bodies through diet and exercise to keep them in line with the *status quo*. It also represents a sexualization of society, where being sexually attractive is equated with social acceptability.

Webber is known for his use of leather and luxury fabrics, but in recent years he has gradually moved towards technologized fabrics. 'I collaborated with Motorola to create an outfit that looked at one possibility of future communication by integrating electronic matrixes into clothing. That's where I see fashion and technology heading. As for technology and the body, it seems that the recognised image of the body is almost irrelevant, because as technology becomes more sophisticated, people can manipulate the body by training specific parts or getting implants.'

The inspiration Webber finds in anatomical drawings and botanical dissection seems to suggest that he is actually taking the body apart and putting it back together again. His work addresses the power that medical science already has over constructing our bodies, acknowledging that science and medicine have a prominent role in defining the body in terms of its acceptable, productive and predictable use. As Webber explained: 'If I can use clothes to start redistributing the balance of the body, the function of the body and its structure, perhaps it's going to set up propositions for future physical adaptations. Right now medical science is experimenting with gene technology to replace implants, pigmentation creams and hair coloration. If genes can be modified to contour the body, change hair and skin colour, then make-up and hair products, implants and liposculpture will eventually be redundant.'

As the 1990s unfolded, fashion moved towards a new body consciousness not seen since Christian Dior presented his dramatic New Look. The voluptuous female that obsessed designers in the 1980s gave way to a harder, leaner form as fashion imagery focused on thin, often waif-like women, or toned, powerful amazons. The message to women was clear: 'Eat less, exercise more'. Extreme forms of exercise, like body-sculpting or body-building, assigned women the attributes traditionally associated with masculinity, making the toned female body an expression of power, authority and control.

Body images like these are reflected in the modern icons of visual culture, which range from the super-heroines of comic strips and action films, to sylph-like super-models and cosmetically enhanced pop stars. As fashion designers exploited the iconic fantasy of perfect proportions, 1990s fashion became characterized by clothes that blatantly revealed the anatomy more than any other era. 'People are much more comfortable with sheer clothing than ever before. The taboos around wearing skimpy clothing don't exist to the same extent that they used to, although a lot of men are still reluctant to dress in a body conscious way. I like the fact that women have more confidence in wearing less, because it displays a certain empowerment. Men don't have the same confidence,' Webber explained. Describing Webber's clothes as body conscious would be an understatement, but his garments are not blatant exhibitions of naked flesh or clichéd expressions of the plunging neckline and the sexy skirt. Webber's proportions highlight and reveal the anatomy by tracing its contours in soft leather; tightly tailored trousers and transparent tops are cut to mirror the skeleton underneath, while jackets are fitted like a second skin.

Webber's designs are among some of the most thought-provoking, understated and desirable clothes in British fashion. A 1997 MA graduate from St Martin's, Webber, like

McQueen and milliner Philip Treacy, was championed by Isabella Blow, who helped secure financial backing and a place on the London Fashion Week schedule. His intellectual leanings and uncompromising determination gained him a reputation as a designer with the potential to have serious impact on the fashion landscape.

Webber's collections are complex, rich in references and nuanced on many levels. Like McQueen, he uses red to signal the body's internal structure. A flash of red in a leather belt, skirt or tailored jacket is used to evoke a visceral content. Mirroring the sliding panels in Chalayan's Remote Control Dress, Webber dislocates panels of fabrics to reveal the skin underneath, referencing the muscle groups exposed when the skin is peeled back. Webber's combination of soft fabrics and glossy leather garments is reminiscent of Azzedine Alaïa's Bondage Dress that transformed the classical evening dress into an erotic device of body consciousness. Webber's attention to the outline of the body recalls two of the greatest women of fashion: Madeleine Vionnet and Madame Grès, who both believed that the only real fashion in the world is that which remains simple and enhances the body's contours.

Though both Webber and McQueen explore the body by going beneath the surface of the skin, Webber's approach respects the integrity of the body rather than suggesting mutilation. Whereas McQueen probes the body by slicing it open and closing it with a safety pin, and paints microscope slides the colour of blood, Webber references dissection to understand how the body moves and distributes its proportions. Both designers acknowledge the power that science ultimately has over the body as life, death and even beauty are inexorably linked to medicine.

Parallel to Webber's anatomically tailored forms runs an interest in science fiction and the future evolution of the body. His 2000/1 collections featured silhouettes that he described as 'futuristic super-heroine', resonating Thierry Mugler's mixture of leather, glamour and high-tech hardware that transformed women into space-age dominatrixes. The clothes were charged with the efficiency of a high-tech world, and his vision for the body anticipated the woman of the future, who appeared as a highly sexual woman, a mixture of female gladiator, seductress and warrior.

Webber is inspired by the science-fiction myths predominant in contemporary visual culture, which have a profound influence on his approach to fashion now. 'The idea of nanotechnology for example, implanting small devices and implements into the body, has a major impact on our perception of what is going on around us,' he said. 'Using these theories in my work is a way of introducing science fiction to it, and moving towards future ideas.' Webber likes to interpret science fiction as social fact, whereby the interventions of technology enable us to achieve images and identities: 'We absorb the science fictional elements that are around us so these become an inherent part of our personalities and also of our visions and ideals.'

The *Idoru* collection (spring/summer 2000) was inspired by William Gibson's sci-fi novel *Idoru*, which takes its name from a Japanese derivative of the English word 'idol', reinterpreted to mean someone regarded as a 'superficial media personality'. The lead character in the novel is superficial to the extreme, even to the point of being a virtual entity rather than human. Webber's references to fashion stereotypes are heavily laden with irony, as his work continues to react against the clichéd images of women in the fashion industry. 'The modern idol is a combination of the historic Sei Shonagon, who wrote *The Pillow Book*, with her knowledge of art, literature, politics and culture, and a modern figure able to manipulate others through her superficial charm.'

Webber designs for what he describes as a 'hyper-breed' of women, who transcends superficial fashion imagery. He explained: 'I don't believe in the "real woman" at all,' Webber said with reference to the traditional woman of fashion. 'I think to start designing for the real woman as she's recognised means denying many aspects of the person you are creating clothes for. I'm not designing for a glamour goddess to map my desires and fantasies onto. I design for women regardless of their physical scale, women who are proud of their intellect and their potential. I'm not producing an elitist race that nobody can attain – I'm attempting to heighten the kind of person you are,' he explained.

Webber recognizes that the modern woman is often portrayed as assertive to the point of being predatory. 'I wanted to explore this idea by doing research on insects, sharks, and animals that hunt as a communal pack. The coding in the clothing has become more subtle because these predator mentalities are internal and biological rather than character-based,' he said. 'A hyper-breed would use biotech to adapt the body and heighten its senses and attributes, becoming more animal in nature but much more refined in look.'

Webber's work is pulling together different strands of body thought. His anatomically inspired clothing reveals the influence that medical science has over our bodies, and makes a powerful response to the widely accepted uses of exercise and plastic surgery. In calling for a new hyper-breed of women, he is making a valid critique of fashion's beauty ideals, and broadening the range of body types permitted in fashion and modelling. With his ability to challenge fashion's ideals, Webber promises to develop into a seminal and far-reaching influence in the decades to come.

Alexander McQueen

Fashion has always been a cruel mistress, and in the world of Alexander McQueen, it still is. No other designer illustrates this point so perfectly as the one who shackles his models in leg irons and distorts their faces with mouth and eye jewellery. Indeed, Alexander McQueen's work often seems to torture and contort beauty, by dressing gorgeous women up in spiky tailoring or restraining them in debilitating outfits.

The principles behind McQueen's work take on an additional charge as they redefine the experience of the fashioned body. Feminine beauty, in McQueen's work, is negotiated in terms of aggression and brutality, assigning each woman the ability to wound and attack. They can be characterized by their extended presence beyond the borders of the human body, or their confinement in painful corsets, metal skirts and dresses made from razor-sharp materials. The McQueen woman is also a warrior, armed with 'weapons' of jewellery and accessories that equip her with technical extensions of aggression, self-defence and alienation. In fact, it always seems that she is 'being added to'; McQueen's women are styled to look complex, serviceable and mechanical.

McQueen's fascination with Aimee Mullins's prosthetic limbs explored the limits of fashion's ability to equip the body with wearable mechanisms that facilitate protection and adaptation. Mullins, a twenty-two-year-old Paralympic medal winner for sprinting, was born without fibula bones in her shins and had to have both legs amputated below the knee when she was a year old. McQueen met her on a photo shoot he directed for *Dazed & Confused* magazine, shot by Nick Knight.[5] The pictures that resulted from this project are among the most ground-breaking fashion images ever published. McQueen demonstrated an acute sensitivity that undermined societal beliefs in what beauty is. The shoot featured models with pronounced physical disabilities, dressed in designs by Hussein Chalayan and Comme des Garçons, and in McQueen's designs for both his own label and Givenchy.

The images rendered moments of poignant beauty. These individuals, traditionally marginalized by the ever-widening cult of body fascism, presented a sense of strength and inner fulfilment rarely seen in the pages of a magazine. Mullins, and the other models, were portrayed as beautiful because of their disabilities, not in spite of them. McQueen created a mood that resonated the unease expressed in Helmut Newton's photographs of Jenny Capitän dressed in a full-leg cast and a neck brace, photographed in a shabby room at the Pension Dorian in Berlin.

In one image Mullins is captured sitting on the studio floor, holding her head in her hand in a melancholic, moody pose. Her gaze is fixed, staring downward; her hands are held in an unusually rigid position with fingers splayed apart and fixed to the floor and to her body. Her colouring seems unnaturally pale, her blonde hair fashionably unkempt, the historical allusions of the crinoline and the exotic contortions of the wooden fan mantle fusing together to create an image of a Victorian doll. The image's colouring resembled sepia or monochrome prints from a bygone era, also suggesting a previous period.

Mullins is dressed in garments that extend beyond the borders of the photo, as if she had been squeezed into the frame. Her own artificial limbs have been substituted by the lower legs of a display mannequin, which appear to be old and stained, but with painted toenails. The seams joining them to Mullins's kneecaps are visible, resembling the joints of plastic dolls. The effect of Mullins's depiction as a beautiful doll evokes a neglected toy abandoned in an empty corner.

The poignancy of the image makes a strong contrast to the violence and aggression that often characterize McQueen's work. The image immediately connotes the pain that typifies McQueen's models, this time epitomizing the sense of isolation sublimated by the female warrior. Here, feminine beauty is negotiated in terms of innocence rather than brutality, positioning the model in line with the sublime imagery usually presented in fashion. The images seem inconsistent but fascinating; in the mergence of living flesh and plastic limbs, Mullins looks like she is half woman and half doll.

Mullins embodies the fascination of the 'other' – the exotic, the unfamiliar and the exalted, while at the same time her representations hover on the edge of her lived experience. She does not remain the other of a conventional model, but draws us closer. It is interesting to note that the mannequin legs take on the same interpretation as the other fashion items – the British media described Mullins as 'in' them, rather than 'wearing them.'[6] This reading is also supported by Mullins herself, who campaigns in the United States for more attractive prostheses to be made.

In another image Mullins is captured at a party, laughing amongst a group of people. The prostheses that she is shown 'in' here are not the ones worn in the image mentioned above: they are the high-tech steel springs that she wears in her sports tournaments, which bear no resemblance to human limbs. These prostheses are metallic, almost robotic in appearance, and bend backwards rather than forwards, bringing truncation to mind rather than amputation, implying superior mobility. As seen in popular depictions of the cyborg, these addenda introduce something strange, foreign and other to the basic ingredients that denote 'human'.

High-tech prostheses such as these can be seen to have a dual function in visual culture. They act as markers of difference, but also function as seductive invitations into the same form of embodiment given to a superhero. This echoes McQueen's fascination with the warrior woman – powerful, invincible and 'added to' in order to heighten her strength and resistance. This example of duality has long been referenced in publicized accounts of amputee fetishism – an emerging subculture centring around the sexualized and fantasized absence/presence of a limb.[7]

McQueen had engaged with another truncated body in a photograph he directed for *Visionaire* in 1997, creating a surreal vision of the flesh body. The model is dressed in a geisha-like style, shown against a white backdrop. The girl is Western, but her hair is combed into a traditional Japanese style, and her pale pink dress has an oriental floral motif. The collar is stiff and upright like that of a Japanese kimono, framing her face and head. Her forehead has been sliced open and fastened with a safety pin; tiny pink blossoms sprout out of the incision. Like the image of Mullins, the limits of her real body have been obscured, and here technology was used to create a composite fashion body.

Around the time of the shoot for *Dazed & Confused*, McQueen was articulating his take on prostheses in a more sinister way. His *#13* collection (spring/summer 1999) included the 'Prosthetic Corset'. Made in moulded leather and sewn together with crude 'Frankenstein' stitching, it transformed the typical feminine laced corset into a monstrous contraption.[8] The corset encased the length of the torso, running from the hips to the top of the throat, leaving one arm and shoulder bare, fitting the other one with a capped sleeve. The lacing crossed the front in two diagonal lines, from neck to armpit, and armpit to waist. 'Prosthetic' recalled tragic violence and dismemberment, where the body's head and limbs were pieced back together and bound in the corset. 'Prosthetic' does not allude to a missing limb, but, sinisterly, to a missing torso.

McQueen invited Mullins to model for the *#13* collection, this time sending her onto the catwalk. This time Mullins wore artificial legs carved from wood made to a design by McQueen himself. McQueen took pains not to sensationalize her part in the fashion show; styled in the same way as all the other models, she passed unnoticed to those who did not know she used artificial legs. McQueen later said Mullins's participation helped reverse a fixed idea on beauty. 'I wanted to show the beauty that comes from inside,' McQueen said to *Le Figaro*. 'If you see her walk, you would understand . . . she is simply magnificent.'[9]

'Woman-as-doll' is a theme McQueen has explored in a number of works, most markedly in his *La Poupée* (spring/summer 1997) and *What a Merry-Go-Round* (autumn/winter 2001) collections. The *La Poupée*[10] collection was inspired by the dolls crafted by Han Bellmer in the 1930s, which were fitted with miniature panoramas in their abdomens. The viewer could look through a peephole in the doll's navel and see a collection of miniature objects that reflected the dreams and desires of a young girl, illuminated by a tiny bulb.[11] Bellmer dismantled the dolls for a series of photographs to reveal the miniatures inside them. *La Poupée* was not a literal interpretation of Bellmer's work, but an expression of the theme of probing and exploring the body's interior that recurs often in McQueen's work (later discussed with regard to his 'Red-glass Slide and Ostrich Feather Dress').

The models waded across a catwalk submerged in a shallow trough of water. The collection featured manacle-like devices and jewellery that encased the body in metal frames, to the extent that one model could only walk in slowly articulated crab-like movements. Reportedly, McQueen thought that the restrictive body jewellery would produce the jerky movements of a mechanical doll. In McQueen's choice of the doll as subject, his models became artificial ladies on the margins of lived experience, suggesting that their bodies were wholly or partly artificial, a hybrid of living woman and mechanism.

What a Merry-Go-Round (autumn/winter 2001) featured a nightmarish toy cupboard filled with manic nodding dolls, giant teddy bears and cobwebbed toy soldiers. From amongst them stepped a 'doll' wearing a ball gown of black and orange taffeta, her face obscured by balloons attached to her dress. The stage was constructed with a carousel decorated with the trappings of a Victorian toy shop. The circus atmosphere was mirrored in the clown-like make-up of the models, whose hair was twisted into spikes or unicorn shapes. Rather than move in conventional catwalk formation, the models danced their way around the carousel, swinging from its supports and simulating erotic pole-dancing on the carousel's uprights. The dolls and toys featured in *La Poupée* and *What a Merry-Go-Round* were invested with a strong suggestion of fantasy and role-playing; live dolls could be interpreted as the submissive 'living dolls' of fetish ideals.

McQueen had not articulated fetishism this intensively since *The Hunger* (spring/summer 1996) and *Dante* collections (autumn/winter 1996).[12] Even the mannequin horses were sexualized; covered in fetishistic latex, they emphasized the subcultural dimension of the glossy fabrics used in the collection. Collars of spikes and black pearls were worn with miniskirts or leather trousers polished to a high gloss. Militaristic and menacing, models stalked the stage in shiny jodhpurs, military caps and long belted officer's coats adorned with black-pearl epaulettes.

The jewellery McQueen commissions from Shaun Leane redefines the body's intervention in the space around it. Rather than hugging the body, Leane's jewellery is typically designed to renegotiate the boundaries of the body. As the pieces of jewellery lift away from the contours of the body and continue outwards, they symbolically extend the body beyond its confines. The jewellery adorns the body with necklaces, armbands and earrings that resemble spears, spikes, barbs and tiny thorns; or mouthpieces that protrude from the lips like snarling tusks or sinister fangs – every bit as deadly as they are elegant.

Some pieces, like the body jewellery commissioned for *La Poupée*, are designed to change the movement of the body by constricting the arms or legs. Facial jewellery is intended to disrupt the symmetry of the face or highlight the eyes, the nose or the lips. The 'eyebar' is designed to slot in between the eyebrow and cheekbone, opening up the eye socket and giving it a different look. A mouth bar was included in the *Untitled* (spring/summer 1998) collection that was clenched between the model's lips like a horse's bit.

Other jewellery pieces serve as prostheses, like the mouthpieces that protrude from the lips like human tusks or vampire-like fangs. Leane's mouthpiece was worn in a Jean-Paul Gaultier advertising video, in which a woman was chased by ferocious dogs. She suddenly turned and snarled at them, brandishing it between her teeth as she crouched to attack. The dogs whined pitifully and ran away.

Facial jewellery engages with games of sexuality, suggesting that erogenous zones in the face and neck are off-limits, or that the pieces of jewellery are implements used to arouse and heighten the pleasure of another. It highlights the fatal threat presented by sexualized femininity, also raising questions about the vulnerability of the body and contemporary anxieties about the potential dangers of its visual and physical possession.

Apart from earrings, none of the jewellery is made for piercing. 'I don't make jewellery for body piecing or for lasting body modification. I like creating illusions,' Shaun Leane explained. 'Jewellery can also be used to highlight different parts of the body.'[13] Shapes like spears, barbs and tusks are unusual in Western fashion, more reminiscent of tribal influences that recall a carnal sense of the exotic. 'The spear earring can actually be worn in a normal ear piercing. The illusions I create accentuate the body in a way that looks as though it has been dramatically modified,' Leane said.

McQueen subverts the traditional use of fashion jewellery as a signifier of femininity. Instead, he uses it as an index of inner angst and political repression, much like the Punks did. 'The type of work I do for McQueen is aggressive,' Leane said, 'it breaks away from the classical style of jewellery.' Leane's work takes on characteristics of the

Shaun Leane's jewellery redefines the body's intervention in the space around it. Rather than hugging the body, Leane's jewellery is typically designed to renegotiate the boundaries of the body. His mouthpieces and tribal rings show that jewellery can be as menacing as it is elegant.

chaos and destruction expressed in the collection as a whole, and disrupts the usual fantasy of perfection presented in jewellery. Leane pointed out that the jewellery is also inspired by McQueen's insight into beauty and danger: 'A rose is protected by thorns, but the thorns themselves are quite beautiful. Lee [McQueen] loves their dangerous edge that is so elegant as well.'

McQueen's fascination with abused and violated bodies has resulted in accusations of misogyny and exploitation. In his defence, McQueen recounts the memory of a brutal attack against his sister by her husband that he witnessed at the age of eight. 'I was this young boy and I saw this man with his hands around my sister's neck, I was just standing there with her two children beside me,' he told *The Independent*'s Susannah Frankel. 'Everything I've done since then was for the purpose of making women look stronger, not naïve.'[14]

This story mirrors a theme that runs through most of his work. McQueen explained: 'I am constantly trying to reflect on the way women are treated. It's hard to interpret that in clothes or in a show because there's always an underlying, sinister side to their

Alexander McQueen's choice of jewellery subverts the traditional use of fashion accessories as a signifier of femininity, using it like the Punks did as an index of inner angst and political repression. Here, Shaun Leane's 'Yashmak' turns the wearer into an urban warrior.

sexuality because of the way I have seen women treated in my life. Where I come from, a woman met a man, got shagged, had babies, moved to Dagenham, made the dinner, went to bed. And that was my image of women. And I didn't want that. I wanted to get that out of my head.'[15] But this image appears to stay with McQueen, haunting him as he strives to reconcile the physicality of abuse, and transpose it into the language of revenge. His garments reconfigure the passive as well as the active, stressing that a woman may be subject as well as object, agent as well as possession.

McQueen's woman-as-warrior can be traced back through each collection he has done for his own label, to his first fashion show, *Highland Rape*. The collection drew inspiration from the English occupation of Scotland. McQueen described the historic bloodshed as 'nothing short of genocide'[16] and used the collection to highlight the violence and oppression of the era that culminated in the Jacobite rebellion. This heralded what was yet to come in his departure from the traditional references to Britain's past depicted by designers like Westwood and Galliano, who often combine historical influences with exaggerated ornamentation, recalling a glorious era filled with pageantry and splendour. McQueen's grasp of true historical events is just as tenuous

From his first show, McQueen's woman-as-warrior can be traced back through each collection. McQueen's use of a headdress crafted from feathers and Tahitian black pearls recalls a female gladiator.

– the drive to interpret both historic and current events according to his own instincts is a principle that McQueen adheres to with obsessive persistence.

One of McQueen's most outstanding collections told the story of a lone warrior. *Joan* (autumn/winter 1998) took its inspiration from the historic figure of Joan of Arc. The show began with a model dressed in a short silver dress that resembled chain-mail armour. Almost every outfit was red or black, signifying saintly aestheticism or blazing hellfire. A black corset was laced tightly over shimmering red trousers, invoking vestiges of fetishism and 'blazing' passion. A red lace dress enveloped the neck, face and head to render the wearer sexually provocative and anonymous. A male model dressed in red and black seemed to represent an executioner, who cued the fiery demise of the last model. Pausing on the catwalk, she was enveloped in flames as a ring of fire erupted on the floor around her.

The criticisms of misogyny are fuelled by the way McQueen's women contradict the sublime image of offering typically presented in fashion. Caroline Evans[17] argues that the aggression inherent in McQueen's depiction of women seems more representative of his wider view of the world than a drive to abuse women. One interpretation of his women is to see them as invincible and uncompromising; but beyond that their aggressive sexuality makes them dangerous, even deathly to male desire.

The pain of abuse is literally acted out across the bodies of McQueen's models, under a prevailing mood of silent anger, seclusion and melancholy. Undercurrents of sex and violence are nothing new to fashion. High fashion in the 1970s in particular was characterized by such a strong undertone of sado-masochism, eroticism and violence that Edmund White described the style as the 'new brutalism'.[18] The photographs taken by Helmut Newton and Guy Bourdin in this era were imbued with fascination and fright, which surfaced again during the 1990s in magazines like *The Face* and *Dazed & Confused*. As brutality became a legitimate theme for fashion editorial, a trend grew for depicting models in abusive scenarios that echoed crime scenes: brutal attacks, rape and even murder.

Feminine beauty, in McQueen's work, is negotiated in terms of aggression and brutality, assigning each woman the ability to wound and attack. His metal corsets and metal skirts plate her body in armour; his jewellery equips her with lethal weapons.[19] Part victim, part adversary, the clothed body is presented as an artefact that has been reclaimed from oppression and decay, empowered through self-destructive and defiant acts against the forces that restrain it. Conversely, flaunting what most women are afraid of – violence, loss of control and fears of the body itself – does not offer a break from the imposed mask of beauty and seduction. In this structure, female sexuality is somehow privatized, closeted, controlled and contained within the arena of violence. McQueen uses fashion to constrict and fetter sexuality, inviting advances while simultaneously deflecting them.

McQueen destabilizes the usual affinity between fashion and material – a sensual relationship that invites both wearer and observer to touch, feel and stroke the sumptuous textures of fabrics. Using non-traditional materials that have rough, sharp and even dangerous surfaces pushes the observer away, maintaining critical distance from the wearer. Almost inherent in fashion is the masochistic drive to withstand suffering as a cosmetic practise, but the pain built in to the construction of garments like these forces the wearer to have a heightened awareness of suffering far beyond the usual fashion 'cause'. For the wearer to withstand the extreme discomfort of such materials, she requires a body tough enough to resist pain and injury. But to suggest that the wearer endures this pain for the sake of fashion alone would be misleading; as power and resistance are inexorably intertwined, her wilful engagement with these clothes signifies her protest. As Gilles Deleuze states in *Coldness and Cruelty*, 'masochism gives primacy to the ego and to the process of idealisation.'[20]

This dynamic is especially evident in McQueen's 'Red-glass Slide and Ostrich Feather Dress'. The lower half of the dress is made from ostrich feathers that expand outwards into a crinoline-like shape, while the upper part of the dress is constructed from two thousand microscope slides layered from hipbone to throat. Ordered from a surgical supplier, each slide was hand-drilled and individually painted red to suggest scrutinizing the body under a microscope. The dress also inverts the relationship between the visual and the tactile, the surface and the visceral; senses often associated with distance and nearness, respectively. As the dress replaces the tactile characteristics of fabric with segments of glass that could instantly shatter into a cascading razor's edge, the seductive materials that caress the skin are supplanted by shards that slice it open. McQueen wants to get a closer look at the body, even going beneath its surface. Employing the microscope as an agent of technology to do this invokes the power that science ultimately has over the body. Pleasure and pain, life and death are inexorably linked to science; once in its control the body can be penetrated to look within it. It is unclear whether it is McQueen himself peering inside, or empowering women to reclaim control by giving them a voice to speak about their bodies.

McQueen refuses to provide themes that camouflage the flaws of the body. He finds beauty in imperfect flesh, in exotic juxtapositions of pleasure and pain, and in the examination of destruction and decay that fashion tries to mask. McQueen recognizes that while traditionally focused on the surface of the body, fashion unconsciously reveals the anxieties of the flesh beneath it. This is exemplified in his 'Razor-shell Dress' (spring/summer 2001), constructed from sharp, overlapping sea shells that form a full-length impenetrable sheath around the model's body, who also wears a bandage-like underlayer wrapped around her torso and head. As she moves, the brittle shells knock together, fracturing and breaking apart as she walks. Her arms must be held akimbo to prevent them from being sliced open by the shells, effectively imprisoning her in the dress. The wearer would find it hard to control the fear and inner chaos caused by the mortal danger of the dress, yet only be able to react in slowly articulated movements that prevent the shells from splintering even more.

In a rare vision of a McQueen model appearing passive and defenceless, Shalom Harlow wore a dress designed to be a blank canvas in the finale for McQueen's *#13* collection (spring/summer 1999). Two paint-spraying 'robots' designed to paint cars were programmed to squirt yellow and black paint onto the dress's white fabric as Harlow paused on the catwalk. The 'White Sprayed Dress' – which resembled a skirt and crinoline pulled up over the torso – was a voluminous white cotton gown secured under the arms by a wide leather belt. The model stood passively as two robotic arms stretched towards her and fired jets of yellow and black paint onto the dress as she stood on a circular platform that slowly rotated. When the robotic arms finished spraying and retracted, the model turned and marched off the catwalk – her dress made complete.

McQueen created an eerie mood in *The Overlook* collection (autumn/winter 2000), which derived its name from the haunted hotel in *The Shining*, a film that culminates in Shelley Duvall's victimization by her violent husband.[21] Basing the collection on this theme cued the audience for the thrill of sinister and violent events, but McQueen slowly transformed the ghostly overtone into a strong winter wardrobe. The catwalk resembled a dark winter landscape, covered with mounds of artificial snow and bare trees. *The Overlook* is considered by many to be McQueen's signature collection, and one characterized by a sense of loneliness and solitude. The show expressed as much about the feeling of isolation as it did about the clothes; a white mask was painted across each model's eyes and forehead to render them expressionless and anonymous.

Even beyond his radical body ideals, McQueen's contributions to fashion have been considerable. He has moved British fashion forward and created a renaissance in British fashion not seen since John Galliano left London. As Galliano left Givenchy to head Dior, McQueen immediately appeared to be the obvious successor. But as he brought fresh vision to the Givenchy collections, the Givenchy boutiques, advertising campaigns, fragrance and cosmetic lines refused to move forward to meet his new aesthetic; his clothes were light years ahead of the image of the label as a whole. He still continued to show his own label in London and New York, though his company remained critically under-funded.

McQueen's extravagant collections have only been possible by attracting major-league sponsorship from outside the fashion world. American Express has consistently sponsored McQueen's fashion shows, reportedly spending over $1 million on the cost of showing his collection in New York. As you can imagine, the relationship between a financial conglomerate and one of fashion's most confrontational designers has not been completely without conflict. The *Untitled* collection had originally been named 'The Golden Shower', but American Express protested against its sexually explicit connotations. McQueen backed down and dropped the title, but defiantly refused to find another name that would satisfy both his sense of provocation and appease his sponsor. McQueen later designed a series of American Express Gold Cards to be offered to five hundred VIPs, featuring one of his sketches from the autumn/winter 2001 collection.

Even before McQueen's tenure at Givenchy ended in December 2000, he had sold 51 per cent of his company to the Gucci Group, solving his financial problems. He

McQueen's designs for the American Express Limited Edition Gold Card feature his sketches from his autumn/winter 2001 collection, literally 'fashioning' the technological systems that underpin international credit exchange.

landed an incredible deal with Gucci which, according to *The Sunday Times Magazine,*[22] is reportedly worth around £50 million. With Gucci holding such a big interest in his own label, there are plans to build the McQueen brand; a four thousand square-feet McQueen store is scheduled to open in New York, with fifty more shops to open worldwide. McQueen's deal with Gucci is thought to have paid him 10 per cent of the total investment in cash, with the remaining 90 per cent being tied up in shares. On top of this, he is said to be receiving a retainer of around £750,000 from Gucci. With appropriate funding behind him, he moved his own collection to Paris and began designing his first collection for Gucci (spring/summer 2002). It was a collection that appeared to celebrate female warriors; McQueen introduced a new kind of woman to the Gucci catwalk: his own.

McQueen's success is a rare phenomenon in the fickle world of fashion. He has certainly come a long way since his Savile Row apprenticeship, and has had more obstacles to pass than most. Even before his deal with Gucci was made public, many of the designers and critics interviewed for this book predicted that he would eventually lead the industry on a worldwide scale; some envisage him to be the most successful British designer of all time.

By turning fashion shows into theatrical productions McQueen revolutionized catwalk presentation like no other British designer has been able to. The sets for his catwalk shows were no less dramatic than the clothes presented in them, and each show was enhanced by the introduction of a theme illustrated in the collection and mirrored in the art direction of the show. The scenery displayed an array of curios ranging from crashed and salvaged automobiles that spewed caustic smoke from their bonnets, to caged ravens, water troughs and merry-go-rounds. McQueen's models have been sprayed with paint, placed inside refrigerated glass tunnels with ice and snow, had their heads encircled by a haze of white net swarming with live butterflies, or encased in a cage of moths. 'Most of the time, I try to provoke people,' McQueen explained. 'I've always said if someone leaves the show and vomits, or has a feeling of "what was that all about?" then I've done my job.'[23]

Hussein Chalayan

Hussein Chalayan approaches the body as a site of exploration, investigating its physical and metaphorical relationship to the world around it. Chalayan's clothes are futuristic in their ability to use the body as a site for both formal expression and experimentation, transforming it into a vehicle for meditations on fashion, design, physicality and on the kind of intangibles that fashion rarely addresses. The conceptual and theoretical inspirations behind his garments are each played out across the body, often inverting traditional views of sexuality, eroticism, embodiment and proportions. 'The body, in some respects, is the biggest symbol of tradition,' Chalayan said. 'That is why I am interested in re-animating certain thoughts around it, because you can alter the idea of the body in the way you present it.'[24]

Chalayan had been exploring the interaction between the body and technology for some time, expressing it on the catwalk in his *Panoramic* collection and several seasons later in his *Echoform* collection (autumn/winter 1999). The Altitude project was based on exploring the relationship of the body's inherent mobility on the creation of forms that give it speed. 'With Altitude I wanted to recreate environmental systems that mirror how the body moves. Thinking of speed led me to focus on car interiors which generated the idea of ergonomically amplifying the body's own speed and movement. I saw speed as something created by technological means to enhance the body's natural capacity to move quickly,' Chalayan explained.

As Chalayan's work engages further with technological systems, he is pioneering garments that place wireless technology, electrical circuitry and automated commands directly onto the body's surface. His Remote Control Dress (spring/summer 2000) was a high-tech triumph that married fashion to technology and technology to the body, establishing a dialogue between the body and the environment. 'The dress expressed the body's relationship to a lot of invisible and intangible things – gravity, weather, flight,

Chalayan's 'Remote Control Dress' suggests technologized sexualization of the body. It reveals and conceals erogenous zones while equipping and manipulating the body to conform ideals of sex appeal.

radio waves, speed, etc,' Chalayan said. 'Part of it is to make the invisible tangible, showing that the invisible can transform something and say something about the relationship of the object – the dress in this case – between the person wearing it and the environment around it.'

The dress, like those in the Aeroplane series, was designed by means of the composite technology used by aircraft engineers, mirroring the systems that enable remote-control aeroplanes to fly. It is made from a combination of glass fibre and resin, moulded into two smooth, glossy, pink-coloured front and back panels that fasten together with metal clips. Each panel is encased within grooves, two millimetres in width, that run throughout the length of the dress. These seams create the only textural variation in the dress, revealing interior panels made from translucent white plastic, accentuated by lighting concealed within the solar-plexus panel and the left side-elevating panel. The dress is designed to remain on the ground, and the principles behind it also mirror the 'intelligent' systems controlling and regulating the functions of modern buildings. This establishes a new affinity between the human and the environment, mediated by clothing designed to be intimately involved with the wearer's activities.

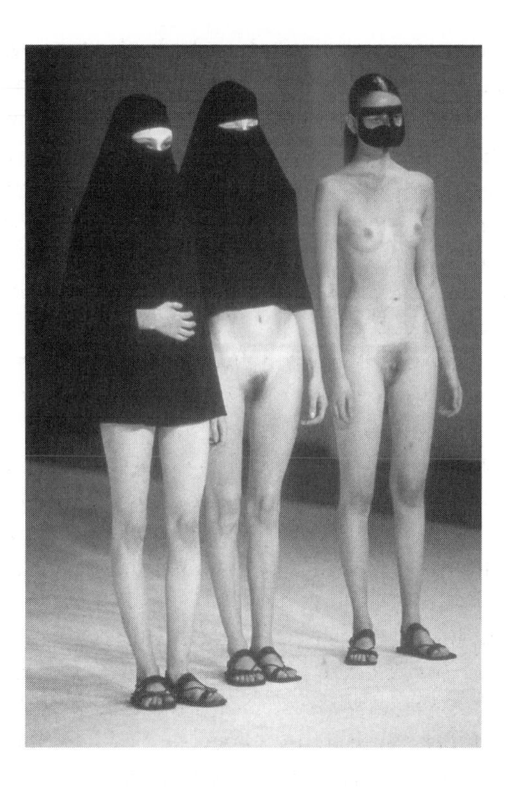

In 1997, some of Chalayan's models wore black chadors of varying lengths and nothing else, alluding to fashion's continual shift of erogenous zones around the female form as body ideals change.

Starlab, the now-defunct research laboratory pioneering technologized clothing, developed prototype garments that could be programmed to anticipate and respond to the wearer's needs by communicating wirelessly via remote systems. Charmed Technology, a research organization exploring the potentials of wireless clothing, conducted similar research with wireless technology to adapt it for fashion (detailed further in Chapter 5). Although their prototypes featured state-of-the-art technology that provided the wearer with a broad range of functions, they never evolved into a fully-functional model. Chalayan's Remote Control Dress, though less sophisticated, was the first wireless device to be presented as a fully-functioning fashion garment.[25] The Remote Control Dress is a ground-breaking achievement on many levels, not least because it showed that the technological principles behind it could be applied to fashion as well as science.

Chalayan described the dress's cyborgian attributes as 'something of a side effect'. The Remote Control Dress was not designed specifically to explore the relationship of technology to the body, but to examine how the form of the garment could evolve around the body in a spatial relationship to its environment. 'If you alter the way the body comes across in the space around it, then the body alters everything in the space that affects it,' Chalayan explained. 'The dress can also be transformed invisibly by the environment. The idea was a technological force between the environment and the person.' Extending the function of a dress beyond clothing is central to Chalayan's work, and the Remote Control Dress demonstrates that garments are capable of interaction with other humans and computerized systems distant in time and space.

The Remote Control Dress lines the body with computer devices and remote-control communication that aligns it to other systems. This reveals how technological enhancement means that the wearer must allow technology to come uncomfortably close to the body, all the while knowing that the systems themselves are capable of many contradictory uses. As the wearer puts on the Remote Control Dress, it literally becomes a cog in the machine. Through the technology in the dress, the body could then be linked to other machines, and linked to other bodies also linked to machines. This would connect the wearer to larger bodies of people, businesses and governments by means of wireless communication technologies. This gives the axis of fashion and technology another dimension, signalling the integration of the constructor and the constructed.

The concept of the human cyborg[26] resulted from Manfred Clynes and Nathan Kline's theories of how humans could survive in extra-terrestrial environments by being equipped with medical implants and prostheses.[27] More recently, Donna Haraway has expanded this definition to suggest that cyborgs represent more than the classical distinction between nature and artifice, as 'a hybrid of machine and organism, a creature of social reality as well as a creature of fiction'.[28] In Haraway's thinking, those surfing the Net, designing virtual bodies or operating equipment can be considered cyborgs, since their own nervous systems operate in direct connection with the artificial intelligence of the machine.

The cyborg body is a paradox of technological power and control, mirroring how the fashioned body is also determined by the ideals and values of a wider society. As scientists define the categories of cyborg bodies, the attributes of the fashioned body can also identified in their studies.[29] In cyborgian thought, technologies of the body can enhance it in four categories: they can be *restorative*, replacing lost functions, lost limbs and failed organs; *normalizing*, creating a generic aesthetic while imposing technologized bodies as social or aesthetical norms; *reconfiguring*, like the performance artist Stelarc, who equips the body with additional limbs or communication systems; or merely *enhancing* by increasing vision, optimizing mobility, hearing, etc. In fashion terms, the cyborg body is for the most part *reconfiguring* and *enhancing* through products like sunglasses, spectacles, mobile phones, palm pilots and even performance sports shoes.

In addition to containing the principles of the *reconfiguring* and *enhancing* categories, the Remote Control Dress suggests *normalizing* properties as it charts the techno sexualization of the body. In its ability to reveal/conceal erogenous zones and shape the body into a uniform feminine silhouette, the dress forecasts the future means of equipping and manipulating the body to conform to body ideals and dynamics of sex appeal. The structural architecture of the Remote Control Dress echoes the attributes of a fashioned body rather than an organic body. The structure of the dress forms an exoskeleton around the body, incorporating elements of body consciousness; its contours mimic the curves of the fashioned female body, arcing dramatically inward at the waist and outward in the hip region, echoing the silhouette of the corset and the crinoline. This gives the dress a defined hourglass shape that incorporates principles of corsetry in its design, emphasizing a conventionally feminine shape, while creating a solid structure that simultaneously masks undesirable body proportions.

As the dress's panels and components are activated to open and close, it evokes the allure of exposed skin and flesh, while concealing the body underneath its lining. 'I made a tulle dress to be worn under the Remote Control Dress, so that's what you see when it opens. I don't show erogenous zones in an obvious, clichéd way,' Chalayan said. 'Sexiness doesn't come from what you wear, or from your physical appearance – it's all to do with feeling good about yourself.' The sensuality associated with revealing and concealing the body is central to Chalayan's work, which challenges the way fashion defines erogenous zones, and avoids creating clothes that scream sex appeal. Chalayan views these pleasure centres as highly individual; zones to be explored and identified on individual bodies rather than dictated by fashion. In 1997 he sent models onto the catwalk wearing black chadors of varying lengths and nothing else, alluding to fashion's continual shift of erogenous zones around the female body in response to changing ideals.

The Remote Control Dress confronts one of the most profound issues raised by new technologies: the possibility that human identities would take on the properties of machines or be at their mercy. Though the wearer can access external systems via the remote-control device, inherent in the dress is a sinister reversal – the potential for those systems to control the wear. The interface of flesh and technology is both thrilling and terrifying: technology holds the potential to override the body's commands and take control of it before the wearer is able to escape.

As a technologized object the dress is loaded with symbolic value: it is a tool of communication, a man/machine hybrid and a hallmark of scientific progress. For fashion, it achieves innovations never thought possible, and amplifies the potential fashion has always had to interact and communicate. As the dress interacts with its immediate environment, or performs manoeuvres originating from a command centre, it enables the body to extend its range of movements and control beyond arm's reach. The dress makes it clear that the fashioned mechanization of the body can be integrated into a larger technological system to produce a whole new range of practices, possibilities and aesthetics that transgresses the body/machine boundary.

This marks a radical departure from a world where distinctions between body and machine, body and dress, present and distant, natural and artificial, once seemed clear. This illustrates how, as Michel Foucault described, social and cultural discourses construct our bodies in a way that makes us as analogous to a machine as possible.[30]

The design of the dress is imbued with technologies that make interaction efficient, productive and empowered, akin to the machine-like principles of controlled automation. The presence of high-tech systems in fashion fuses its body conscious ideals with a belief in automation, speed and accuracy as the means to achieve it.

While, historically, fashion has defined the human body according to social values, technological progress is radically changing the way it is perceived. As Chalayan's work reflects these changes, his Remote Control Dress represented what science could not yet represent: the icon of the technological age. The Remote Control Dress reminds us that we are always embodied, while showing that future choices of embodiment, like choices of clothing, may not always be simple. As Chalayan continues to expand his thinking behind these representations, his clothing requires a body with confidence to carry off clothing still heavy with the thought process that created it.

The new body ideals explored by Webber, McQueen and Chalayan read as a desire for new forms of embodiment, and re-evaluations of the traditional meanings of embodied experience. Every age has had its mythical figures that transgress the boundaries of the human body: from the living statues of the ancient world and the morphing god Zeus to the werewolves and shape-shifters of European folklore, the idea of acquiring capacities beyond the boundaries of the individual body has become a cultural legend. Through engaging with these registers of continuity and tradition, these designers use fashion and technology to redefine physical experience in terms of hyper-breeds and cyborgs. Their search for new body forms is generating fresh approaches to body differences and even physicality itself. As the twenty-first century dawns, so does the potential for new body ideals to emerge out of fashion's mythical desire for the perfect figure.

three

Surveillance

Our visible and invisible worlds are continually monitored by visual technologies. Surveillance is the gaze of technology itself; forced and distorted, recording our every movement and playing it back to gratify our endless fascination with watching others and ourselves. The visualization of people and events pervades the whole of society, as the presence of closed-circuit television (CCTV), the popularity of webcams and the 'Big Brother' genre of television programmes make us painfully aware that surveillance is not the exception, but the norm.

Surveillance systems, we are told, were developed as mechanisms of protection and defence, which today have evolved into a global network of sensors that record human activity in real time. Britain alone has an estimated 200,000 video surveillance cameras, many of them continuously monitoring streets and shopping centres, apparently making it easier for police to identify criminals. There is something sinister about their panoptical properties, making us wonder if we are actually guarded, or policed. As these systems spread, the search for 'real' enemies becomes a part of urban mythology, as technologies now monitor an unseen, invisible, unidentified and non-specific threat both within and outside the boundaries of the Western world. Whether 'real' enemies are apprehended or not, the presence of surveillance technology creates a virtual enemy, just as potent in generating paranoia.

Fashion's engagement with surveillance places emphasis on visibility; a concept essential to the consumption of fashion but often underestimated in interpretations of it. Clothes, being the form in which the fashioned body is made visible, give the wearer a public identity while fostering the construction of the self. The gaze of visual technologies makes the experience more intimate and more exotic, amplifying the function of clothing as both boundary and margin in the ever-narrowing gap between public and private personae.

The visual exchanges of life now take place in a culture of hypervisibility. The presence of television cameras, medical cameras, satellites, military aircraft and digital cameras ensure that we never escape the scrutiny of the lens. Fashion exploits these media to instil the desire to be seen, be visible and even pursued. Being captured on film is to be glamorous and chic; putting oneself under surveillance is tantamount to exhibitionism. The 'I know you're watching me' facet of the fashion experience reads as a willed pathology of surveillance. As the body becomes increasingly monitored by the fashion world, it creates a parallel culture of self-surveillance, in which individuals must also scrutinize themselves to monitor their social acceptability.

Not everyone in fashion is sold on the idea of being under surveillance. As cameras continue to overexpose us, fashion provides the solution to reinstating our anonymity. Simon Thorogood's couture garments are designed with principles of visibility in mind, constructing his clothing with panels that can become high collars or hoods that mask the wearer's identity, using stealth tactics to be rendered anonymous, yet not faceless or genderless. The hip London label Vexed Generation also create garments that are reactions against surveillance. Using strategic design tactics, their clothing rebels against the widespread acceptance of video-surveillance by using visors and hoods to render the wearer anonymous. They give fashion the power to invert and deflect the political agendas that promote electronic surveillance as a means of social control.

The intelligence expert and fashion technologist Katrina Barillova was covertly recruited into her country's espionage training programme to learn secret-agent skills of self-defence, reconnaissance and surveillance. Once she realized that her stealth expertise could be used to integrate high-tech surveillance systems into fashion, she co-founded Charmed Technology in 1999 with Alex Lightman, an MIT graduate with a specialist interest in satellite technologies. Her designs are significant because they equip the wearer with the technological means to survey the environment and the activities of others, both near and remote.

The work of these three designers engages with the vast areas mapped by surveillance technology, and the power it can exercise over the individual. Fashion's relationship with hypervisibility is investigated further as their work explores the extent to which clothing has the potential to react against surveillance, and how technology can equip fashion with the means to cheat surveillance systems. As new visual media redefine the meaning of visibility in our society, fashion is making a clear response.

Simon Thorogood

Simon Thorogood possesses a focus for authenticity and purism that is more about the philosophy of fashion than fashion itself. He has done what others strive to do but seldom achieve: he rethinks fashion starting from a point in the future and then backtracks to the present. Thorogood breaks with traditional ideas of body and dress to reconstruct conventional proportions of body and space. 'I'm not really interested in retro styles of dress or previous eras,' he explained. 'I'm much more fascinated by

While the hoods and extended sleeves of Simon Thorogood's garments allude to anonymity, their futuristic lines, shiny fabrics and rich metallic colours give the wearer a strong identity.

things like developments in aviation. That's what lead me onto stealth technology, and the new stealth bombers that are still on the drawing board,' he said. 'I saw parallels in how Le Corbusier focused on the ships, cars and aeroplanes of his day for his own design work.'[1]

Thorogood's garments are arrestingly modern, beautiful and breathtaking in their simplicity. They possess a subtle spirituality; at once ecclesiastical in their extended sleeves, capes and hoods, but undeniably futuristic in their clean, simple lines, shiny fabrics and rich metallic colours. It would be hard to overlook the transcendental properties of the garments themselves, which soothe the boundary between maverick identity and ethereal anonymity. Is he trying to define the spirit of the future? Does he consciously incorporate surveillance elements into the clothes? Do the clothes interface between fashion and technology? The answers are, apparently, yes, yes and yes.

Thorogood rose through the ranks of the 1990s London fashion scene virtually overnight, and was labelled by the fashion press as a rising star in the new 'Brit Couture'. Thorogood maintains an uncompromising commitment to couture principles, preferring to present his work in private shows rather than participating in Fashion Week. Rather than express his style in commercially appealing terms, Thorogood preferred to present his work as a static fashion installation rather than recruit investors to fund a catwalk show. 'When I started off I had to make a lot of decisions about how I would play the game. I knew that being a regular fashion designer would mean following a well-trodden path because fashion is a commercial industry. I didn't want to get myself involved in that, I decided that I wanted to do it my way and not start compromising,' he explained. Saying no to Fashion Week has enabled him to present his work in a much richer context, leading to presentations at the Victoria & Albert Museum, the ICA[2] and Judith Clark Costume Gallery in London, the Künstlerhaus in Vienna, and in the *London Fashion* exhibition curated by Valerie Steele at the Fashion Institute of Technology in New York.

At a time when some of the best fashion ideas have resulted from collaborations between couturiers and artists; new and innovative positions in fashion are often interpreted in the same language as art criticism. But despite Thorogood's fine art background (he received both his BA and MA from St Martin's) the cliché of the singular, isolated romantic artist does not adequately reflect the multi-faceted alliances he fuses between technology, music, architecture and fashion. 'I came to fashion by mistake. On my arts foundation course we had to choose subjects. The sculpture and painting courses got filled up, so I had to choose something else. Eventually I decided on a fashion degree because it was a medium that I could use to express my interest in graphics, technology and three-dimensional forms. I never had a desire to be a fashion designer and still struggle with seeing myself as one today,' he said.

Stealth technology, according to Thorogood's numerous books on the subject, is actually a complex design philosophy. Constructed of radar-absorbent materials, the aircraft's body features smooth, polished surfaces, irregular angles and undulating contours. Most of the radar signal is absorbed into the body of the aircraft, or dispersed over its surface. The aeroplane's low radar cross-section reduces the range at which radar is able to detect it, making it invisible on the surveillance screen. As a by-product of its functional design, the contours and geometry create a sleek aesthetic.

Thorogood does not necessarily see the Stealth aeroplane as a design innovation that will revolutionize fashion, but discovering its mysterious beauty forged a futuristic direction in his work. 'Surveillance is about more than Stealth aircraft or even technology; it has a lot to do with principles of visibility and new ideas about construction,' he explained. 'I tuned in and got excited by surveillance because the Stealth opened up a whole new chapter in aviation design, just like it opened up a new direction in my work.'

Whereas conventional aeroplanes have air intakes and exhaust ducts articulated on their surface, the Stealth conceals them underneath insulated panels to deflect heat-seeking missiles. Thorogood's designs play on the idea of concealing the body in similar manner, inverting Western notions of concealing and revealing in dress. 'Surveillance is mostly expressed in my clothes in the way that I adorn the body in oblique ways. Most couture garments are careful to cut the sleeve at a particular length and design a revealing neckline. I lengthen the sleeve to conceal the hand and wrist completely, unless the wearer pulls the fabric back herself. My garments come up and hide the neck, or I design hooded panels that conceal the neck and head from a particular viewpoint. I took this idea directly from the Stealth's design, which is radically different to other aeroplanes,' he said.

Stealth aircraft are sexy. Their metallic curves and extraordinary, otherworldly shapes, together with the official secrecy that surrounds them, almost give them cult status. They are a metaphor for the thrill of avoiding detection, and generate a Lacanian fantasy of a self-contained psyche hidden away for secret observation and discovery. 'In them I find extraordinary shapes with beautifully blended surfaces, faceted planes and strange motifs,' Thorogood said. These are explored in complex and configured exercises on the pages of Thorogood's notebooks. When sewn together and worn on the body, the garments project a silhouette that designates the body as a superstructure beneath them. 'I tend to look at shapes and designs in different fields, whether it's engineering, aircraft design or music. I suppose it's a very "boy" thing, being drawn to mathematical systems, which I have great empathy with. I am still fascinated by the Stealth aircraft because it turned over a new leaf in aviation by being a blend of different materials. Visually, they are like fine examples of minimalist art,' he said.

Though the inspiration for his collections are technological, Thorogood works with traditional materials and methods. 'The reason I felt drawn to silk was because in a sense it is very ancient, a traditional couture fabric used for wedding gowns and that sort of thing, yet it has a modern feel to it, there's a paradox to it. It looks metallic, and you don't usually print on it, but the marks I print on it are almost invisible. On some pieces, I use very small facets of resin and Perspex, or fragments of wood. And often, these are just ideas from things that spill off the pages of a sketchbook,' he explained. 'Drawing is the fundamental starting point of everything that I'm looking at or feeling or thinking about. They gradually morph into colours, perhaps into three-dimensional forms, or into writing, and I enjoy putting together sketch books'.

Thorogood's entire practice is set up as a couture studio, where clients come for informal meetings and fittings. The type of clients he attracts dispels the notion that couture fashion revolves around ladies who lunch. Thorogood made a conscious decision to move away from the traditional woman of fashion and clichéd approaches to femininity, to appeal to a women who is utterly contemporary in her vision. 'It tends to be a culturally aware person who wears my pieces, but that's certainly not the only person I'm aiming for. I'm aware that all my cultural interests and current ideas come across in the clothing because that's what inspires me to make them that way.' Thorogood's patrons range in age from young, career-minded professionals, to mature women considered to be the upper echelons of the gallery and museum world. Thorogood's clients are normally referred to him by word of mouth, or have come to him as a result of recent exhibitions in London and abroad.

'I cut according to couture principles, using only pure duchesse silk dyed to create colours that are unique and individual,' he explained, 'which adds an element of luxury and elegance to the collection.' Each garment is made for an individual client during at least three fittings. 'There is a need to see people engaging with your work and it's great to see people wearing the clothes. Once the garment ventures into the public domain, it becomes a hybrid of them and me. So there is often a spiritual connection there, which is partly why they single me out from other designers in the first place.' Because Thorogood regards each garment as an interactive work, the wearer is not only the direct object of the work; she is an active part of the set of conditions that create it.

Thorogood also draws inspiration from minimalist architecture and experimental music to interpret the complex abstraction of the body. The fabric, as if it were an industrial material, is contemplated in terms of its surface area, then cut and constructed to engineer symmetrical planes and architectural proportions. 'I'm interested in traditional processes of making, but the way I work with duchesse silk means I have to back it with various fusings and interlinings and treat the fabric to make it do what it wouldn't ordinarily do. So, there's something technologised about the process of making pieces that I enjoy,' he said.

Though drawing inspiration from architecture, Thorogood's work moves away from the built environment. The references he makes to stealth and surveillance are expressed with transcendency in mind, suggesting a refusal of the urban world and a shift towards the microcosm. 'The garments, like architecture, are designed with considerations for the inside and the outside. I place importance on the inside of the garment as an environment within itself, mirroring the detailing on the surface in a secret interior world made only for the wearer. What I'm dealing with at the end of the day is clothes, but I'm experimenting with the idea that it can be more than just garments, in the same way that music can be much more than a melody or a hummable tune,' Thorogood said.

Each piece has a strong dynamic of its own, made to accommodate the individual rather than forcing a generic blueprint upon them. As Thorogood explained: 'By scrutinising things made in a functional context without any previous aesthetic or intellectual value, you can suddenly make a real aesthetic or intellectual discovery. To me the aircraft are charged with new significance, communicating new ideas which I then translate into fashion to create something that is unique in its look and the way the wearer can relate to it,' he said.

Thorogood is aware that the aesthetic qualities of his Stealth garments are so distinctive that it has practically become his signature style. 'When you look at my work, in a sense, you are also looking at limitations. Part of the reason the garments have an architectural quality is because a lot of the shapes in my work were line drawings, taken from the panelling of not only the Stealth but of various aircraft. I wouldn't try and achieve a flowery feminine look because I know I wouldn't be particularly good at that. It's actually my limitations and my strengths that are my signature, not the Stealth. But, they can be my undoing because there is a danger of repetition,' he said.

Thorogood's *fascia* exhibition at Judith Clark Costume Gallery in London received acclaim by the Press, the art world and fashion critics. The installation featured nine *fascia* constructions shown alongside two garments from his spring/summer 2001 collection, expanding on the idea of clothing as a wearable home. 'As much as my design work involves a fascination with stealth aviation, it seemed logical to derive bands from sections and panelling of current and new-generation stealth aircraft,' Thorogood said. 'In exactly the same way the words were fused together so would sections from a wing and the fuselage be fused resulting in a series of strange and abstracted shapes. These forms were then scaled up to create freestanding sculptures that would dramatically range in size and colour. These would not only interact with one another but also generate interesting relationships with the viewer, creating simple fashion compositions,' he said.[3]

The *fascia* theme resulted from an earlier project, where Thorogood had been commissioned by The British Council to produce a body of work for the *Personal Space* exhibition shown in a London gallery. As Thorogood was researching the theme, he considered the different elements of the body and individual space. The words fashion, architecture, signs, colour, interior and apparel came to mind, which he merged into an acronym; 'fascia'. He discovered that it also existed as a real term, meaning bands of fibrous tissue between groups of muscles, or a distinctive band of colour on an insect or plant. Thorogood replicated some of the panels in the Stealth aircraft's design and fitted them together in freestanding sculptures so that the viewer could walk around them. 'I thought of these pieces as "suggestibles" of clothing; visitors to the exhibition could wander around them and complete them as garments in their imaginations,' he said.

The technological influences that pervade Thorogood's design processes and presentation formats run parallel to his stealth aesthetic. Thorogood is also using electronic music systems – which are even less tangible than stealth – to forge new directions in his work. 'The music is about taking an aspect of something else into the realm of clothing. I'm completely absorbed by covert systems in music, and the way people like Brian Eno, John Cage and Stockhausen compose very specific recipes to create sounds or textures. In my work I have been trying to build up a visual framework from those systems and ideas, working with musicians and composers,' he said. Through his collaboration with Stephen Wolff, the composer known for his digital artworks and interactive scores that blur the boundaries between composer and performer, Thorogood is involved in creating computer software that reconfigures ambient noise and converts it into a two-dimensional wave pattern. 'I'm excited about the progress we're making because I'll be able to take a musical score and turn it into a three-dimensional garment by transposing the sound through the computer programme,' he explained.

Part of Thorogood's inspiration for basing garment designs on music is to engage with the composer's work and give it another dimension. When music is interpreted through the body, it most commonly takes the form of dance, but Thorogood wants to take it to another dimension by expressing it on the body as form. 'I've always been fascinated by someone like John Cage, who was interested in handing over co-authorship to a third party. I'm trying to explore that in fashion, getting beyond the last word, starting the ball rolling in a new direction,' he said.

Apart from his collaboration with Wolff, Thorogood join forces with other innovators to participate in an impressive range of projects. 'The basis of my work is interactive and about a shared framework. On one hand it means that things can be tough, but on the other hand I get to work on lots of interesting projects,' he said. Thorogood produces music with the digital art group Spore, presents his collections with the design collaborative known as Grey Area (detailed further in Chapter 4), and lectures at universities in England and abroad. 'I was influenced by a book called *Global Paradox*, written by John Naisbitt, highlighting how businesses in the future may become more niche or more commission-based because of shifting patterns of work; being both local and global at the same time. I began to see how I could carry out my work patterns and projects according to these predictions,' he explained.

Throughout the 1990s, the value of couture was questioned by many cynics who dismissed it as an archaic institution without a future. The brilliance of designers like Thorogood, with such a vested interest and dependence on couture, is a strong indication that the creative and magical elements of fashion will continue to thrive in this tradition, sustaining a philosophy that is lived rather than consumed.

Vexed Generation

When it comes to counteracting surveillance, Vexed Generation are the ones to watch. For more than a decade, Vexed Generation have crafted clothing from bullet-proof and

Vexed Generation's hooded jackets were created as a commentary on the prevalence of surveillance during the 1990s. Designed in response to the political climate in London throughout the decade, the look protects anonymity but facilitates a public presence.

slash-proof materials for an urban lifestyle that counter the problems of modern life. Their collections pioneer new materials and construction methods, combining principles from sportswear, high-performance protective clothing and cutting edge street style. They work with fashion not to mimic the latest trends, but to use it as a form of communication and resistance that can initiate long-term changes to the social infrastructure.

One of their most famous garments is the 'Vexed Parka', which they created as a commentary on the escalation of surveillance during the 1990s. The parka was designed in response to the political climate in London at that time, but relates to a universal narrative. Adam Thorpe, who owns Vexed Generation in partnership with Joe Hunter, explained: 'It was 1994, and there were the surveillance cameras going up at the time. Now there are cameras everywhere but at that time it was just starting and nobody was discussing it. So we put that on the agenda as well.'[4] The Vexed Parka is characterized by a sinister hood and collar that covers most of the head and face, closing over the mouth and nose but leaving the eye area open. 'We made the parka in 1994 and

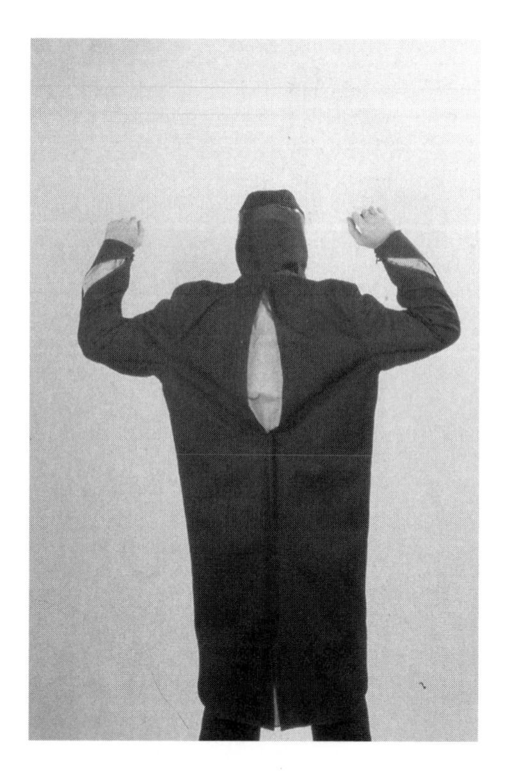

Vexed Generation pioneer new materials and construction methods, combining principles from sportswear, high-performance protective clothing and cutting-edge style.

launched it in 1995. It sums up all the ideas and concepts we had about fashion and social surveillance, which we include in most of the other clothes we have designed since,' Thorpe said.

During the 1990s, the British government and private industry are estimated to have spent around £3 billion to establish surveillance systems and equipment. 'For a fraction of the cost we made it pretty much redundant as the person wearing the parka can hide his face,' Thorpe said. 'The area in front of the mouth and nose is formed so it can take one of the filters normally used in special neoprene cycle masks.' Though the mask was designed to look and function as a filter, it also concealed the lower half of the face.

The political climate at this time was characterized by protests and civil disobedience in response to the controversial British Criminal Justice Act and the government's implementation of poll-tax reforms. 'At that time we felt that civil liberties were attacked. Freedom of expression, the rights to demonstrate, assembly or party were strategically cut short. Particularly during the poll tax riots it was apparent that although holding an equally valid proposition or opinion, people were confronted with riot police wearing protective kit,' Thorpe explained. The parka embodied the difficult

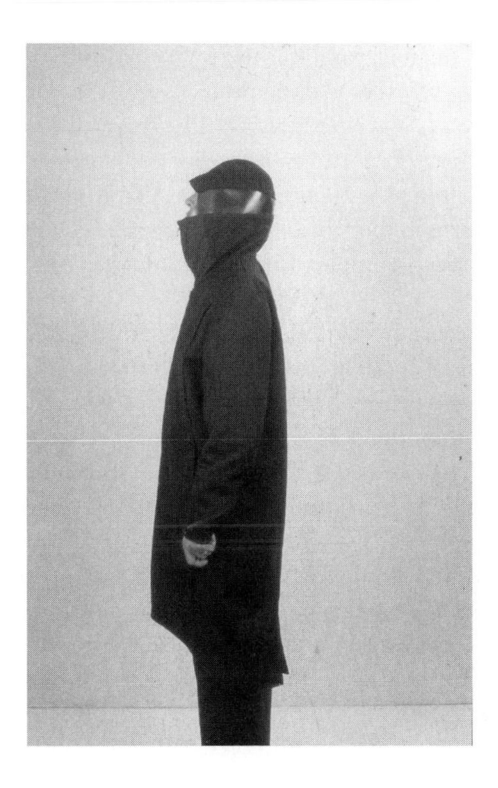

Vexed Generation's 'stealth utility' line updated street style with hoods, visors and technologized textiles, creating a new urban look for Londoners.

juxtaposition of civil liberties and CCTV, becoming a confrontational parody of police riot gear that protected the wearer. 'We were interested in the possible sartorial links between the extremes. For us the garment was a kind of modelling of social situations,' Thorpe said. This enabled the wearer to maintain a public presence and gather social and political information first hand, while remaining anonymous. Thorpe said: 'Our clothing is about communicating what we think is essential or important. We give people enough protection for them to be able to go out and be active, more involved with their environment in a secure fashion and be more individual.'

Anonymity and visibility against the urban landscape became considerations expressed in each garment Vexed Generation make. As they began exploring materials with different properties, the functions of the jackets extended beyond concealing to include weatherproofing, physical defence and environmental hazards. 'As well as making garments for our own conceptual reasons, we are also making clothing that people want to wear for practical reasons,' Thorpe said.

Vexed Generation choose technologized materials like Kevlar and ballistic nylon for the strength and durability that makes them slash-proof, providing a shield in the event of a knife-wielding attacker. 'When we first started using Kevlar you could only get it in Britain, where it was manufactured for use by the Ministry of Defence and security companies. We had to say we were making protective clothing to get it, so we told them our company name was "V G Security",' Thorp said. He began buying other technologized textiles from factories in Switzerland, America and Italy. Using high-tech materials created a unique aesthetic almost by default, because the densely textured surfaces and subtle patterns in the fabric have real impact. The properties of non-woven textiles are ideal for creating complex forms, due to their strength and ability to hold their shape.

The aesthetic this created became known as 'stealth utility', because it defined the wearer against the public space, concealed their identity and constituted a multi-functional design. Other streetwear labels soon began to update their look with hoods, technologized textiles and multipurpose designs. 'We never intended to become part of any fashion trend, but have noticed that much of the clothing that we originally made in 1994 and 1995 has ended up becoming a new sort of urban utility look,' Thorpe said.

Investing their garments with stealth significance has in some ways contributed to the social mythology that generates the 'Big Brother' paranoia associated with surveillance systems. But as Vexed Generation's range of customers grew they attracted people who liked the stealth aesthetic for its practical value, rather than the surveillance principles behind them. The concepts and social principles behind their clothes remained in place, but their designs evolved to included garments less radically concealing. 'While the first pieces we did were single statements, allowing people to shut themselves off from their surroundings, now we also make the "A4 Crombie" styles that appear much more conventional, tolerant and open,' Thorpe said. The danger with the principle of self-sufficiency is that sometimes the wearer closes off to the environment they are in, relying on the clothes to filter the input and stimuli from outside. 'I agree that if the comfort zone goes to a point in which people become too dependent on technology or where people become too distant from reality there is a concern there. I think the boundaries of natural and synthetic should not be forgotten; once they are forgotten we start getting into trouble,' Thorpe added.

The coats in the A4 Crombie range are tailored like traditional overcoats, echoing classic Mackintosh styles. Made out of high-performance duramix wool, the A4 Crombie range combines the resilient outer shells with a waterproof, breathable coating. They are less menacing than the Vexed Parkas, but elements of their stealth aesthetic still remains. With a few discreet zips the hood covers the face and a mouthpiece is revealed, a look that turns from stylish urban fashion into fully functional protective gear. 'If you want to hide from a camera you still can, because we've put in a tinted visibility strip so you can still look around and remain anonymous. We use high performance cloth that can last and be durable and can cope with all those outdoor things that are thrown at you, whether it is the weather, or an uncivil civilian. We are trying to make clothes that will stand the test of time, including the styling,' Thorpe said.

The use of temperature-regulating materials in Vexed Generation's winter collections ends the need for bulky layering. Phase Change Material, a substance originally developed for NASA, is used in the lining to equip coats with built-in thermometers that act as personal thermostats, keeping the body temperature constant while journeying through transitional spaces. 'Phase Change fabrics like Outlast have tiny paraffin capsules embedded in the fibres to create a climate controlled atmosphere,' Hunter explained. 'When the body heats over forty degrees centigrade the paraffin molecules react and absorb the heat. When the temperature drops below thirty-seven degrees centigrade they expand to release the heat they've stored and warm up the wearer.' The material produces a comfort zone by maintaining a constant temperature for the wearer both inside and out, bringing the temperature under the control of the individual, following the same principles of the fifth season created by urban air-conditioned environments. Their semi-tailored suit/bike jackets are streamlined even further by the use of Corwool, a fabric with the warmth and appearance of wool, without the bulk and shapelessness of an anorak.

Almost everything that Hunter and Thorpe do is inspired by the London scene. Like the skateboard labels that emerged as a part of urban subculture, Vexed Generation's range of clothes paralleled developments in urban youth culture. 'We started in response to the English street environment because we thought that that was the environment we knew about and where we were placed ourselves,' Thorpe said. When Hunter and Thorpe decided to go into business together they were equally drawn to the idea of starting a music label, because Thorpe had the experience of working for a London record company. 'When we got together we were all on the dole and couldn't decide if we wanted to do music, design, fashion, whatever,' said Thorpe. 'We made some records first and eventually decided to have a go at fashion, which we made based on new ideas and materials,' he added. When they lost access to the recording studio they were using fashion seemed to be the easiest option, since Hunter had the experience of having previously produced his own fashion label.

The London fashion scene is characterized by social contrasts, with a wide gap between insider and outsider. Coming into fashion virtually by default highlighted this divide; working outside fashion conventions proved to be to Vexed Generation's advantage. The concept behind their shop and showroom was set to break down the insider/outsider boundaries, by presenting fashion in an open forum rather than through insider PR events. Rather than just watching fashion shows, the public can be in dialogue with the clothes, look at them close up and try them on. The showroom was in Soho, accessed via a spiral staircase, where the latest collections were hung on dress forms suspended from the ceiling. Thorpe explained: 'We put all of our energy in communicating the ideas through the space, through our shop because it is open all year long, anyone can walk in and experienced it. Meanwhile, if you do a catwalk show you rely on the press or on those who attend to communicate what they've seen or they've felt to other people.'

The showroom's interior design expressed their clothing concepts in architectural principles. While in architecture things are usually built to be longer-lasting than they are in fashion, the concept behind the showroom inverted this. The technologized textiles they use mean that the clothes are almost impossible to wear out, and more durable than the paint, carpet or wallpaper, while the shop's décor was made to constantly wear away. The Plasticine floor in the gallery space started off as a pure blue surface that would be worn down with each footprint, recording the traces of each visitor and accelerating the process of erosion day by day. 'We were interested in its weathering capabilities and in concepts of quality and tradition and longevity,' Hunter explained. 'It was also our Ludite approach to surveillance, because we were tracking people without using digital technology.'[5]

Rather than fitting heating insulation, they padded the shop's interior with the type of quilting they would pad their garments with. 'We did that to slow things down,' Thorpe explained. 'Before that people could scribble their names and orders on the wall, but we put the padding up so that they could embroider their names, which took them longer to do. Later on we printed out labels for each order that had the customer's name on it. One was sewn into the clothes, the other was sewn up on the wall, mimicking the way big retailers build a name and address database to keep records of their customers,' he said.

Vexed Generation's uncompromising perspectives on the standards and values of their designs is a rarity in both conventional and cutting edge fashion. Vexed Generation tend to invert superficialities like marketing clothing for its sex appeal, capitalizing on short-term trends, notions of exclusivity and product branding by placing emphasis on protection and durability. They also innovate by guaranteeing high performance standards for their clothes, achieved through high-tech textiles and functional design. 'With our garments, and as a philosophy, we go against the mainstream of production where the products are designed to last a determined period of time through concepts of cheapness and disposability. We are fundamentally against that and that's why our garments are intended to endure and keep their qualities. We'd like to think of our garments going into second-hand shops and yet, being in perfect shape,' Thorpe said.

More recently the stealth utility concept has been extended to a range of garments designed to be worn on a motor scooter or bicycle, called the 'See and Be Seen' line. 'We use a lot of technological developments because we appreciate the utilitarian values of them and because when we use motor scooters, we know how it feels to be in the freezing cold and have aching knees for at least four hours after you come off your bike. We made them [the See and Be Seen range] to be worn on the scooter but also to look like an ordinary day coat. When you wear it on the scooter, you unzip sections to show reflective panels inside. Other parts unzip to give you the expansion you need in a scooter coat to hold that position of leaning forward on the handlebars,' he explained. 'So I guess they're not so ordinary after all.'

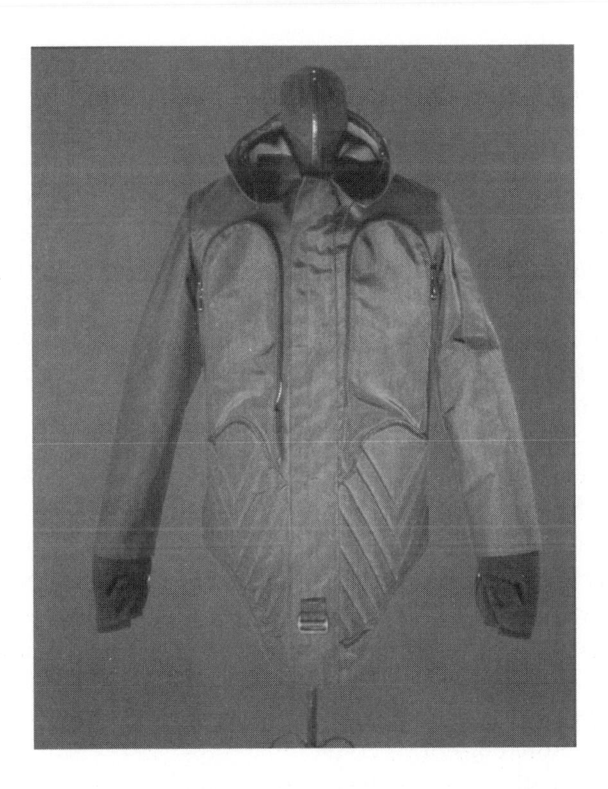

Vexed Generation give protective clothing insectoid padding and streamlined tailoring. Worn on a motorcycle, sections unzip to reveal reflective panels and expand comfortably as the wearer leans forward to grip the handlebars.

Katrina Barillova

Listening to Katrina Barillova's life story is like watching a James Bond film. At the age of ten, a test given to all students at her school in Slovakia revealed that she had an IQ of 140. Once the Czechoslovakian government found out, they secretly recruited her into an espionage training programme to learn secret-agent skills: self-defence, stealth and surveillance.[6] The programme was so top secret that not even her parents knew she was being trained to work as a spy; they read about it in the *New York Times* years later. Apparently, leading a double life was just part of the training for the undercover work she would do later. 'I would make a good actress because I had to develop acting skills for my undercover work,' Barillova explained. 'The difference between movie acting and acting in a sting operation is simple: If you don't perform correctly as an undercover agent, you die.'[7]

Barillova said her 'cover' had been to work as a fashion model, while in reality she was studying six languages and training in the latest surveillance technologies. 'Being a model was good cover because if someone tells you they are a model you don't expect much brain activity, and they become less threatening to you,' she said. With the fall of communism and subsequent collapse of the Czech regime, Barillova was out of a job, so she caught a flight to New York. 'I didn't know anyone in New York and barely spoke English. Some people I met on the plane helped me get a place to stay, because I didn't have any money either,' Barillova said. Her excellent physique – perhaps a side-effect of her rigorous secret-agent training? – good skin, and height landed her a job as a fashion model in New York, so she gave it a whirl until she perfected her English. Barillova then moved on to private security firms specializing in undercover work and industrial espionage, who reportedly placed Barillova on a number of assignments that took her around the world.

Today Barillova has in-depth knowledge of most communication systems, computer programming and audio-visual technology. Building her own body rigs for spy missions required a sound understanding of complex technology that could both transmit and receive information without being detected. Barillova used to conceal the equipment within her clothes, jewellery or handbag, so she knew how to adapt these systems to be worn on the body. Barillova's high-tech approach to stealth is a literal one, interpreting communication and surveillance in unequivocal terms. 'You have to be really smart to avoid detection and conceal your identity,' Barillova explained. 'Just wearing a hood isn't enough – you need to be equipped with systems that tell you if you are being monitored or not.'

Barillova's work with Charmed Technology combined her knowledge of video-capture capabilities used in CCTV with the rise in popularity of the mobile telephone and the Internet.[8] 'I could see how surveillance technology could help to solve problems in everyday life, and how this would move technology forward into the future,' she said. Barillova's next mission was to partner surveillance with mobility and interaction, so that portable surveillance technology could be worn by anyone without looking conspicuous.

Charmed's research of wireless Internet access, wireless video relays and wireless interfaces opened up possibilities for new types of systems and unprecedented access to information wherever the user is. 'Having the technology with you all the time would let you be online whenever you wanted and access people and databases whenever you wanted,' Barillova said. 'This type of access would be provided through the Internet, at least initially, where you could send and receive video files and watch things in real time that other people are experiencing in another place. You could use the Internet to go beyond what information there is around you, because true surveillance is being able to look beyond and challenge the reality of what you think you see,' Barillova explained.

Surveillance can mean, paradoxically, that in order to see you have to be seen, moving and operating in detection systems outside your own. Personal access to surveillance systems, in Barillova's view, is a way of turning 'Big Brother' inside out: you are tracking the environment, rather than the environment tracking you. Having this sort of information available when you need it means you have a better chance of avoiding the hidden cameras now commonplace in the urban landscape. 'There are a lot of hidden cameras used the United States but people don't notice them or talk about them,' Barillova said. 'I usually detect them immediately and say to my friends, "There's a camera, here's a camera – hey look, there's a camera right over us" and I think I may be making some of my friends a little paranoid by now.'

In Barillova's experience, stealth and fashion do not mix. Clothing identifiable as being technologically equipped attracts attention and could make the wearer a walking target. This is why Barillova believes in systems that can be concealed within jewellery and accessories. 'Technology is now evolving faster than fashion trends, and for the time being, it's pointless to try and confine it to a specific dress code or type of garment,' she said. And from Barillova's perspective, a fashion garment designed to incorporate wiring and interfaces is already redundant, because her technology is all wire-free.

As a spy, Barillova's clothing and even her looks would have had to change from mission to mission, or several times a day for an incognito operation. Because communication activity can be tracked and traced, it makes it more difficult for the wearer to escape detection. Devices, unlike clothing, can be dumped quickly to prevent compromising information from getting into the wrong hands. Intelligent clothing that integrates fashion and technology is not always practical from a surveillance point of view, though it has applications for other kinds of communication and information technology.

Barillova's familiarity with the sensors, cameras and microphones inspired her to investigate the feasibility of planting sensors on people. Communication and video technologies are much bulkier than sensors, so one of the initial phases of Charmed's research was aimed at reducing their size. 'If you look at the diameter of an ordinary pen, we can even make cameras smaller than that. They can be fitted into clothing easily,' Barillova explained. This is a difficult process, because just reducing them in scale does not work, as not all technologies are easy to downsize. A microphone-bugging device is easy to make wearable, but it would take a lot of work to reduce a mobile phone to the size of a tiny earpiece, and even more skill to craft them as fashionable earrings.

Making technology fashionable is a big part of what Barillova is trying to do now. Stealth is a good description of the way her technologies work; their futuristic aesthetic gives contemporary fashion a subtle twist and enables the wearer to do things most others would not expect. Barillova is confident that it will work as a 'look', and eventually appear normal, perhaps even attractive. 'The idea of stealth in fashion is sexy, the technology itself can make you look sexy,' she said. The wireless prototypes Charmed demonstrated in 2002 featured metallic curves, unusual contours and futuristic shapes, and are discreet in size.

Charmed's headset displays, transmitter earrings, necklaces, bracelets and rings are ultimately made in a functional context. Technological products rarely have any aesthetic value in the fashion world – but Charmed is inverting this norm by designing

Surveillance may mean that in order to see you have to be seen. Charmed Technology disguise surveillance systems as fashion accessories and sunglasses.

products to be clothing accessories rather than 'wearables'. Barillova feels confident that Charmed's products will engineer a symbiosis between technology and fashionable dress, and give technology new significance in the fashion world. 'In the technology I find beautiful shapes and they can look very fashionable. Our vision is to make computers that resemble everyday fashion objects,' Barillova said. 'Only then will people stop fearing technology.'

Once Charmed's prototypes were up and running they decided to present them in fashion shows rather than confine them to static exhibitions. The *Brave New Unwired World* fashion shows were staged in London and Berlin at Internet World 2000. Charmed presented male and female models wearing futuristic clothing and demonstrating the prototypes on the catwalk. 'They made you look sexy and powerful, the kind of thing fashion designers are trying to achieve anyway,' Barillova said. The shows featured products like 'The Communicator', a wireless broadband Internet device designed to be activated by voice, a hand-held remote and a wireless keyboard. An eyepiece allows the user to see the equivalent of a full computer screen right in front of one eye, yet still have peripheral vision. The Communicator provides video technologies that relay the wearer's vision back to base, or receive images relayed from a remote source. This two-way transmission was played back to the audience on the catwalk's screen backdrop.

Surveillance is also possible without cameras. Charmed are developing a bracelet/armband that acts as a wearable body monitor to relay data about the wearer back to a central base. The device can contain sensors that monitor the wearer's vital signs, or track their physical movements. In a corporate environment, employees could be tracked by systems like these, and even their brainwaves monitored. A communicating badge is being pioneered that simultaneously transmits and receives information through filters programmed to match the wearer's criteria. The badge will even be able to monitor people in a social environment by locking on to their coordinates.

Barillova's vision makes it possible to wear your life on your sleeve, or even outsmart CCTV systems when you need to. Thorogood and Vexed Generation may be able to provide sophisticated camouflage to obscure identity, but will fashion ever be able to antidote the type of surveillance mediated through information technology? As social control shifts to data systems, visual surveillance is becoming outmoded by sensors and key fobs that track access to buildings, and credit-card transactions that can be relayed at a speed that pinpoints an individual's location before they have had time to leave the shop. Perhaps fashion's engagement with surveillance will one day be considered purely nostalgic, heralding a desire to return to an exclusively visual world.

four

Cybercouture

There is nothing more cutting-edge in fashion today than the pooling of minds into an immense, interdisciplinary collaboration. It is already widespread in art, design and architecture; now contemporary fashion designers are taking the new opportunities that come with developments in multimedia technologies and systems of mass telecommunication. Cyberspace, as a realm of intersecting practices, presents designers with a forum where fashion can be represented digitally, or shown on an interactive platform. As technology continues to evolve, so does the potential to take the consumption and presentation of fashion in a new direction altogether.

Cyberspace is a concept that 'names the space of information exchange that already exists in the flow of databases, telephone and fibre-optic networks, computer memory and other parts of electronic networking services.'[1] In one sense, cyberspace is an intangible construction that identifies a horizon of contemporary thought, but in another it is regarded as a 'real' space on the fringe of mainstream culture. It is here that fashion is becoming directly aligned with information technology, visual representations and interactivity, creating a fashion ethos known as 'Cybercouture'. Moving away from retail boutiques, couture showrooms and catwalk events, individual garments or whole collections can be webcast on the Internet or viewed through digital technology. Fashion is now interfacing with the evolving subculture of computer-generated realities, science fiction and far-reaching visual technologies.

Fashion's new affinity with cyberspace reflects a gradual shift away from traditional methods of designing, presenting and selling clothing. Emerging and established designers alike are beginning to eschew the norm of the Fashion Week catwalk show, gravitating towards cinematic, webcast, or installation-style presentations. Pia Myrvold has explored the breadth and depth of presenting and creating collections in cyberspace, while designers such as Julian Roberts, Russell Sage and Simon Thorogood chart the possibilities of cinematic fashion shows and digital installations. As the work of these and other designers is explored, fashion's break with traditional systems and processes unfolds, as does its future in a landscape of visual technology.

Pia Myrvold

The manifesto of fashion's future could have been written by Pia Myrvold, whose fashion collections turn the icons of modern technology into wearable couture. Originally from Norway but based in Paris for several years before launching her label in New York in 2001, Myrvold gives a technological twist to contemporary fashion by bringing cyberspace into the fashion arena. Myrvold is not a 'techie' or a systems expert – she is a trained painter and musician turned fashion designer who finds inspiration in the possibilities offered by cyberspace. She operates within the traditional horizons of fashion design and manufacture, but reconfigures them into her own system of Web interactivity. Working within cyberspace allows her to pioneer new relationships between fashion, technologies and social narratives, as well as giving her a platform to challenge traditional ideas about the fashioned body, cultural concerns and methodology.

Myrvold creates her innovative range of couture-inspired clothing via her website, www.cybercouture.com. This departure from conventional fashion resulted from her mission to circulate the ideas behind her collections – essential to grasping what each garment represents – simultaneously with the clothes. Myrvold's fascination with multimedia and information technologies led her to the interactive potential of the Internet. Web interactivity, though still dependent on photo-based media, makes this new information-based approach to fashion possible.

'The Internet had none of the limitations of other media; sound, image, film, text or voice could overlap freely and create new contexts,' Myrvold said. 'I also realised that a truly interdisciplinary universe could be linked by technology to the clothes and from the clothes into practical reality.'[2] Myrvold is emphatic that she uses the Internet because of its practicality rather than its novelty. In fact, she operates in a manner that is almost antithetical to novelty. She usually uses the same platform and format for each collection, changing only the garments and range of prints, and the texts that accompany the collection. Myrvold's method of presenting her collections interactively is still ground-breaking, and seems to satisfy the media's fascination with novelty. With every development in her fabric technologies, software, or textural collaborations, the media had something to report, but frustrated Myrvold by focusing more on the garments than the message behind them. 'Journalists simply accused me of being "too difficult to understand",' Myrvold said. 'The fashion Press, which first seemed impressed by the originality of the clothes, had great problems relating to the larger issues that lay behind them. Journalists needed to simplify the message in order to make it less threatening to themselves and a scattered public that was buying fewer and fewer fashion magazines.'

For Myrvold, cyberspace is both process and agent. Through the Internet she has established a forum in which to merge fashion with ideas reflecting art, architecture, philosophy and music. It also allows her to operate outside the traditional fashion system, and the space to produce collections that confront unethical workshop conditions and beauty ideals rather than reinforce them. 'My challenge was to try to produce and compete within this reality while not representing its false ideals,' she said of the fashion industry. Myrvold consciously designs for a range of body types and body shapes; her cybercouture is made in accordance with the wearer's measurements to render any fit they require. She resists advertising her clothes in campaigns that would specifically target the 'tall, thin and beautiful' stereotypes that dominate visual culture.

Parallel to the fashion collection is the editorial space on her website, titled 'Clothes as Publishing', that expands her ethics and concepts textually. Myrvold invites 'prominent leaders in the various media to contribute,' consisting of artists, writers, musicians and philosophers who wish to communicate their ideas through the clothes or open a dialogue about a current issue. Myrvold hopes this type of discussion will provide an antidote to what she feels is the irresponsible behaviour of mainstream fashion and the fashion media. According to Myrvold: 'They don't concern themselves with issues that scream for attention in our time; no questions asked, no solutions offered, just sell and survive, by any means possible.'

The interactive, or fashion-as-message approach is also used by other designers to voice protests or communicate resistance. New York design label Imitation of Christ, for example, also reacted against the values of the fashion world by using non-conformist methods of producing appropriated, recycled or regenerated clothes. Imitation of Christ, designed by Matt Damhave and Tara Subkoff, incorporated handwritten manifestos, such as 'Hold no brand sacred', 'Do not worship false idols', 'Gucci is greed' and 'No justice, no pleats'.

Myrvold describes her clothes as a 'blank page' – an interactive project which her clients can participate in through the website. A new collection is launched each season which clients can scan through quickly, and with a click and a drag of the mouse, decide how they would like their choices put together.

Each garment is initially displayed in white; once selected the image rotates three-dimensionally to display the garment's construction and detail. Clients can browse among the current range of prints, or drag them onto the garment to get a scaled view of how the pattern will look on their choice of garment. While they are 'shopping', clients are free to experiment with a range of options. Some garments can even feature several different prints – the sleeves can be made in one print and the body in another. Each order must include the concise measurements of the client, as each piece is made to a custom fit. The clients then email their orders to Myrvold's centralized workshop, where the garments are cut according to specification, printing the selected patterns via a heat process. Skilled craftspeople then sew the garments together and ship them to the client more or less immediately.

Myrvold's texts describe her personal views about a wide range of issues. She believes that making them available to her clients reduces the traditional degree of separation between designer and wearer. In fact, her entire design method draws the wearer closer

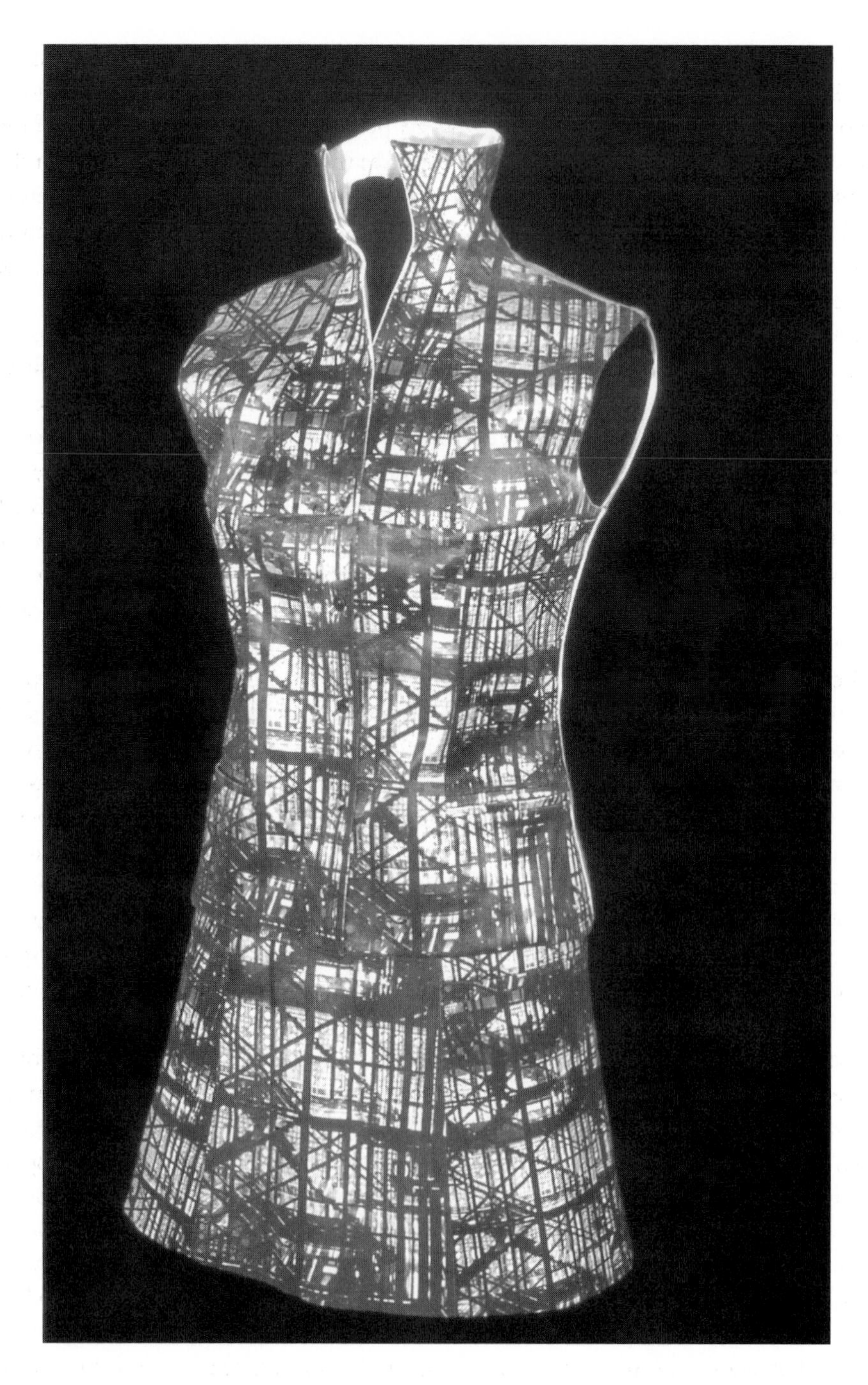

Pia Myrvold's interactive collections are constructed on her Web portal and shipped to the purchaser. Each garment is initially displayed in white; once selected the image rotates three-dimensionally as it is customized by patterns and images.

into her design process as they construct their own garments within the range of materials that she creates. This invokes questions of authorship, where the designer no longer assumes responsibility for the finished product. In a sense, the wearer's direct involvement in the garment's construction makes the interactive platform a hands-on creative process. Part of the process is to dislocate the immediacy that characterizes traditional fashion, giving the wearer a forum to individualize their clothes according to specific tastes. While conventional collections can limit the wearer to one range of mass-produced looks, Myrvold's approach emphasizes individuality.

The clothes themselves defy the boundaries of streetwear and daywear, formal and casual. Organic fabrics are gently stitched or woven to produce gossamer knitwear, while the nylons and industrial plastics are precisely tailored in streamlined silhouettes that suggest a utilitarian or futuristic identity. The clothes are functional and original, and designed with a high degree of comfort in mind. In fashion shows they are worn with a range of communication devices to emphasize their interactive potential. The *Dada Memory* and *Body Theory* collections (1997) interfaced interactivity with the built environment, characterized by sound and image loops activated by models talking into their communication transmitters and pushing buttons in the clothes while walking on the catwalk.

The prints featured in the *Female Interfaces* collection depict radios, record players and telephones as 'interfaces' of a bygone era, suggesting that these artefacts had been incorporated into the fabrics they were printed on, redefining the body as a machine interface. The *Female Interfaces* garments were equipped with interactive technology; it was so advanced that the models required special training to operate the audio-visual relays, video loops and broadcasts. Myrvold equipped the garments with communication technology to demonstrate how recent developments in technology could give clothes the means to function as Internet portals, cellular communication devices and computer software. While these advances are often shunned by traditional designers, Myrvold sees the interfaces as a shattering premonition of what clothing will become in the future.

'I bring the role of the models into the work,' Myrvold explained. 'They introduce themselves and talk about what they're wearing and experiencing, like "Hey, I'm Lisa, I'm from Brazil and this is what I'm wearing . . ." like they are rapping along with the music.' This performance pushed the boundaries of fashion's communicative properties even further, heralding a new way of receiving and processing information, and illustrating Myrvold's new information-based approach. Myrvold uses models as personifications of creative thought and action; not merely a face, but a creative unit.

Myrvold presented her autumn/winter 2001 collection at New York Fashion Week. The collection was simply titled *Cybercouture*, and was well received by the Press. Images of the cybercouture.com website were projected alongside the catwalk, broadcasting Myrvold's video, *Interference*. The show commenced with dancers from the Norwegian National Ballet moving dramatically down the catwalk *en pointe*. The show was graphic and strikingly modern, with colours and prints depicting urban and architectural details

Pia Myrvold equips garments with communication technology to show how recent developments in technology could give them the means to function as Internet portals, communication devices and computers, illustrating Myrvold's vision of what clothing will become in the future.

from Paris, New York and Bergen (Norway). One pattern was based on images of the Institut du Monde Arabe in Paris designed by Jean Nouvel, another uncovered Bergen manholes. Zipped jackets, wrap skirts and tailored coats were simple and linear, sporting printed images of the old and the new economies. Myrvold juxtaposed the images of an old-fashioned typewriter and industrial wheel cog against high-tech mesh scaffolding and a pattern of CD-ROMs.

The collection attracted the interest of Karim Rashid, resulting in their collaborative prêt-a-porter collections, *Hypermix* and *Cyberware*. The collections include one-off pieces featuring a range of Rashid's graphics, distributed both by Myrvold's website and retail boutiques. 'Working with Karim meant I needed to change my process. Using email and graphics technology means we can create one-off pieces in a collaborative way without being in the same studio together to do it. Now I scan my designs into Photoshop or Illustrator, and email the images to a factory who print out a pattern for each garment. They are then sent to the workshop to be cut and sewn together,' Myrvold explained. The garments are made in five sizes with a choice of

Pia Myrvold creates prints that link artists and designers in different disciplines and circulates their concepts in the world of fashion.

twelve different designs to choose from. *Hypermix* includes Rashid's 'Morph' graphics and images chosen from his design vocabulary.

Myrvold's choice of prints reflects themes that transport images from the world of media into the world of fashion: 'My idea linked artists from different disciplines and distributed their ideas through fashion. The garments publish the work, the contributing artist's name and, for the time being, an e-mail address.' The 'artists', Myrvold is referring to are actually musicians, writers, or architects like Jean Nouvel and Bernard Tschumi who contribute blueprints, drawings, photographs and writings that become the prints transferred onto her fabrics. Myrvold's collaboration with Tschumi began in 1992, when he commissioned her to create an installation as part of an architectural event held at Parc de la Villette. Myrvold stretched scaffolding and textile panels for five hundred metres along the canal in an interactive structure that viewers could move through.

Website clients can choose from renderings of a Nouvel building or a Tschumi park, or a musical compilation depicting DJ Dimitri's *Sacre Bleu* notations. Myrvold's collaborations with musicians or artists working with the spoken word use recordings of their voices, which are processed digitally in Photoshop into a pixellated image, then transferred onto the fabrics. Myrvold intends to blur all notions of authorship and reinforce the idea that clothing can be a communicative device with many voices. 'I always had the sense that fashion was about communication because the messages it carries impact profoundly on the way we live,' she said.

Myrvold trained as an artist before becoming a designer, and this probably accounts for her theoretical approach to fashion and her ability to interpret it as a conceptual tool. Myrvold's interests in expressing issues through her work evolved during the 1980s as she began exploring interdisciplinary art practice. She became interested in theories of Deconstruction and Post-Structuralism which were already being discussed in architecture, and decided to move away from art and interpret fashion through these theories. As a conceptualist, Myrvold never felt that working within the confines of the conventional fashion system would fully enable her to express herself. 'As I had to defend my move from artist to fashion designer, I became interested in clothes as a medium for communicating ideas, that is, ideas other than the ideas of prominence, success, beauty and the need to belong, that dominated – and still dominate – the marketing of fashion.'

Creative freedom and the space to explore and experiment are only truly possible when the designer's output is not directed by marketing demands or production methods. 'It was difficult to keep the intrinsic value of the design of the clothes, as factories demanded "streamlining" of the product and did not want to cope with spontaneous variations in a series of garments,' Myrvold explained. 'The element of chance was not allowed in the design, unless it came from carelessness in production.'

The difficulty in negotiating the line between design and commerce reinforces the designer's profile as a 'creative' rather than a businessperson. 'At first, my art career had not prepared me for the obstacles of production and distribution,' Myrvold said. 'I started out to learn everything I could, all the multiple factors that could go wrong from the time of order until the day the shipment arrives and the clothes are in the boutique. Even then, more things could go wrong; clients failing to pay, changes in the currency exchange rate, and a myriad of other unforeseen circumstances. Even this process was, for an already established artist, quite ridiculous and time consuming.' By selling directly to clients on the Internet, Myrvold is able to manage production, distribution and cashflow more effectively, and detect potential obstacles before they get out of control.

Because fashion is structured in accordance with an established commercial system, it may take time to expand her client base through the Internet. In the meantime, Myrvold continues to use the fashion system as a vehicle for the distribution of both her clothes and her ideas. The presence of her clothes in boutiques, fashion shows and magazine photo shoots throughout the world will, she feels, broadcast her ethos within the clothes themselves. This is partly why Myrvold shows some of her collections on the official schedule during Fashion Weeks in Paris and New York. By capitalizing on fashion's ability to reach the mainstream public, she decided to use the shows as a

Myrvold's spring/summer 2003 collection 'The Bridge' also launched the eighth edition of her 'Clothes as Publishing' project. Myrvold used digital technology to 'publish' a range of Karim Rashid's motifs on the surface of her designs.

vehicle to introduce her philosophy to the fashion world. 'Rather than showing an installation in a gallery or lecturing at a university, I attempted to bring these ideas into the clothes and into the fashion shows that large numbers of people around the world perceive on intellectual and subliminal levels,' Myrvold explained.

Myrvold's philosophy extends beyond her website to engage with communities to address and improve a wide range of societal issues. The production workshop that makes her clothes is not a normal factory, but an integrated part of the cybercouture infrastructure that encourages the workers to have creative input into each garment they make.

As an example of how she envisages the role of the cybercouture workshop unfolding over time, Myrvold recalled a proposal she made to relocate her workshop to Kirkenes, a small village in the northeast of Norway. Kirkenes is situated on the Russian border, which is an important strategic location for the North Atlantic Treaty Organisation (NATO). The local mining industry had closed down, and few employment opportunities existed for the ten thousand people living in the community.

Concerned with the depopulation of this area, the Norwegian government encouraged initiatives to promote new industry. A women's group contacted Myrvold and asked if she wanted to base her workshop there, in line with the government's incentives to attract new industry to the area. Excited by the prospect of opening a workshop as part of an urban renewal scheme, Myrvold drew up a business plan for a 'cultural factory' that would manufacture and ship custom-made clothing ordered on her website. Her plan was to form a local investment group to set up and equip a workshop where workers from the area could combine art and craft skills with the design and pattern-cutting techniques necessary to print fabrics and sew garments. As a result, Myrvold hoped to unify the construction and philosophy within the garment, avoiding the kind of production and distribution problems she had experienced in the assembly-line methods of conventional factory production.

The women's group recognized the potential of Myrvold's proposal to create a cultural centre, where locals could find inspiration and new ideas by having direct access to Paris from Kirkenes, even sending young people on internship placements in Myrvold's Paris studio. Myrvold's prophetic vision is to make it feasible for cyber-couture workers to operate under an ethos that is more creative and less commercial than traditional fashion production. Unfortunately, a local committee voted against Myrvold's proposal, opting instead to build sheep farms. Nevertheless, Myrvold's proposal presented an inspiring vision of how fashion can be used to spark economical or cultural revitalization.

Like Myrvold, other conceptual designers are known for finding alternative routes to the traditional methods of fashion presentation. As early as 1996, Walter Van Beirendonck was presenting his collections on the Internet and on CD-ROMs; the CD-ROM even gave instructions on how other designers could copy his garments. In 1998, Helmut Lang showed his entire collection on the Web during Fashion Week rather than produce a catwalk show. Jeff Griffin showed his collection on the Internet the same year, being one of the first British designers to do so. Victoria's Secret unveiled its spring/summer 2001 collection by live simulcast from their website, tapping into the cyberspace obsession of millions worldwide, generating unprecedented media hype by giving the public access to an exclusively 'private' event.

Victor & Rolf presented their spring 2001 collection on a CD-ROM, which was handed out to buyers and journalists. Using the Web or digital means can transcend the boundaries of time and space and overcome the problems of geographical distance. This makes a collection available to more spectators than could ever be accommodated at a fashion show. The Web-based collection also provides a platform for showcasing experimental design or tangential projects that the designers may not be able to explore in a live show.

Without the benefit of history, it is not easy to predict how cyberspace will affect the way designers present their collections to the world. Undoubtedly, it will have a revolutionary role that extends far beyond that of the boutique, showroom or private fashion show. With each advance in technology, pioneers like Myrvold are able to engineer connections and interfaces that may bring the fashion world online for good.

nothing nothing

Julian Roberts is an unpredictable designer: cerebral, where other designers are radical; non-conformist in the face of tradition; a leader of innovation rather than a follower. Perhaps his approach is more typical of a filmmaker – he draws heavily on the principles and practicalities of film production in his fashion work, because he makes films in between collections. In fact, he spends a lot of time making films about the collections themselves.

That said, Roberts's fashion shows have more in common with the art world than the film world. Cinematic presentations of his work are more akin to video installations or film screenings than a catwalk show. This is fine with him; Roberts is happy to churn out film after film. Over the years he has made a number of films in 35ml, super-8 and digital video (DV) which he exhibited at art events, and produced music videos for underground pop groups and British bands.

Roberts's label 'nothing nothing' has always been considered avant-garde and highly creative. 'I called it that because that's all I had to start it with,' he said cynically.[3] But those in the know nicknamed Roberts' label 'everything everything', because of the big ideas and ambitious projects he had in mind. By the time he started his own label, he had received an MA degree from the Royal College of Art, survived a two-year stint working alongside Jasper Conran (a period he describes as 'very frustrating'), and accrued enough business acumen to attract financial sponsorship. nothing nothing quickly gained acclaim on the London fashion scene, and began showing on the Fashion Week schedule a year and half later. And just as soon as he achieved this, Roberts decided it was time to move in a new direction.

'I'm trying to push fashion forward,' he said simply. 'London's got this reputation for being an innovative place, with lots of interesting fashion. Yet, the designers here keep showing their collections exactly like designers in Paris, New York and Milan do. We need something else,' he said. Mainstream fashion of the last fifty years has done little more than make stylistic changes within an existing matrix. True innovation in fashion is rare – a radical change in direction even more so. Though fashion is an industry that praises innovation more than others, most of the industry do not welcome it or encourage it, and few designers know how to produce it.

While Roberts was rethinking the presentation of his work, he made a film about the next collection, and decided to screen it at his Fashion Week show instead of having a catwalk. 'There are a lot of restrictions imposed at Fashion Week,' he said. 'The British Fashion Council don't recognise cinematic presentation as a legitimate fashion show, so the film projection had to be made off the official schedule.' As an added blow, he

Frustrated by the restrictions imposed by catwalk shows, Julian Roberts made a film about his collection instead, and screened it as a colossal video projection at London Fashion Week. The video was projected directly onto the façade of the Natural History Museum.

later discovered that newspaper picture editors would not publish film stills or photographs of a film installation in the fashion pages.

'Actually nothing nothing is not just a fashion label – it includes projects in other media that aren't fashion based,' Roberts said. Staging an off-schedule show gave him scope to present the label as he envisaged it, rather than limiting the presentation to the collection alone. 'I was looking for new means of mediating and communicating which don't have to be in a magazine and on a catwalk,' he continued. Roberts felt that producing a catwalk show limited his range of expression, because he had to delegate so much into the hands of other people who may want to show his work in a different light. 'It's hard to control the catwalk presentation of the collection. Once it starts going on you have a high-pressure situation where you have input from stylists and show producers, and you have models to worry about. You get more control of the show if you film or photograph it, then edit it yourself and project it.'

The catwalk audience generally assume that the show they see is a direct message from the designer. In the case of a large-scale Fashion Week show, technicians and producers get involved to make it all happen. The show brings together commerce and culture on the catwalk, which the media project to an audience fascinated by image and identity. 'After all, fashion is a communication process,' Roberts explained. 'Designers make clothing, which is then interpreted by a stylist. PR people reinterpret what the stylists make of the clothes, then put their spin on it to convince an agent it's the right image for their celebrities. The celebrities then wear it to send their own message, and the public then interpret it in association with other things.'

Each nothing nothing collection centres around a basic design vocabulary of twenty signature garments, which reappear each season in different forms. Part of Roberts's ethos is to work within these existing designs, progressing them and finding new expression in them rather than basing new collections on emerging trends or retro styles. 'I'm not caught up in this cycle where each collection has to be a new trend or based on something new. I like to keep working with my basic designs and find new ways of cutting them and new fabrics for them, then show new versions of them each season,' he explained. 'The clothes I make for nothing nothing are created through a complicated process. They are limited editions – I do it once, and that's it.'

The *One of One* collection explored the theme of duplication and replication to investigate the links between fashion multiples and one-of-a-kind pieces. Because the garments would never be reproduced, Roberts was free to use limited-edition fabrics and elaborate processes that could not be used in garments created in mass production. nothing nothing's reverence for the one-off is not a criticism of designer multiples, but a means of communicating a message of individuality. 'Everyone who buys fashion wants to be part of an image, so the one I show here is about individuality rather than a generic look,' Roberts said.

'All of my designs are very simple shapes to start with, then transform as I work with them and explore the fabric. By the time I get to the final version, the original shape has replicated itself several times to evolve into a complex design. The final versions are therefore complex designs that morph out of simple shapes,' Roberts said. *One of One* included the 'Virus Print Dress', featuring a motif that resulted from myriad replications of an original. Virus Print consists of a pattern of desktop folder icons found in Photoshop software. The folder icons were duplicated thousands of times through the software, then made into a digital print. 'The first folder I created called itself "original" by default, then the second one called itself "original copy one", the third "original copy two" and so on,' Roberts explained, 'so you can see how far away from the original idea you get when you copy it over and over.'

British fashion, at the beginning of the millennium, seemed to be in a state of flux conceptually as well as geographically. Most of the young design talent that gives British fashion its 'cutting-edge' hallmark were showing their collections in the East End of London, or online, and Fashion Week began to have the staid feel that it had before Galliano and McQueen appeared on the scene. Roberts's off-schedule shows had received publicity and press acclaim, and the British Fashion Council wanted him back. Roberts had been planning a large-scale outdoor projection that season, so plans were made to present it on the official schedule. The Natural History Museum[4] eventually

Each nothing nothing collection centres around a basic design vocabulary of twenty signature garments, which reappear each season in different forms. Rather than basing new collections on emerging trends or retro styles, new expression is found in existing designs.

agreed that Roberts could project a film onto the building's façade, so he made plans to project a 150 square-foot image.

The British Fashion Council predicted that the event would boost media attention, so Roberts used the presentation as a forum to launch his second label, 'JULIAN AND'. 'My new label JULIAN AND defies definition because each season I work in collaboration with a different designer,' he explained. 'As a second label it gives me a chance to work with other people and progress that way, plus produce a ready-to-wear line. Because nothing nothing is about one-off designs JULIAN AND will give me a chance to reach more people.'

The film's soundtrack was a musical score composed by Japanese recording artist Ryo-co, performed by a live band. The film was produced to create a mood of what the label represented, rather than leave viewers with an impression of a new trend or new look. 'The film was made to deconstruct the perfect moment of "the pose" captured in a fashion shoot. I wanted to show how contrived that moment is, by filming everything else going on; the build up to it, the tension it creates, and the relaxation afterwards,' Roberts said. 'I organised a two-day photo shoot and filmed it, so there are photographs of the filming and film footage of the photography.'

Working with film led Roberts to explore the use of digital technology in fashion, which in turn influenced the type of work he did. 'The digital stuff I learned in film is crossing over into the fashion. I'm using it to manipulate pictures and print them onto clothes by heat transfer or silkscreen, and using digital film stills as prints,' Roberts said. 'For the *One of One* collection the print was scanned digitally and sprayed onto the cloth by digital inkjets filled with dye, then the fabric was steamed to fix the print.'

Both nothing nothing and JULIAN AND are communicated through the use of film, drawing and text, in a method that reveals the process of their construction from initial idea to finished product. This suggests a deconstructivist dimension to nothing nothing's design, without the tearing and shredding characteristic of the deconstructivist style. In essence, they appear to be more reconstuctivist, because the process of their creation is shown as a chronology, rather than dismantled to expose how they were made. 'I'm not deconstructing or reconstructing,' Roberts said. 'What I'm doing is structuring and constructing – I'm interested in showing the structure of garments and the process behind making them, behind the catwalk, behind fashion itself. To show the process I have to use media outside fashion, so I use film, video and photography for that.' Roberts is also keen to explore how digital technology and computer programmes can factor into the process. 'My pattern construction would be much easier if I could work with a programmer and create software that would guide the cutting and folding. That way other people could use it too,' he said. 'It would be such a big advance in pattern cutting. Because you are working two-dimensionally and have to try and imagine how it looks three-dimensionally, it would save a lot of time.'

'There is a big movement to return to using vintage and antique fabrics but I usually source synthetic fabrics that hold shapes well. I am always on the lookout for supermodern fabrics because I use microfibres a lot. I like mechanical polyesters that have bounce, because I need fabrics that have tactility and lightness,' Roberts said. The technological development of textiles is driven by high-volume fashion companies that want to engineer high-performance materials that are substantially cheaper than woven fabrics. Some smaller design labels prefer classic fabrics because they become an emblem of their originality, others do not have a choice. 'It can be quite tricky to buy supermodern fabrics,' Roberts said. 'The factories try and tell you the minimum order you can place is 300 metres when you only need five, and then getting them into the country past customs isn't always easy.'

Roberts relates the process of a garment's construction in terms of lived experience, as though each garment developed its own sense of identity during the construction process: 'In the process of designing and making the clothes and presenting them to the public they become imbued with all those sentiments along the way to reaching the wearer.' He wants to communicate this sense of the garment's history, which fashion normally takes steps to erase. His film presentations usually juxtaposes the garment's construction with the finished version. Roberts places static models dressed in the collection alongside the film installation, so that spectators can interact with them physically. 'I like what Pia Myrvold is starting but I would never want to do a webcast collection or a digital collection alone. Virtual environments lose human contact, and human contact is what you need in fashion,' he explained. 'I think a lot of collections shown on the website don't sell because of that – that's why so many fashion.com sites went under. Clothes need touch and feel, and that requires a human factor.'

Grey Area

Grey Area is a design collaborative established to pioneer new and innovative ways of progressing fashion. By resisting the traditional platform of the catwalk show, and focusing on revealing the design process, the designers want to demystify fashion by bringing the audience closer to its reality. The group was founded by Julian Roberts and British fashion designer Russell Sage, who set up Grey Area following the successes of their mixed-media presentations. Sage has long been acclaimed for his unconventional fashion shows, and his collaborations with film and other media. Roberts and Sage came together to acknowledge a 'middle-ground' between fashion, video, music and art, which, according to Roberts, was the inspiration for the group's name: 'It's called Grey Area because it hasn't really defined itself yet.'

Part of their agenda is to create a platform for other designers interested in using digital technology and film-making techniques in the presentations of their collections. Roberts and Sage hope their impact will change the current format of Fashion Week shows and make them less routine and restrictive, and expand beyond the fashion scene. 'We expand the whole idea of what fashion is, because we show that it doesn't end at clothing,' Roberts said.

Artistic control is important to Roberts and Sage, because their expression of fashion clearly extends beyond the clothes themselves. They see the garment, the medium, the message and the concepts behind each collection as one means of interrelated expression. Dislocating any one of these from the other would dilute the message of them all. 'Usually for a catwalk show the trend is for the designer to work with a show producer, stylists or an art director, meaning it can be harder for them to keep things going the way they want it to,' Roberts explained. 'When designers work with film, they have complete artistic control. As they set it up, film it, edit it and produce it they are extending the creative process. It enables them to create a mood but also create exactly what they want.'

Grey Area's exhibition at the ICA in London for the spring/summer 2001 collections was a fashion first. The event included four fashion collections, five film premieres and one interactive digital catwalk show. Roberts and Sage presented work alongside fashion designers Simon Thorogood and Ebru Ercon, and a short film directed by Anna-Nicole Ziesche. Thorogood presented his collection in the form of a 'Digital Runway', a computerized catwalk show that used virtual models. Each item in the collection was projected onto a screen controlled by the audience, giving viewers scope to interact with the running of the show. The catwalk was built with a layer of pressure-sensitive padding which viewers were encouraged to walk on. As the pressure-sensitive pads were triggered, the projector activated images of different garments.

Ercon and Sage used live models in their fashion shows. Ercon equipped each model with a sound transmitter that changed frequency as they crossed paths with each other. Micro-cameras in the garments relayed the chaos backstage in real time, projected onto a screen in the audience. The cameras revealed a madhouse of naked women, discarded dresses and frantic stylists, juxtaposed against the tranquillity of the slow movements on the catwalk. Sage famously filmed the descent of his own parachute jump from an aeroplane, then used the parachute itself as the fabric for his spring/summer 2001 collection. Using live models against a backdrop of his film, Sage's work made powerful statements about fashion and society; danger, risks and survival; and transforming cast-offs into beautiful new shapes.

Anna-Nicole Ziesche's film explored the life cycle of clothing. The film featured an image of half a garment reflected in a mirror to create the illusion of a full shape. As a woman undressed, quickly pulling off layer after layer of clothes, the colours and the mirror image created a kaleidoscope effect. The film was projected as a continuous loop, creating the illusion of a never-ending garment that morphed into new garments.

Roberts screened three films, presented as a cinematic triptych. The films were projected simultaneously, positioned side by side along the vertical axis of the screen. The first film recorded a journey around London on a sightseeing bus, played at high speed. The second film was made collaboratively with digital architect John Jong to render a three-dimensional virtual model of the ICA's theatre, where the collection was presented. The third film showed models wearing the collection underwater, in an otherworldly dreamscape that could have been the mythological Atlantis or a surrealist painting. The three films merged into one spectacular image that represented an aesthetic journey of clothes and states of consciousness. 'The films weren't made to take you anywhere in a narrative sense. I like approaching video as a visual phenomena,' Roberts said. Eight garments of the twenty made for spring/summer 2001 were worn by static models, each one positioned on a podium alongside the screen and lit from above.

As Grey Area make high fashion available to a wider audience, they are also promoting a new way of interpreting fashion. The cinematic dimension entices viewers into a world beyond their field of vision, altering fashion's visual grammar. The more remote in time and place it is, the more surreal it seems – activating more ideas and possibilities about the individual garments and the atmosphere the designer is creating. The response Grey Area received from the 'seen it all' fashion pack has generally been a positive one, apart from complaints that there was no seating. 'We have had some dramatic reactions in the past because people came expecting to see a catwalk show but got film instead. I'm always surprised at how the Press react by not getting the format they are used too,' Roberts said.

Expectation is everything in the fashion world, where catwalk shows are often viewed as entertainment events, generating the same excitement as the opening of a new play or the premiere of a film. Asked to describe what she thought about New York Fashion Week one season, Liza Minnelli reportedly quipped, 'Fantastic . . . fashion is the new theatre.' In 1984, Thierry Mugler staged his *prêt-a-porter* fashion show as an enormous rock concert. With the help of a rock impresario, Mugler orchestrated a cast of fifty to perform to an audience of six thousand. Mugler broke the tradition where only invited guests could attend a fashion show, by making most of the tickets available for sale to the public.

Grey Area's installations draw large audiences from the worlds of art, film, fashion and media, but also attract students, members of the general public and passers-by. This group is the opposite of the typical fashion show audience, who number themselves among an elite few. 'A fashion show is more difficult for an ordinary person to relate to – a model and a catwalk isn't a part of lived experience,' Roberts said. 'When you make a film, almost anyone can relate to it because everyone goes to the cinema and watches television.'

Interpreting the presentation in terms of cinematic structure makes it more complex because the viewer is influenced by *mise en scène*, editing and location. 'Some people may judge the collection like they are critiquing a film,' Roberts admitted, 'But most of them see it as something new, an innovative expression of different media.'

After four successful catwalk shows, British fashion designer Jeff Griffin decided to move away from the catwalk concept and explore new directions through interactions with designers from other disciplines. His fashion installations express as much about the space they were shown in and the people he worked with as they did the clothes themselves. Griffin began using a static format in 1995, producing a sculptural, technological installation for the Design Council in London, which was also staged in Tokyo. For the autumn/winter 1999 collection, Griffin produced a short film with Donald Christie, which was broadcast on Channel 4 during London Fashion Week. The film depicted the lifestyle of a fictitious pop star waiting in an airport. While waiting for the plane, he gradually became cocooned in his clothing, making a statement about Griffin's remit to use clothing as shelter and protection (Griffin is discussed further in Chapter 6).

Showing on-schedule at an official Fashion Week event is prohibitively expensive for most designers, whether they show in London, Paris, New York or Milan. For designers who show off-schedule, the cost of model's fees, venue hire, stage design, lighting and staff overheads are still overwhelming. Monetary restrictions and regulations imposed by the Fashion Week management make it difficult to realize abstract ideas in that format. Like the performance artists of the 1960s and 1970s, this structure pushes designers on alternative paths to find new platforms for showing their work. It has been suggested that fashion collections shown in this context should be entitled to Arts Council funding.

This is part of the reason that digital shows are becoming more and more popular, because they can be produced at a fraction of the cost of a live show. This gives designers the flexibility to present the collection in an unconventional space, or webcast the collection over the Internet instead. Presenting collections off the beaten track can make a strong statement about the designer's influences, particularly since conceptual designers, as Grey Area illustrate, often connect their collection to the worlds of film and music.

Simon Thorogood launched his acclaimed *White Noise* collection in an east London art space in 1998. 'First of all, it cost a lot of money to have a show at Fashion Week, and if you want to transform it into something really exciting, it's very expensive,' Thorogood said.[5] *White Noise* was a *tour de force* in collaboration with, Spore and the electronic musicians, Barbed. 'Working with a composer and having a band at the opening was a way of interacting with other artists. The "sampledelic" and "collage" sounds they played said something about the clothes beyond the space itself,' he explained. The installation featured garments suspended from the ceiling that rotated along with a synchronized light and music production. Forty computer monitors displayed key inspirations behind the collection, ranging from images of early computer graphics to the musical wizardry of Brian Eno. 'I see fashion as a site for many infinite variations and permutations. Like a band uses a producer to cut an album, I take different influences and edit them into a single,' Thorogood continued. 'Fashion, in its broadest definition is about flux. So in terms of representing movement or sculpture it can embrace all sorts of things, which I think is truly exciting.'

The off-schedule fashion event addresses an ever-growing need for young designers to present their work and ideas outside the conventional catwalk show. Martin Margiela began exploring offbeat presentation in his early collections. In 1989, he showed in a basement disco, opening the show the public and even placing an advert in the free newspaper *Paris Boum Boum*. The following season he showed on an urban wasteland, inviting local children to participate in the show. In 1991, he sent a handwritten telephone number, instead of an invitation, which connected callers to an answering machine giving the time and address of the show. Recently, he has also removed both models and catwalk from his presentations, and showed his clothes on video screens, and even suspended on hangers held by assistants in white lab coats.

Rather than being driven by the demands of the fashion media, as is the case with catwalk events, these designers do not create shows merely to be marketing ploys. The designers who work according to conceptual inspiration are generally marginalized by the mainstream Press, attracting the attention of edgier publications like *Dazed & Confused*, *Purple*, *Tank*, *Merge*, *Flaunt* and *Surface**. Inter-media collaborations often result between conceptual designers and 'edgy' publishers, particularly since many of them do not trust mainstream magazines to style their clothes as they were made to be seen.

While some designers view Web-based fashion platforms and digitized design methods as harbingers of vast beginnings, others think that fashion's alliance with technology signals the death of fashion as we know it. They recognize a danger that it may eventually become just another high-tech phenomenon, propelled and defined by the parameters of technology instead of designed and conceived spontaneously.

Digital technology and cyberspace are the newest and perhaps the most alien manifestations of fashion in the contemporary world. From the innovations we have seen here, the twenty-first century promises to be a time where fashion designers will ignore rules and traditions, and invent themselves a new future. Cyberspace holds the potential to be a wonderful landscape of designer collections that express new concepts and lead the fashion establishment in a fresh direction. While it make take time to transcend traditional design methods and presentation platforms, fashion looks set for a course through cyberspace, which may prove to be its next frontier.

five

Intelligent Fashion

Whatever you think of Geek Chic, you have to give the techies credit: they have embraced the world of fashion a lot quicker than the fashionistas have embraced technology. Hardly any of the new 'intelligent' fashion has yet made its catwalk debut, but these visionary styles are predicted to revolutionize fashion forever. To fashion techies,[1] a dress is no longer a dress, but a wearable computer interface. Their goal is to take the concept of clothing as we know it to its very limits – integrating software, communication devices, sensors and speech-recognition systems into garments to make them think for the wearer. Systems like these would give garments the capacity to surf the Internet, make telephone calls, store and retrieve computer files, monitor the wearer's vital signs and administer medication without the wearer even noticing. In what technologists hope will be a seamless merger, high-tech computer systems will soon be a part of the everyday wardrobe, giving these 'prêt-a-portal' garments an active role in how we interface with the world around us.

The vision of these technologists promises a future so rich in wireless systems that we may not even realize technology is there at all. But the key to making this possible depends on the extent to which the industries of fashion, communication and information technology can forge an alliance and work towards the same goal. While the fashion industry would have to embrace new production technologies in order to create intelligent clothing, communication platforms would have to converge and create a network that can relay a broader range of signals. New research and developments in these areas not only indicate ground-breaking possibilities and future directions for these and related industries, but also question the future of fashion itself. Will it be possible to reject intelligent fashion and still lead a productive life professionally and socially? Will the choice of fashion be health-based, if, for example, a techno textile is prescribed as medication or skincare? Will it be possible for the wearer to create a personal style?

The applications intelligent clothing presents for businesses and the workplace are infinite, but paradoxically they create just as many obstacles to overcome. While integrating diagnostic systems into clothing could revolutionize the health care industry, the potential health hazards associated with wireless devices means it will take some time for researchers to assess the risks. The military have established projects to research intelligent garments that would enhance the protective properties of combat gear and equip them with telecommunication systems. In the initial prototypes the weight of the batteries necessary to power them makes them impractical for long-range missions until an alternative energy source is developed.

Integrating fashion and technology could also pave the way for fashion to interact with home products, furniture and architectural accessories, and eventually integrate them into the built environment. If invisible sensors could be embedded almost anywhere, then shoes could announce to the house that they are approaching the front door, and doorknobs could recognize the occupant's touch. Clothing and household devices will also be connected to the Internet, enabling you to email a recipe to your kitchen and have it automatically cooked for you. Voice-recognition software will activate doors and gates to open, eliminating the need for keys and entry codes. Living in intelligent houses and wearing intelligent clothes is predicted to lead to living in an intelligent world.[2]

Fashion has not been chosen as a vehicle for technology because of any inherent intelligence of its own, but because, as a medium, it is versatile, mobile, universal and adaptable, and can act as a conduit for a body area network, which provides the backbone for intelligent clothing. The network allows the transport of data, power and control signals within the wearer's personal space. Modular devices with functions shared by different applications can be connected to it: for example, a single display can be used for mobile-phone communication, email and audio track selection. Intelligent software ensures that the devices cooperate in an efficient way: muting the CD player when the mobile phone rings, for example. This modular network system and a user-friendly design make it possible to configure the system to match the wearer's choice of interaction, rather than requiring the wearer to adapt their behaviour to accommodate the system.

The possibilities for technologized clothing have expanded due to the availability of smaller, cheaper and more powerful electronic components, and the availability of wireless communication and portable computers. These have already been used in jackets containing partially integrated mobile phones and music systems, and in wearable data ports developed for use in factory production. Although most of the products like these seriously stretch the 'intelligence' label, researchers are optimistic that these gadgets will carve a path through consumer scepticism that intelligence wear can one day exploit. The sophisticated garments described by the terms 'smart clothing', 'intelligent wear' and 'clothes that think' are mostly in development stage, or exist as prototypes that are not yet commercially available.

Wearable technology first appeared on the retail fashion market in September 2000. Levi Strauss claimed to have identified a group of consumers they called 'Nomads', who move between vehicles, offices and airports, and need to be in communication at all times. Levi Strauss collaborated with Philips Electronics to design four jackets in an 'Industrial Clothing Design' range branded as the 'ICD+' label. Phillips developed the technology behind ICD+, while Levi's fitted jackets made from water-repellent, metallic-coated nylon with a simple body area network, integrating wires into their designs but not specifically into the fabric. The network interconnected a unified remote control, earphones, a Philips GSM[3] mobile phone and a Philips Rush Digital MP3 player. The remote-control network included a microphone in the jacket's collar for 'hands free' telephone calls, and a wireless remote to stop, play, fast forward, or skip music tracks on the MP3 player. Music from the MP3 player could also be played through the telephone connection. Rather than carry around three separate pieces, the wearer could buy a jacket in which they were fully integrated.

Massimo Osti, the Levi's designer behind the ICD+ range, created four models: the Beetle, the Mooring, the Producer and the TRC, a fleece vest.[4] Osti said the range was targeted at consumers who expected design and style with functionality and performance.[5] Each jacket was developed to meet three criteria: to be adaptable, to pioneer new forms and fabrics that provide protection from the elements, and to integrate the latest communication technology into its design. For Levi's, the launch of the ICD+ range signalled 'a return to its roots',[6] suggesting that the ICD+ range reinstated their original workwear aesthetic. For Philips, who had been researching the idea of wearable electronics since 1995, the launch represented their first step towards integrating low-tech technology into fashion.

French fashion designer Olivier Lapidus has been showing his collections in Paris since 1989, often showcasing the potentials of technologized clothing in his couture range. Lapidus designed a solar-powered parka lined with Mylar in black-and-white silk, complete with micro-lithium batteries and voltaic mono-crystalline solar captors. His designs often mix traditional fabrics, such as organza and silk, with glass and carbon fibres, and he has even developed a tweed woven from rubber yarn. Lapidus has also designed tweed suits with hologram insets, and abandoned conventional stitching in favour of glue bonding. As Lapidus experiments with adapting communication technology for his *haute couture* creations, the interest in his work indicates that the incorporation of high-tech materials is catching on in high fashion as well as streetwear.

The gap between fashion and sophisticated technology is being bridged by research laboratories dedicated to exploring intelligent fashion's immediate and future possibilities. Research into intelligent clothing seemed to rise parallel to the 'dot com' phenomenon in the late 1990s; as that industry declined, so did the funding behind the research organizations, causing several to terminate their research projects or close down altogether. The most prominent of these research laboratories are MIT's Media Lab, who were the first to explore computerized clothing; Starlab, who collaborated with the fashion designer Walter Van Beirendonck before closing in 2001; Charmed Technology, under the direction of Alex Lightman; and International Fashion Machines, known as IFM, spearheaded by Margaret Orth and Joanna Berzowska.

The research of these organizations is oriented towards 'fashioning' technology by developing electronic textiles, expressive software, interactive design, industrial design and micro-technology. Their combination of skills, fashion expertise and intellect is transforming new and existing technologies into beautiful, practical and innovative garments and fashion-based products. Ultimately, these researchers are not only developing technology that is wearable, but fashionable.

MIT's Media Lab is probably the most famous breeding ground for new technology and eccentric sci-fi ideas. They began researching ways to invisibly embed technology into garments, arguing that computers should not be self-contained machines on desks, but systems capable of communicating with humans via the sensory methods we use by nature: touch, speech and vision.[7] In 1993, the scientist and researcher Thad Starner wore his portable and accessible IT system for days at a time to identify the pros and cons of using a wearable system.[8] Other MIT scientists designed a computer with a half QWERTY keyboard and display modules to be worn on the wrists; strapped to the operator's forearms, text could be entered by bringing the wrists together and typing. Steve Mann, also a scientist, began transmitting images from a head-mounted camera to the Internet, then went on to develop the Wearable Wireless Webcam. This transmitted images in real time from a head-mounted analogue camera to a silicon graphics base station via amateur TV frequencies.

These experiments proved that computer systems could be made wearable and still operate efficiently when worn on the body, although their bulk proved to be uncomfortable, limit mobility and interfere with other daily tasks. Taking the project to the next stage, Rich DeVaul and Steve Swartz focused on developing a 'clothing computer', but one that could be worn with everyday clothing rather than requiring a specific outfit. 'MIThril', as the project was dubbed, developed a high-tech electronic system encased in a vest-like garment. The batteries, hardware and circuitry were housed in special pockets, connected by a cabling system that integrated power and data delivery. MIThril used a MicroOptical digital display that resembled an ordinary pair of glasses; the display itself was actually a small cube in the middle of one lens, operated by a small electronic module positioned on the earpiece. Using the display, the wearer could surf the Internet, read text or look at images. MIThril have since been able to reduce the system's bulk and adapt it to be worn comfortably on the body, and the project continues to make progress towards miniaturizing the wireless wearable components into virtual invisibility.[9]

Starlab was established to move beyond MIT's research, developing wireless systems that aligned clothing with sensors embedded into the built environment. Starlab was founded in 1996 by Walter De Brouwer with funding from a range of commercial sponsors, including Adidas, France Télécom and Levi Strauss Europe. From Starlab's headquarters in Brussels, sixty of the world's leading scientists, chemists, health experts, systems designers and engineers worked together to develop networks of sensors for intelligent clothing that could alert the wearer to specific stimuli, or monitor their movements and vital signs. These were developed to perform in four key areas: in the home, at the office, in mobile professions and specialist occupations. De Brouwer abbreviated intelligent wear to 'i-Wear', giving this name to the prototype garments they went on to produce until Starlab was forced to declare bankruptcy and close down in June 2001. The official receivers collated and catalogued Starlab's research, making it available as intellectual property that could be sold to repay the company's debts.[10]

Charmed Technology was established in 1999, describing itself as an 'MIT Media Lab spin-off established for the research of the smallest most economical platform for Internet products, services and technologies'.[11] Their vision is to incorporate Internet access into fashion, lifestyle and health applications by creating inexpensive wireless devices that allow individuals to access the Internet wherever they are. The wireless technologies that Charmed are developing mimic fashion accessories rather than clothing: transmitter earrings, necklaces equipped with sensors, and data screen sunglasses are designed to enhance or substitute conventional fashion accessories. Charmed view fashion accessories as the most appealing vehicle for wireless systems, as it feels that individuals will be reluctant to wear fully technologized garments.

Charmed present their products in fashion shows as an alternative to static trade fair exhibitions. On the catwalk, models wear jackets, badges and belt buckles enhanced with mobile telephone technology, or surf the Internet behind visors and sunglasses that double as a computer screens. The shows illustrate Charmed's concept of 'Wireless Everywear', devices that enable wearers to go online without plugging in to any terrestrial systems. 'Charmed Earrings', for example, are prototypes of a net-connected fashion accessory with embedded lights that blink or play tunes when an incoming email is received. A vocoder is built into the necklace that allows the wearer to dictate messages through voice-recognition software. Charmed's bracelets and rings are also being engineered to perform these functions.

i-Wear

The i-Wear project got under way with the production of conceptual prototype garments. In parallel with the conceptual work, design research was initiated to understand and generate the enabling technologies that would bring the vision of intelligent clothing to life. The project was set up as a five-year research commission that produced several generations of prototype garments during its lifespan. De Brouwer and his team developed a prototype garment consisting of multiple specialized tiers intended to supersede everyday objects, such as batteries, mobile phones, laptops and sound systems, by engineering i-Wear to perform their functions instead.

The prototypes were designed in collaboration with Walter Van Beirendonck, the acclaimed Belgian fashion designer who also shared Starlab's vision for the eventual interface of fashion and technology. Van Beirendonck belongs to the group of avant-garde fashion designers known as the 'Antwerp Six', all of who are well established

Charmed Technology present their products in fashion shows. Models wear jewellery enhanced with mobile telephone technology and surf the Internet behind sunglasses that double as a computer screens.

on the international fashion scene. Dries Van Noten, Dirk Bikkembergs, Martin Margiela, Ann Demeulemeester and Dirk Van Saene are the other five.

Van Beirendonck is the only one of the Antwerp Six to express an interest in integrating technology into clothing. Fascinated by computers and new media, he was exploring and using the Internet and CD-ROMs as early as 1996, being one of the first designers to do so. In the past few years, many of Van Beirendonck's designs have been technologized with light and sound effects built into the garments themselves.[12] Van Beirendonck explored this field in greater depth, planning to move beyond wearable devices to garments made with integrated wireless technology. With Van Beirendonck's creative input, Starlab were able to apply fashion principles to the i-Wear aesthetic.

Van Beirendonck's collaboration with the team of technologists generated a multi-disciplinary approach that required them to question each other's assumptions about fashion. Contradictions had to be resolved – from Van Beirendonck's perspective, the integrity of the garment's fashion design should be maintained, while the technologists were insisting on locating components in areas of the garment that distorted its aesthetic and compromised the comfort of the clothing. In the pursuit of a compromise, both disciplines discovered new, innovative ways of working. This would suggest that other intelligent fashion collaborations would develop principles that could potentially redefine and restructure their respective disciplines.

Finding the right style for i-Wear was a complex process; it was a toss-up between whether it should look futuristic and progressive, creating an aesthetic of its own, or mimic mainstream fashion trends to look as 'normal as possible'. The prototype presented in June 2000 mirrored the classic cut of a man's dress shirt, with a collar, cuffs and buttons, facilitating the same ease of movement and egress typical of a button-fronted shirt. The technology was ingeniously diffused among several interconnecting layers, rather than being confined within one bulky garment. The tier structure was attributed to the influence of Van Beirendonck's *Dissections* collection (autumn/winter 2001), which divided clothes into their basic layers. The decorative effect of using linear patterns to differentiate each layer also recalls the deconstructive elements and compartmentalized systems shown in *Dissections*. The overall aesthetic dictates clarity, simplicity, functionality and economy of line, balancing the independent layers and the overall volume.

Mobility was a primary consideration for i-Wear, which is one of the reasons it was designed to be as lightweight and streamlined as possible. Starlab assigned specific software to each tier, giving the wearer the option of combining individual tiers according to the functions they need, rather than wearing all of them. According to De Brouwer, 'Our philosophy was to integrate very naturally the technology into the clothing. The i-Wear shouldn't hinder people's movements, it should be like normal clothing, but with many new options. It should be a second skin that feels what is going on inside the body and outside in the environment and takes action using that data.'

Each i-Wear combination required the energy tier for power, though plans had been made to integrate an energy source into each individual tier. 'The idea of this layering is that each function can work separately, and we can choose different modules. So, at a later stage, we had planned to combine different functions in one and the same shirt,' De Brouwer explained. 'Another reason we were working with layers is that it reflects reality – people wear several layers: underwear, shirt, trousers, shoes, jacket, backpack. Integrating different functions into these layers and making them communicate, would have been the key to making the whole thing work,' he added.

The energy tier was designed to boost the existing i-Wear systems and have the capacity to divert power supplies to auxiliary devices, like music or video equipment. Starlab explored the possibilities of generating energy from a range of ideas, including the use of wireless interfaces to recharge it with electricity, using kinetic energy generated by the body itself, and washing it in a detergent charged with a conductant source that could convert light to energy as the garment was hung out to dry. As none of these sources proved viable during Starlab's initial research, they also turned to the portable energy relays developed for the Apollo spacesuits, which could be redesigned as a compartmentalized underlayer to house lightweight batteries.

The i-Wearer could access information via a tiny, disc-shaped device with a screen and a few button controls. Nicknamed 'Spyglass', the device is a miniature personal computer (PC) that can retrieve data or operate external speakers and microphones. Looking into the screen is rather like looking through a jeweller's loupe; the image is sharp, but minute. Other research laboratories are developing fabrics that will allow the wearer to designate an area on the garment's sleeve, cuff or lapel to be used as a display screen.[13] As De Brouwer pointed out: 'You could check your email or surf the web, but you wouldn't really want to look at your sleeve all day. What would be much more useful would be to get supporting information during the day or wear special glasses.'

The 'communication' tier was designed to be activated by inserting a digitized SIM-type card containing software into its portal, bringing the i-Wear online to send and receive email, text messages and phone calls wirelessly via Web technology and Internet applications, text retrieval and text enrichment.[14] Voice-recognition software would be activated via microphones in the collar, obeying the wearer's commands to transmit messages or surf the Internet. Other types of SIM cards could turn the jacket into a DECT phone, or sensors could detect where the wearer was geographically and automatically switch between GSM and DECT. The i-Wear sensors would have been interwoven into the fabric, or fashioned into zips, buttons or other ornamentation together with the information-gathering transmitter/receiver that gave the prototype its communication potential.

i-Wear also has implications for the commercial world, which Starlab predicted would eventually be transformed into 'intelligent environments' that have no user interfaces at all. Electronics would be embedded invisibly almost everywhere, so that sensors can exchange information about a number of systems they are programmed to detect. De Brouwer illustrated this by describing how the i-Wearer, upon entering a department store, could connect to the shop's website or intranet site, and begin a dialogue about products and services through the help of a virtual sales assistant, talking to them through speakers positioned in the collar.

This concept is central to the i-Wear project, because the wearer would rely on the relay systems embedded in these structures to receive and transmit information from the environment around them. Interoperation and integration into 'intelligent environments' is a major forum for all scientists pioneering wireless technology, since expanded wireless networks are the key to increasing the possibilities for new and different services. Getting there will involve further research on speech-recognition technologies, advanced sensors and new types of interfaces.[15]

The data collected in these intelligent environments throughout the day would be stored in the i-Wear memory circuits, gradually building up a data bank of the wearer's activities. Over a period of time, it could interact spontaneously with the wearer to establish a routine. Data could also be transmitted to computer systems or other i-Wear clothing. The data could be stored in a separate 'memory' tier, where it would be held on processor chips for future use. It could even search the Internet for travel arrangements, book them and then give periodic reminders that count down the time remaining until the wearer needs to leave for the airport.

You would not have to worry about losing your keys or credit cards, because i-Wear would keep track of them. i-Wear could also be directly linked to any object or individual equipped and programmed to transmit or receive information. Embedding a computer chip in door or car keys, for example, would enable them to be read by the i-Wear sensors, which would alert you if the keys went out of radar range. Low-tech surveillance of young children and pets would also be possible by tagging them with i-Wear sensors, which could map their location on radar by using ultrasonic and infrared sensors. Inter-family 'com' links would allow the entire family to monitor each other's conversation and movements throughout the day.

The design of the 'motion-sensing' tier contained accelerometers for i-Wearers to programme to recognize and respond to particular movements, such as standing, sitting, walking and running by monitoring ambient temperature, movement, sound and light. Each tier was being developed to contain integrated circuitry that would communicate with the other tiers in the garment's infrastructure to determine the best method of 'speaking' to the wearer. The accelerometer could trigger programmes to react to body posture. If it sensed that the wearer was lying down, it could automatically divert incoming messages to voicemail, and play them when the wearer sat up again. They could also make the garments automatically expand when the wearer moves into a sitting position, or adapt to provide extra support during exercise. The 'sound' tier would also function on this premise, being programmed to play different music depending on the wearer's movements – relaxing music would be played when the wearer reclined, and high-energy music played when exercising.

The 'environmental' tier was designed to compensate for changes in the wearer's surroundings. Using microphones and sensors embedded in the collar and cuffs, it would detect and monitor chemicals and pollutants in the air, measure changes in light, temperature and sound and regulate the wearer's environment. By measuring light density, for example, the shirt might lighten up when it became dark and improve the wearer's visibility. IFM's remarkable 'Firefly Dress' and necklace operate according to this principle. The Firefly Dress is not only one of the first techno fashions, it is also one of the most beautiful. The entire dress and elaborate necklace lights up in the dark, made possible by integral fabric circuitry, power distribution planes and sensors. Margaret Orth describes the application of lighting technology as 'a labour of love,' because wiring and connecting each fibre in a garment is still a time-consuming process. 'It's not really feasible at this point to start thinking about mass-producing clothes that light up, but fashion designers can use fibre optics to decorate or enhance a part of the clothing,' she said. Because fibre-optic cables do not generate heat they can be safely worn against the skin for extended periods. The designer Patrick Cox uses them for shoe and boot design, creating a striking effect that can be transformed into a choice of colours.

Electric Embroidery

The Fabric Area Network (FAN), is the wireless network that facilitates communication within each i-Wear tier. The FAN was integrated into each individual tier to provide an infrastructure of interconnecting sensors and data, linked by a conductive thread mixed with stainless steel. According to De Brouwer, the last i-Wear prototype included several intercommunicating layers, made possible by weaving the hardware into the shirt's structure. 'In the long term, we are looking to integrate computing capabilities into the fabric and fibres themselves. The way the threads are woven would create different circuits.'

The type of threads and fabric De Brouwer is describing are not the soft, warm, washable textiles normally used for clothing. In fact, the short life cycle of most clothes is totally unsuited to the incorporation of sophisticated electronics. Even though mobile devices are designed to keep working when used in the rain, normal weather conditions are benign in comparison to the hostile environment encountered inside a washing machine. Washing machines, tumble dryers, steam irons and dry-cleaning solvents conflict with the care of electronic insulation, inflexible connectors and power interfaces. The materials used in electronics, such as copper, are also susceptible to oxidation, and create friction within garments that damages other textile fibres.

This is why IFM, who are also adapting weaving and embroidery techniques to conduct signals, are also concerned about durability. According to Orth, much of the physical technology will have to progress before computer parts can take the sort of

Prototypes like IFM's 'Firefly Dress' and necklace measure light density and automatically illuminate when lighting fades. The entire dress and elaborate necklace light up to improve the wearer's visibility, made possible by integral fabric circuitry, power distribution planes and sensors.

bending and twisting that normal clothes are designed for. 'We're breaking new ground in developing techno textiles as part of what we do, but they have to be advanced further if the clothes are to be durable enough to support the technology.' According to Orth, connectors are the first things to fall apart, so she is currently developing a conductive thread through which an electronic signal can pass.[16] 'Kevlar is one composite fibre we can use, but stainless steel is safe for people and works better with most fashion designs. Choice of conductive fibre is often a design issue, depending on what kind of yarn it is being combined with,' Orth explained. IFM's long-range vision is to use conductive fibres to integrate technologies into furniture, household equipment and architectural systems, collapsing the boundaries between fashion, consumer electronics and emerging technologies.

IFM used conductive thread to create a wearable musical instrument within a Levi's jacket. The 'Musical Jacket', as it is known, features an embroidered keypad, a fabric bus, a mini-midi synthesizer, speakers and batteries to enable the wearer to play a range of sounds using the jacket as a synthesizer. Once the keys have been embroidered using a standard industrial process, the conductive thread connects them to a chip wired to a small midi synthesizer on the shoulder. Charmed Technology have also researched conductive fibres to create 'e-broidery', or 'electronic needlework', which stitches conductive silicon thread into a keyboard that can be embroidered in any fabric. They are exploring a network of embroidered fibres that bypasses data ports by enabling data to be keyed directly into the clothing.

IFM work with a range of fashion designers as part of their 'Technology Trend Services' to consult with them on ways technology or technologized processes can enhance their collections, or revolutionize their design and production methods. 'Right now we are showing clients the potentials of our "animated fashion module" that uses a special design ink to create a moving image. The module is round, similar to a monocle, and contains a moving image inside. A fashion designer could programme it to feature their logo, or an image,' Orth explained.

The animated module can be incorporated into fabric, leather or almost any fashion material. It could also be used as a decorative accessory, like a buckle for a belt or a shoe, or combined with jewellery. One of the advantages it has over a digital display that it is less bulky and can be fitted seamlessly into the fabric to have a flush surface. Each module is powered by a low-grade battery that keeps the animation constantly in motion. 'We are committed to making fashion attractive,' Orth explained. 'And this product wouldn't look good if it was made in a square or rectangular shape. It was worth the extra work to make it circular, and now we can make it in almost any shape.'

IFM plan to use the garment's raw materials to move audio, data and power around the garment relatively easily. Their conductive fibres could also be integrated into knitwear and woven materials, and the conductive inks to create electrically active patterns that constantly morph into new shapes.

The British electronics company ElekSen invented 'ElekTex', a versatile technologized fabric that acts as a malleable sensing and switching system that interfaces the

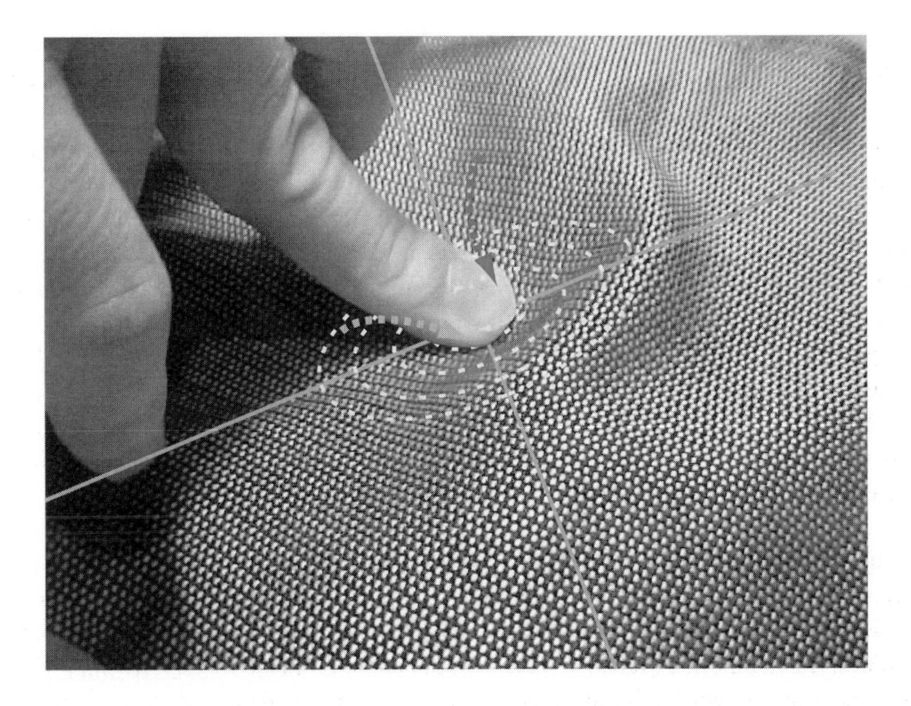

'ElekTex' is a technologized fabric with a fibre structure that interfaces with customized software to process data through the fabric itself. It senses electronic impulses by fabric field and translates them into digital data. When it is touched it recognizes where the contact point is, sending digital signals to control any number of devices.

fabric's fibre structure with customized software to process data through the fabric itself. It can also sense electronic impulses by fabric field and translate them into digital data. When it is touched, it recognizes where the contact point is, and it can use this information to send digital signals to control any number of devices. By combining conductive fabrics with microchip technology, ElekSen have created raised keys within the fabric that give tactile feedback – more or less the same feeling of pressing a button – bringing MIT's vision of sensory technology into fruition. The keys do not move individually, as the keyboard is a continuous surface. The keyboard is also sensitive to input in the areas beneath the 'keys'. This means there is no blank or backside – the keyboard can receive and transmit on either the inside or outside of the fabric. A remote-control mouse can be used as a component in the same product landscape.

Sensory Signals

Starlab were also developing i-Wear to react to hormone release to detect the mood of the wearer, so it could be programmed to indulge the wearer in nostalgic yearnings.

As De Brouwer said, 'I like the idea of clothing as memory, which accumulates part of the impression of the place you are staying, say, on holiday. It would record the freshness of the air, the background noise, it would take snapshots like a tourist. I got this idea from thinking about how we could give garments a heart, a soul and a reason to live. If it could sense the environment, then it could even be worn by someone else to recreate the experience for them.' If i-Wear could be programmed to sense emotions, then feelings like panic or embarrassment could trigger soft, easy music to soothe the wearer. By sensing and recording the wearer's state of mind, a shirt could recreate a mood associated with a particular conversation or a significant moment in the wearer's life.

Jenny Tillotson, Director of the Sensory Design Lab in London, is introducing smell technology to intelligent fashion. Tillotson's research will be used by Charmed Technology to produce the 'ScentBadge'. A wearable fashion accessory, the badge will contain scent suspended in oil or alcohol, which would be released periodically. Tillotson collaborates with perfumers, chemists, olfactory experts, medical technologists and nanotechnologists to pioneer what she refers to as 'electronic nose technology'.[17] Her research combines technology with fashion and medicine – in its broadest sense – by incorporating a system of micro-miniature tubing, pumps and sensors into intelligent garments and fashion accessories. Tillotson explained: 'Fragrances can be actively pulsed electronically through a cabling device system. Mimicking the human senses, in particular the scent glands, in our bodies, the fabric structure will literally incorporate these into it. The system will act as a new platform for delivery, especially for designer perfumes, reducing the application of alcohol on the skin.'[18]

Among the scents Tillotson is developing are 'PsychoScents', which border between pharmacology and perfume. Psychoscents will contain special aroma molecules that affect the brain to change our moods in subtle ways. Pscychoscents would be released through the Charmed 'AromaBadge', a badge triggered to emit scents based on the temperature, heart rate and the state of arousal or excitement of the wearer. As changes in the wearer's mood are detected, the system will be triggered to release aromas and perfumes. Perhaps this system will hold the potential to synthesize the Prozac of the future?

Techno fashion can even help you fall in love. The Charmed 'PheroMate' is designed to help wearers find their perfect partner through each other's scent. The PheroMate can analyse the pheromones of people coming into contact with the wearer, and alert the wearer to those who match their pheromone profile.

Tillotson's research also has applications for the medical diagnostic area, because the technology also monitors the heart rate, temperature and hormonal balance of their wearers. The 'SenseWear Pro Armband', also a Charmed product, is a bracelet-like, wearable body monitor that relays accurate diagnostic data back to a centralized system that could detect any imbalances and alert the wearer. Worn on the back of the upper arm, its sensors continuously monitor movement, blood flow, skin temperature, ambient temperature and galvanic skin response. Corporate employees could one day be required to wear systems like these at work so that their health and efficiency could be charted during office hours.

Jenny Tillotson, in collaboration with Charmed Technology, works with perfumers, chemists, medical technologists and nanotechnologists to pioneer 'electronic nose technology'. Her research combines fashion and medicine – in its broadest sense – to create a wearable badge triggered to release pheromones.

Techno Medicine

Starlab were developing a 'health care' tier to be worn directly against the body. It contains sensors that monitor body functions, administer medications via the epidermis and relay medical data to a physician who could diagnose the patient without a visit to the surgery. Alice Pentland, Director of the Center for Future Health at the University of Rochester, New York, recognizes the potential benefits of using i-Wear in health care. Paraplegics can have serious circulatory problems resulting from clothing that is too restrictive, as can extreme diabetics, who suffer from lack of sensation. Optical fibres worn against the body could alert the wearer to any pressure points inhibiting blood flow so that they could make adjustments to counteract it. Sensors could be placed in socks and underwear, for example, that would pinpoint areas where the pressure was strong enough reduce the light flow and alert the wearer. 'This causes other sensors to buzz or vibrate so that the person would know they needed to adjust the clothing,' Pentland said.[19]

Watches that monitor blood-sugar levels by analysing the chemistry of perspiration are already commercially available. The same technology can also be adapted to identify other chemical imbalances in the body and alert the wearer as they are detected. Alex Pentland (Alice Pentland's brother), of MIT's Media Lab, foresees garments that diagnose and administer medication without the wearer even noticing. 'Why can't the clothing then synthesize the drugs on the fly? Your shirt sensors could detect low blood sugar and then produce the necessary drugs to counter it, releasing them onto the skin where they're absorbed,' he said.[20]

Garments that medicate the wearer are already available in mainstream fashion. Skin patches that use electrical impulses to inject medicine into the body have been on the market for several years. American lingerie designer Victoria's Secret have filed a patent for tights coated with theophylline acetate (THA), a compound they claim can treat cellulite. THA is bound to the fabric with an organic polymer glue that melts when it comes into contact with the body. As the tights are worn, perspiration raises the fabric's pH enough to melt the polymer glue and release the THA onto the skin.

Cancer specialists working in the research department at the Georgia Institute of Technology are developing a wearable cancer diagnosis system that will transmit data to a remote analysis computer via a wireless network. The physicians would scan the patient by wearing a sensor glove that would detect malignant cells or abnormal tissue growth. The remote computer could guide them to target specific areas when X-raying or giving treatment. This breakthrough could allow patients to receive treatment outside the hospital.

An IBM wearable computer is being tested by doctors on their rounds at Duke University Hospital in Durham, North Carolina. The unit has a wireless modem PC card plugged into a standard expansion slot, enabling the doctors to access patients' hospital records and diagnostic reports through an intranet or Internet interface. Completely wireless, the wearable computer is much more practical than carrying around a laptop. Primary input is by voice, with the microphone supported by a headband or attached to the physician's collar.

The joint efforts of Sensatex and Lifelink, two health-orientated research organizations, are conducting research on health-care systems that can monitor patients wirelessly. This would give a new dimension to the capabilities of a hospital gown, or create a special garment that would supersede it entirely. The gowns could be made in fabric woven throughout with copper strands to allow for a continuous flow of current powered by rechargeable batteries.

Hospital administrations are devising methods to shorten hospital stays by initiating more home care, which has led to a growing need for remote diagnostic technology. The wired devices currently in use by bedridden patients or infants are often uncomfortable, and impede their mobility and range of movement. Such devices transmit data only periodically, by using conventional telephone modems. The wireless models under development by Sensatex and Lifelink would be capable of transmitting information in real time. This technology could also be used to monitor high-risk heart patients and subjects participating in clinical trials.

Although the health-conscious might be a big target group for the evolving techno fashion industry, they are also the first ones concerned about the potential health risks of wrapping themselves in technology. One of the concerns about wearable computers and intelligent clothing alike is that they increase the wearer's intimate proximity to all sorts of radiation. To minimize any radiation hazard, Starlab planned to weave i-Wear's communication antenna into the fabric, keeping it away from the head and dispersing radiation throughout the tiers.

With battery-powered technology comes the risk of high levels of electromagnetic energy radiating over the body, even with batteries integrated into the components they power. If batteries are positioned in direct contact with the conductive blood stream, or a major organ, it could have serious side-effects – including heart attack. The environmental impact of equipping entire households and offices with portable batteries could also present a major hazard. The danger of batteries exploding spontaneously is minimal, but the high-level energy density contained in fully charged batteries is powerful enough to trigger a chain reaction of battery explosions. Health issues related to these dangers are being explored by the Human Research and Engineering Directorate Command of the United States Army Research Laboratory, but it may be some time before conclusive test results are ready for publication.

Probably the most extreme danger and complications that could result from wireless technology would be the maladaptation of devices implanted into the body itself. Kevin Warwick, a professor of cybernetics at the University of Reading in England, experimented with an implant that would enable him to connect to the Internet wirelessly at will.[21] Using himself as a test subject, Warwick had the device implanted into his arm, but it had to be removed after only nine days due to complications.

Military Intelligence

The United States Army recently developed a T-shirt made of cotton woven with optical fibres that can monitor the wearer's vital signs and relay medical data from soldiers in the field. Researchers at the Georgia Institute of Technology[22] developed the shirt for a project funded by the United States military, who are exploring technology that can monitor the physical condition of soldiers during battle.[23] The United States military is establishing projects to research further types of intelligent clothing for soldiers, to enhance the protective and communicative properties of their uniforms and combat gear. Soldiers' uniforms could be engineered to change colour to match their surroundings, making camouflage patterns redundant; sense the impact of a bullet and send a signal to the soldier's command base; and even administer medicine, and detect poisonous gases.[24]

Part of the MARSS (Maintenance and Repair Support System) series, the 'bodyLAN vest' is one of the most sophisticated wearable devices ever developed for the military. The multi-pocketed vest has several specially designed compartments to house the software and communication devices and is made of durable high-tech synthetics that contain battery-powered circuits. The systems can switch between different bandwidths, depending on the type of communication they need to make. For example, the life signs from a wounded soldier could be monitored by a distant medic, who could locate the soldier's position via his Global Positioning System's (GPS) tracking device.

Like the bodyLAN vest, the 'VuMan' is a body-hugging computer. It features a circular dial control that displays animations of repair procedures, replacing bulky maintenance manuals with lightweight technology. Soldiers can simultaneously see both their equipment and the computer information through a headset display as they make repairs.

Directions through unfamiliar territory can be displayed on an electronic map, where it is displayed alongside the user's itinerary. Maps can be scrolled or scaled by using voice commands, as well as updated with tactical data radioed from other units. The model is being developed to include artificial intelligence capabilities, enabling it to respond to complex queries, such as 'How do I get to station X from here?'

The United States military are pioneering alternatives to battery power to operate their intelligent wear in the field. Relying on a battery pack presents a problem, because to fully operate the systems on a long mission, soldiers would have to include a set of heavy batteries with the rest of their gear. According to DARPA, the United States Defence Advanced Research Projects Agency,[25] for the soldier to carry a four-day battery supply they would have to leave behind four hundred rounds of ammunition, food rations for four days, or a protective mask and first-aid kit.

The combat technology that DARPA are now developing recalls the type of weapons and technology used by the 'US Colonial Marines' in the 1986 science fiction film *Aliens.* In the film, the soldiers wore helmets containing cameras that transmitted eye-level images to the base commander, who could read a continuously updated display of each soldier's vital signs. Similar systems are now being tested by DARPA, which also contains a miniature Liquid Crystal Display (LCD) to equip the soldiers with video-receive capability.[26]

Virtual Networking

With the computational power of multimedia desktops and laptop computers now reduced to processing units the size of a hand-held organizer, technology is integrating with commercial workwear and uniforms. The research that MIT's Media Lab, Starlab, IFM and Charmed have made available has encouraged others to move towards the goal of interoperability, making the establishment of a single ubiquitous platform more achievable in a shorter time period.

Charmed has even begun a project to maximize networking potential by making business cards redundant. In theory, people wishing to exchange information about their business interests would not even have to stop to exchange their details. At a business function or convention, those wearing the 'Charmed Badge' could communicate as they came into range of each other. The Charmed Badge is an electronic device that simultaneously transmits and receives information through filters programmed to match the wearer's criteria. The Charmed Badge will even be able to locate key people in a social environment by locking onto their coordinates. No physical exchange of cards or documents will be necessary, as any data can be swapped via infrared laser scanners as the badges conduct beaming sessions with each other. Back at the office, the badge can be downloaded into files with the contact data of everyone it communicated with.

The Charmed 'Communicator' is a wearable, wireless, broadband Internet device designed to be controlled by voice, a remote, or linked to a keyboard. The Communicator is made of three separate wireless components: a single half-mirrored eyeglass, similar to a pirate's eye-patch, that displays a computer screen; a handheld touch-controlled mouse; and a hard-drive the size of a mobile telephone that can be carried in a pocket. 'The glasses allow the user to see the equivalent of a full computer screen right in front of their eye, and still be able to regain full vision by shifting focus,' explained Charmed's spokeperson.[27] The Communicator enables the wearer to access and utilize office systems from a distance, conducting field research or working during travel time. The Communicator provides GP3, MP3, digital photography and video technologies and can be customized with additional software and hardware options to suit the individual. The system is designed to run at a lower temperature than conventional software, and supports extended battery life. One of its possibilities is to create a virtual office anywhere in the world, by gaining remote access to office systems and the Internet, and relay images and information about remote environments to other users.

Also based in the United States, the systems experts Xybernaut are in the final stages of developing face-recognition technology that will enable airport security to instantly investigate suspicious travellers. The Mobile Assistant 5[28] is a wearable computer being phased into security personnel uniforms. It will enable security personnel to positively identify a suspect, basing identification on facial symmetry that can be read beyond glasses, facial hair or disguises. This is expected to revolutionize face-recognition technology by providing a positive recognition and vital information quickly to the security officers who have to detain and question suspects. According to Dewayne Adams, Xybernaut's Senior Vice President and Chief Strategist, 'Face recognition requires lots of large cameras running through very powerful servers. The trouble is, when you get a match, you need to be able to get all that information to the person on the floor immediately. With this device, the guard gets the data wirelessly while he is on patrol, he can then see who the person is, walk up and verify the person's information.'[29]

ViA Inc. adapted a wireless PC to be worn as a part of the Northwest Airlines' ticket agent uniform to enable them move beyond the gate and ticket counters. Agents can process tickets as the passengers wait in line or wait at the gate, streamlining the check-in procedure. Researchers at the Georgia Institute of Technology are designing food hygiene uniforms, complete with a 'Hands Free Food Inspection System'. The system allows food workers to make reports on quality and temperature, which are transmitted via a wireless network, without using their hands.

The possibilities discussed here offer a visionary glimpse of what might become reality in the near future. The ultimate vision of these technologists is that people will consider wearable electronics a part of the everyday wardrobe, and that in future all clothes will contain elements that add value to an infrastructure of electronics built into the environment around them. They predict that the clothing of the future will constitute the individual's personal area network, gradually evolving into an intimate network capable of interacting with other systems. The role of the wearer as a systems user will undoubtedly require more adaptation and learning, meaning that shaping attitudes toward intelligent fashion is one of the most important tasks research organizations face. How individuals will react to the health concerns is a big question in the industry – integrating the electronic parts into garments will need to be backed up by a lot of research to reassure the public that they are completely safe.

Developing i-Wear, wireless accessories, health care systems and military equipment is just the tip of the technological iceberg, because the commercial world will still have to invest in new interoperable platforms to make these designs viable. The advances in technology and platform infrastructure described here will require a synergy between the disciplines of computer science, fashion, health care and defence to fully develop. However esoteric the thinking behind the products is, the products themselves will, at least initially, have to be simplified to a set of interactive devices to make them marketable and user-friendly. Despite these challenges, technologists are still committed to pushing the limits in wireless electronics, garment construction and fabric technology, with unpredictable results. One thing seems certain: it will take a while before intelligent fashion becomes our second skin. In any case, the technologists are likely to have time on their side.

six

Transformables

The 'transformable' is the simplest and most minimal fashion statement of all. Though its design may seem complex, the principles behind it bring utility and functionality to fashion, refining and maximizing the wardrobe beyond its wearable potential. For contemporary designers, experimentation with space and construction often provides the richest source of innovation, enabling them to transcend established boundaries and challenge conventions in fashion. The emerging trend for transformable clothing juxtaposes designs from the most elevated corners of the fashion universe, against some of the most impractical and gimmicky products imaginable. A chic raincoat that inflates into a comfortable chair is genius, but converting trousers into a laptop table might be distracting if taken off during a meeting.

Transformable fashions became visible in the urban landscape as the traditional compartmentalized wardrobe no longer sustained shifting social and cultural needs. New changes in lifestyle included regular exercise routines and informal office wear; as dress codes became more fluid, they also became more practical. Mobility and multi-functionality became a key consideration for urban dwellers, who started commuting to work in sports shoes and replacing briefcases and shoulder bags with backpacks. Modular components transformed overcoats into raincoats as hoods and collars were buttoned or zipped into place; parkas with removable hoods and detachable sleeves could be adapted to weather changes. Accessory designers made plastic wallets that opened into raincoats, hats with built-in sun visors and bags that expanded in volume or converted into backpacks.

A true transformable, at least in the fashion world, is first and foremost a garment that can be comfortably worn. Its design must include at least one other construction possibility, which can only take shape through the components made specifically for that garment or for a range of modular designs. After being transformed into its secondary design, it must be capable of being reversed back to its starting point, i.e. its original form. Clothing that meet these criteria can usually be described as one of three

Mandarina Duck's 'Jackpack' is a jacket that transforms into a backpack, encapsulating principles of multi-functionality and transformability that streamline and maximize the wardrobe beyond its wearable potential.

Lucy Orta's Modular Architecture consists of portable, wearable dwellings made up of individual sections, panels or units that can be combined to make a number of different forms, or simply worn as protective clothing.

Hussein Chalayan's interest in techno fashion is inspiring his contemporaries to move forward. 'The fashion audience doesn't really know about technology or architecture,' Chalayan said, 'but they soon will.'

Lucy Orta designs personal environments that can be varied in accordance with weather conditions, social needs, necessity or urgency. Refuge Wear is intended to give refugees some sense of agency and sanctuary as they struggle to mesh their domestic world with larger systems of political mandates.

McQueen uses materials like glass that have sharp and even dangerous surfaces. He inverts fashion's traditional relationship to tactility, ensuring that the observer maintains critical distance from the wearer.

Alexander McQueen styled this ensemble with a mantle of silver thorns and black pearl made by Shaun Leane, indicating a sinister side to elegance as the model strikes a predatory pose.

Techno fashions are often characterized by a trend to build a superstructure around the body. Shaun Leane's 'Rose Corset' for Givenchy plates the body in metal and adorns it with roses crafted from steel.

Although the inspiration for his collections is often technological, Thorogood prefers to work with traditional materials and methods. He cuts according to couture principles, using duchesse silk dyed to create colours that are unique and individual.

Pia Myrvold's collections defy the boundaries of formal and casual, streetwear and daywear. Myrvold uses nylons and industrial plastics to create streamlined silhouettes that suggest a utilitarian or futuristic identity.

The designer Patrick Cox uses fibre optics for shoe and boot design, creating a striking effect. Because fibre-optic cables do not generate heat they can be safely worn against the body for extended periods.

Galya Rosenfeld teams up with photographer Yael Dahan to capture the spirit of her modular fashions. Each of the components shown here can be connected and reassembled to construct a new dress or design a pattern. Modular systems like these may herald a new future for prêt-a-porter and accessories.

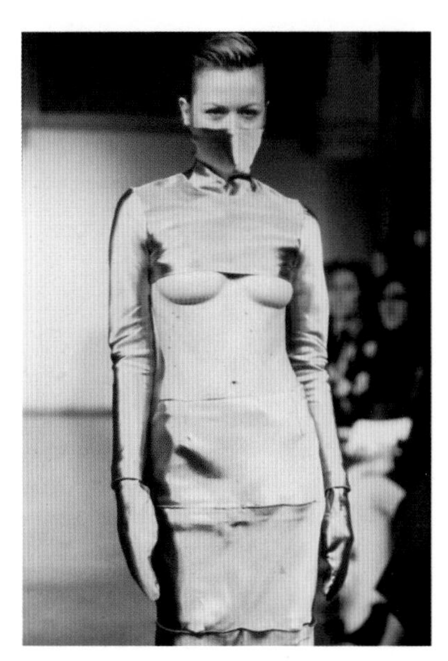

John Ribbe experiments with Velcro to make versatile designs. The panels are interchangeable: the front and back pieces of dresses, skirts, bustiers and sleeveless tops can be mixed and matched to form different garments.

Shelley Fox is fascinated by the ideas hidden in coding, interpreting fashion as a system of subtle symbols. Combining her interest in concepts with her liking for minimal graphics, Fox depicted Morse code as a graphic pattern on some garments, and printed Braille patterns on fabrics.

Shelley Fox explores principles of geometry to create circular silhouettes that challenge conventional fashion thinking. Fox never restricts her work to traditional shapes and simplified lines, but balances clothing construction against the symmetry of the body.

types of tranformables. The first type includes garments that transform solely through the reorganization of surfaces, i.e. reversible fabrics, or linings that detach to transform one garment into two. Sportswear labels pioneered reversible fabrics and detachable thermal linings, a principle also applied in mainstream fashion to coats and winter clothing. Included in this type is the natural transformation in appearance and texture that fabrics undergo in the process of wear-and-tear or ageing, which is becoming an area of interest among conceptual designers.

The second type consists of items that can assume two or more clothing functions. Garments like these are often made in reversible fabrics and feature innovative fastenings. Junya Watanabe expresses this theme in his collections from time to time, designing skirts and handbags that unzip or unfold into jackets or shawls. The Italian design label Mandarina Duck created the 'Jackpack', a jacket that transforms into a backpack. The backpack's straps, fastenings and compartments are integrated within the fabric of the jacket's back panel. The jacket becomes a backpack by taking it off, turning it inside out, folding the sleeves, lapels and fabric lengths into a concise pouch that defines the structure of the backpack, then zipping it closed and flattening it. The pouch contains other zipped compartments for stowing away small objects or other items of clothing.

The third type embraces transformability at its most sophisticated, where function is seminal. Garments can be transformed into objects like furniture, tents and mattresses made for the built environment, or reconfigured into multiple designs through a modular system. The system's components should constitute at least one wearable garment that can be transformed by rearranging its integral parts, or in combination with other parts. London-based designer Patrick Cox introduced a modular system of dressing in his *Pieces* collection, which maximizes the utility of each garment by transforming it into something else, or by giving one design several looks. Modular fashions are transformed by the wearers themselves, introducing a notion of technical skill required beyond the point of purchase.

The beauty of modular clothing is that any one piece can be replaced without affecting the rest of the system. Galya Rosenfeld is the designer behind *G Construction*, the system of tiny modular segments that can be interconnected to create whole wardrobes. They can be rearranged to transform one item into myriad designs, or built in panels that can function as modular sections. As in Cox's *Pieces* collection, worn-out modules can be renewed, and styles can easily be reconfigured by interchanging the modules. Ultimately, products like these are flexible enough to meet the style of individuals, by providing them with standard products that they can customize into a wider range of garments. This could enable designers to offer customers the range of clothing combinations found in a large collection, while only manufacturing several core designs. The economics of mass production make it prohibitively expensive to manufacture small numbers of individual products, yet very cost effective to produce large numbers of a small range. Designers would be able to reduce their production costs considerably, and offer more competitive prices to the consumer.

This is why Vexed Generation developed a range of transformable fabrics for their *tectonics* range. They discovered that it was not viable to produce one-off garments, and the constraints of mass production made it difficult to include enough variations to make each garment unique and individual. Rather than explore modularity, they began looking for a design innovation that would transform the garment over time, and also give the wearer a role in personalizing it.

Initially Vexed Generation attempted to find high-performance fabrics that would change texture or colour with use, mimicking the way that suede gradually turns into smooth leather with wear-and-tear. 'To begin with, we tried making the *tectonics* range in ballistic nylon,' said Joe Hunter 'but the nylon doesn't mould to the shape of the body so we changed to denim instead.'[1] The *tectonics* range includes trousers, jackets, coats and 'mid layers' made out of non-stretch plates of fabric laid out onto a stretch framework. As they are worn against the body they move apart, referencing how tectonic plates operate in nature. 'We were aware that the friction between the two materials would create an erosion in the edges of the cut that would change the garment over time,' he said. Rather than deteriorate with wear, the *tectonic* garments would transform into something new. 'We once talked to Reebok about how to produce a range of clothing based on transformability, because what these people want is to mass produce individuality which is a difficult thing to do,' he explained.

In terms of its aesthetic, transformable clothing hangs in limbo somewhere between Deconstruction and Reconstruction. The term Deconstruction was appropriated by fashion from architecture, where it is used to describe the philosophy behind buildings designed with visible infrastructures, exposed joists and external pipes. In fashion, it describes a technique of creating new clothes from old ones by taking them apart, rearranging the pieces and sewing them back together in a new form. The intention is to uncover, to reveal, to simplify; although the term itself describes taking apart, this process actually shows the garment's construction. This type of work is expressed in the shredded tailoring of Robert Cary-Williams, whose use of zips, fastenings, straps and linings feature as explicit design motifs, and the Deconstructivist chic of Martin Margiela, who reconfigures knee socks into jumpers, and gloves and ball gowns into waistcoats.[2]

Reconstruction is a term characterized by garments that appear to be in mid-manufacture. Like Deconstruction, the process of construction is highlighted, but the emphasis is placed on completing the process rather than destroying it. Transformables encapsulate principles of both Deconstruction and Reconstruction; the zips, snaps and fastenings usually concealed in garments become fundamental devices that make the design transformations possible. As the garment is put together in its secondary design, the process of Reconstruction is ultimately completed because the wearer is the agent of construction.

Though Reconstruction describes a process of transformable fashion, it does not constitute a specific type like the three mentioned earlier. At a conceptual level, designers take a literal object, consider the meanings behind it and construct a new object that recreates them in a different medium. The British design duo Antoni + Alison printed photographs of demolished nightclubs on T-shirts in their *Dead Disco* series, poetically reconstructing and memorializing them through their collection. As discussed earlier, the aesthetic and technical principles behind the Stealth aircraft inspired Simon Thorogood to represent spy planes in fabric form, while Hussein Chalayan also symbolically transformed aeroplanes into a series of dresses. His Aeroplane Dresses mimicked aircraft technology in their design principles, equipping the wearer with a metaphoric vehicle complete with a flight pattern, but keeping them on the ground.

The icons of the transformable trend are the garments that become furniture. In Chalayan's *before minus now* collection, this principle was inverted to produce furniture that became garments, demonstrating the Reconstruction aesthetic. The collection was intended to express displacement and expatriation, but the objects made for the collection also deserve recognition for their design genius. The collection featured five pieces of domestic furniture designed to transform into dresses and skirts, complete with suitcases to pack away the clothes taken off. Chalayan's chairs functioned as both pieces of furniture and wearable dresses, and folded into suitcases by collapsing their frames. The round table transformed into an accordion-like skirt by removing a rounded disc from the table's centre and pulling the inside edge up over the hips and attaching it to the waist.

Chalayan's first transformable garments were his 'Paper Dresses', made out of Tyvek, a synthetic paper whose creased, uneven surface create unusual patterns of shadow and light. The dresses can also function as letters – they can be written on, folded into envelopes and sent in the post – or made into kites. The dresses are spare, clean and constructed to creates volume without adding layers underneath. The most famous of these is the Paper Dress worn by Björk on the cover of her album *Post*. The Paper Dresses are durable enough to be refolded and posted many times, and the Kite Dresses easily transform back into their dress versions again. But unlike the Aeroplane Dresses, the Kite Dresses actually can fly.

Transformable clothing charts a collective shift towards multi-functionality in fashion and an interest in the new innovations made possible by modular design. As this chapter continues to explore the work of designers pioneering this area, Patrick Cox's modular clothing outlines the possibilities created through the combination of metamorphosis and mobility, as does the interlocking couture of Galya Rosenfeld. John Ribbe experiments with precise modularity by cutting clothing in panels that can be constructed in a multitude of designs, and garments that can be expanded by the wearer. C P Company counter a world in transition by charging transformables with functionality and utility to create some of the most high-performance fashions ever designed. Kosuke Tsumura pioneers the transformation of clothing into mini-environments designed as intimate homes for the individual, in which to find refuge from modern life. Design-conscious urbanites can find chic clothes with unexpected twists in the collections of Jeff Griffin, whose coats become sleeping bags, and jackets transform into lightweight mattresses.

The icons of the transformable trend are garments that become furniture. In his before minus now *collection, Hussein Chalayan inverted this norm by producing furniture that became garments, demonstrating a Reconstruction aesthetic. A round table became a skirt when a model stepped inside the table's centre and attached it to her waist.*

Bits and Pieces: Patrick Cox, Galya Rosenfeld and John Ribbe

In 1999, Patrick Cox produced his *Pieces* collection, extending his footwear range to include a line of clothing. The collection is a complete wardrobe of shoes, clothing and accessories designed with the millennium in mind, centring around a futuristic concept of functionality and versatility atypical of stylish clothing. Each *Pieces* item was constructed modularly to make it multi-functional and create a unique range of transformable clothing.[3] Zips and snaps open to reveal extra lengths of fabric, or zip away completely to remove sleeves, trouser legs, collars, hoods and dress tiers. The range is coloured in subdued tones of taupe, terracotta and muted greys, in five fabrics constructed to be reversible, or finished in contrasting details.

The collection was not designed with the urban nomad in mind, but the efficient traveller who considers packing an art form, and strives to maximize the performance of each garment. Travelling as light as this limits the number of combinations made possible through mixing and matching. But *Pieces* is unlike typical travel gear because each garment is cut in slim lines that adhere to the body, emphasizing definite forms rather than generic shapes. The style is modern, informal, unexpected and unconventional; part of its appeal is that its basic tailoring and detailing are the properties that make the clothing transformable.

The womenswear garments are tailored into streamlined shapes that are attractive and body conscious. A form-fitting, long-sleeved red dress becomes a sleeveless khaki one, by unzipping the sleeves and turning it inside out. On a trip away it could be worn as a khaki shift by day, then adjusted to become a long-sleeved red dress by night. Similarly, a long skirt has tiers that can be unzipped from a knee-length version into a miniskirt. The tops unzip to become short-sleeved or spaghetti-strapped, while one has a torso that zips away to change it into a bra top. Even the coats can be pared down: a calf-length raincoat transforms into a biker jacket by zipping away the bottom length and unzipping the collar and hood. Each item in the range folds into its own zip-up pouch, which either comes away from the garment completely or remains as an integral feature.

The bags may also be worn – the bottom of a deep shoulder bag could unzip to become a loose-fitting dress. The bag's handles become the dresses' shoulder straps – making exact sizing difficult – but the design succeeds in creating a wearable shift. Carrying the *Pieces* wallet means you will always have a bag when you need one, because it unzips to become a shopping bag. The flat-soled men's boots unzip laterally to turn into mules, while clever zip detailing on the sandals removes the heel strap so they can be worn like flip-flops.

The menswear garments combine urban utility with comfortable, weatherproofed fabrics cut wide for freedom of movement. The trousers and jackets contain more zips and pockets than the womenswear, mirroring the practicality of high-performance

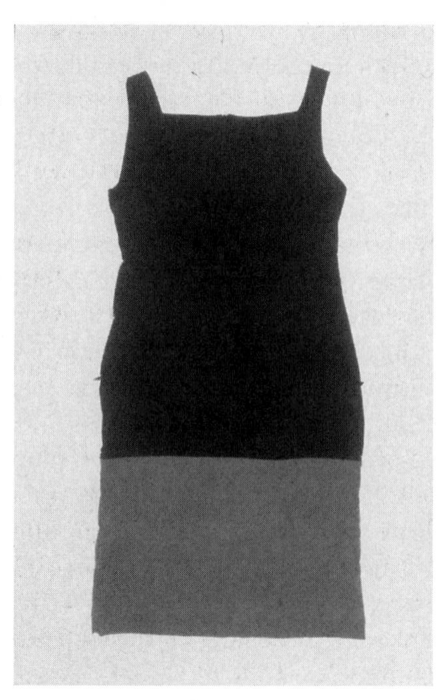

Patrick Cox's Pieces *collection is a complete wardrobe of shoes, clothing and accessories with functionality and versatility atypical of stylish clothing.*

labels like Carthart and Caterpillar. Snug parkas transform into sleek waistcoats as their sleeves, collars and hoods zip away. A classically cut blazer is fitted with snaps to become a sleeveless zip-fronted vest, while long-sleeved shirts become short-sleeved tops or sleeveless vests. Trouser-legs zip away to make shorts out of trousers, then store away in the zipped pockets.

The shoes, garments and accessories are packaged in individual pouches. Cox considered selling them in vending machines as an alternative to a retail environment. This would take the concept of utility a step further, even impacting on conventional retail display and purchase points. For those who eschew shopping, buying clothes from a vending machine would make an ideal alternative, but for the majority of shoppers who prefer trying clothes on before buying them, machine-sold clothing could be a nightmare. That said, the success of mail order, where clothing is sold by pictures rather than tactile experience, suggests that vending machines could one day provide round-the-clock fashion for shopping fanatics.

Transformability is at the very core of American designer Galya Rosenfeld's modular fashion line *G Construction*. Rosenfeld relates to 'pieces' in the most literal sense of the word – her clothes are not composed of standardized modular units, but interlocking 'bits' that form the structure and shape of the garment. Something about her clothes signals a return to a happy childhood, where playing with a set of Lego kept you entertained but also prepared you for making beautiful clothes in adult life. Rosenfeld's collections feature ready-made clothing that can be taken apart and reassembled, or adjusted by unlocking the segments to open and close vents, adjust sleeves, change hemlines, or rearrange necklines. The structure Rosenfeld explores creates a new technical system for making clothes, which could one day become the Lego of the fashion world.

The pieces are made out of dense fabrics like ultra-suede and felt, but crafted to contain a certain degree of flexibility that fits the wearer comfortably and allows for movement. The genius of Rosenfeld's design is that she has devised an entire system of clothing that can be constructed without a single seam or stitch, yet each garment has a shapely, stylish look that contours the body. Each module has two tabs and two slots that enable it to interlock with the other modules around it. So that small items like coins do not slip through the slots, Rosenfeld's handbags have a special lining cut to attach to the modules' tabs from the inside, and lock them into its surface to create a seamless interior.

Rosenfeld's system allows the garments to be constructed randomly or abstractly, in different colours or monochrome, that can instantly adapt to several basic designs for use in changing seasons or climates. Rosenfeld bases the system on two types of components: basic bits that form a repeating modular pattern to create panels and lengths of fabric, and special bits that lock into place where seams normally would be, allowing them to construct a sleeve joint or redefine the neckline.

The symmetry of the components forms a geometric pattern, while the tabs on the garments' surface create a richly textured relief. 'I used mathematic and geometric

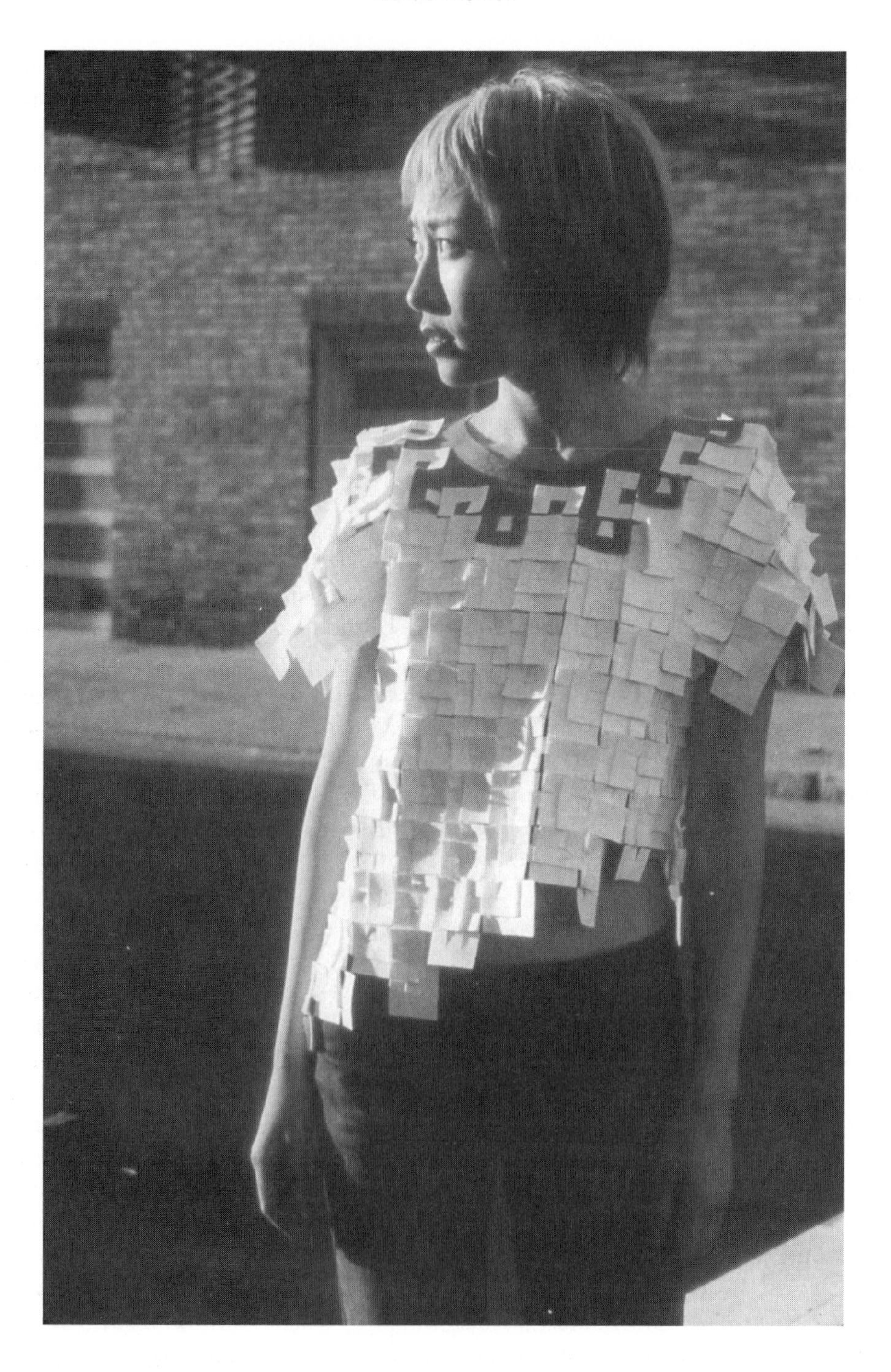

Galya Rosenfeld's system of interconnecting modular segments can be rearranged to transform one item into a range of other designs without a single seam or stitch.

principles to figure out how the pattern could continue and interconnect. Here is something that is really technical that can be expanded on a two-dimensional plane if you keep building it like a puzzle. As you add and remove pieces you can change the shape and how it fits the body,' Rosenfeld explained.[4] The overall effect is a juxtaposition of geometric precision and fragile form that camouflages the garments' modular structure.

'Object Un Dress' is a geometric spiral around the body. Using a single zip, some 315 feet in length, Rosenfeld constructs an entire dress, complete with capped sleeves and a high neckline. The zip locks into place around the neck, then zips down and around the body, over the shoulders and around the torso, continuing to circle around the hips and thighs. At this point the zip gradually expands into a voluminous crinoline shape, giving the dress an elegant silhouette that allows the body to move freely within it. Rosenfeld regards the zip as both a technical device and a modular piece that can define and transform a garment's length and volume. Object Un Dress has the potential to divide a garment into tiers of varying lengths; each tier crafted from a single zip.

Rosenfeld's range also includes dresses made solely from snap tape, a traditional haberdashery material sewn inside fabric joins to provide invisible fastening. She also regards this material as a modular system, because it can be combined according to length and colour to create a variety of tops and dresses. 'In modular clothing the garments can be continually changed or taken apart, and the modules can be made into something new,' she said. 'The wearer can continue the design life of the piece. In the snap series I didn't intend for the wearer to construct the garment, and I don't recommend that they take them apart – it will be very hard to put back together!'

Snap tape is a cotton-twill ribbon studded along its entire length with evenly spaced snap buttons (also known as pop studs). The snaps themselves comprise metallic male/female, or positive/negative, interlocking parts. The ribbons are studded with one half of the interlocking parts, connecting together with lengths containing the other half of the interlocking part when fastened. Snap tape can be compared to the warp on a weaving loom as it is stretched onto the body, then intersected by the tape containing the other halves of the interlocking parts, which is superimposed across them at a ninety degree angle, rather like the weft woven through the warp to make fabric. Once they snap into the other half of the interlocking part, a grid is formed that resembles a web when worn on the body. 'I expanded on this since the angle in the grid is flexible due to the fact that the positive parts of the snaps rotate in their negative clasps. This is how an essentially two-dimensional puzzle can be built to fit a three-dimensional body. It is interesting how this affects the movement of the whole textile when all the snaps rotate in unison. This was actually my starting point,' Rosenfeld said. This enables her to construct an entire dress using only two corresponding lines of snap tape, without a single stitch.

As with the modular bits, the snap tape incorporates a certain degree of flexibility that expands and contracts, accordion-like, to fit the contours of the body. The structure of the garment is calculated into the grid, stretching into shape once it is worn on the

Galya Rosenfeld regards the zip as both a technical device and a modular piece that define and transform a garment's length and volume. 'Object Un Dress' zips into varying lengths.

body. 'I like the continuity and functionality of modular systems,' Rosenfeld said. 'Every time the wearer decides to change the design a new process begins – the garment is never finished *per se*. I also like the fact that it can be fun to experiment with the pieces and create your own designs. Isn't it fun to have fashion you can actually play with?'

Paris-based designer John Ribbe has explored the potential of modular clothing for nearly two decades. The transformation of shapes and the reinvention of fabrics and patterns have always been recurrent themes in his collections. He creates contrasts, movements and patterns through his mix of colours, fabrics, layering and modules. Ribbe has gained a reputation for creating innovative shapes and construction techniques, and his use of surprising materials: knitted metal, embroidered vinyl, artificial grass, paper and plastic-coated lace. He even creates patterns by making clothes out of dollar bills and embroidering evening dresses with bottle caps.

Ribbe charges his work with an impressive international pedigree. He lives in Paris but was born in Hamburg, educated in England and the United States. Ribbe graduated from the Fashion Institute of Technology in New York, where he worked for Liz Claiborne and a number of other American designers, before moving to France in 1988. He designed for several French fashion houses before launching his own collection in 1993. Parallel to his main line, he later introduced a secondary collection called *John Ribbe – Zwei* (from the German numeral 'two'), which is produced in Japan.

The theme of modularity was notoriously expressed in Ribbe's 'Half Shirts' from his spring/summer 1999 collection. The shirts were constructed in panels assembled with buttons and snaps; which covered only one side of the body, leaving the model's breast exposed, or concealed the breasts and revealed the abdomen. 'Modularity is about the body,' explained Isabelle Peron, who worked with Thierry Mugler before becoming Ribbe's right-hand collaborator and wife. 'You either wish to reveal it or not. In these clothes is the means for the woman to decide for herself what she reveals and when. There is a lot of freedom for the body in that.'[5]

Ribbe's 'Mummy Dress' (autumn/winter 2000) was equally provocative. The body of the dress is constructed of panels that spiral down the body. Fully assembled, they cover the body from head to toe; the unusually high collar can be turned upwards to hide the lower half of the face. As the panels disconnect, they 'unwrap' the body, exposing the legs as the hemline is made shorter, revealing the torso or the arms as those panels are removed. The entire dress can be dismantled and worn as four separate pieces: a long skirt, a short skirt, a shirt and a bustier. Other pieces in the *Mummy* series are shirts that become dresses, coats that become jackets, and jackets that become shirts.

The 'Changing Colour Dress' (spring/summer 2001) is a simple monochrome sheath fitted with contrasting layers of white, yellow and red. All three layers can be worn to create a structured dress, or detached and worn separately as lightweight cotton shifts. Ribbe's 'Paper Doll Dresses' are also reversible, with different coloured panels that allow one dress to transform into three. 'This is an idea that we will continue to pursue,' Peron said. 'We want to make clothes that have many possibilities, but at the same time keep them very simple. There is potential to combine the idea of changing colours with the other modular idea to make a new system of fashion.'

Ribbe's modular system borrows from principles of sportswear and the tradition of fashion separates. In the 1930s American designers promoted the idea of interchangeable separates as the essential wardrobe for the modern woman. Claire McCardell developed a system of wool jersey separates that could be worn as daywear of formal eveningwear, while Vera Maxwell's 'weekend wardrobe' created multiple looks from five basic items.

Ribbe also experiments with modularity using Velcro, which provides the means for his designs to be worn and constructed in a multitude of ways. The panels are interchangeable so the front and back pieces of dresses, skirts, bustiers and sleeveless tops can be mixed and matched to form different garments. Velcro closures make it possible to tighten or loosen sleeves, open panels on trouser legs or skirts, cinch the waist of a jacket and adjust its sleeve length, or remove them completely. The Velcro pieces are made with detachable outer layers of yellow, pink or turquoise chiffon, to further emphasize the blend of materials and contrasting opaque and transparent fabrics that characterize Ribbe's work.

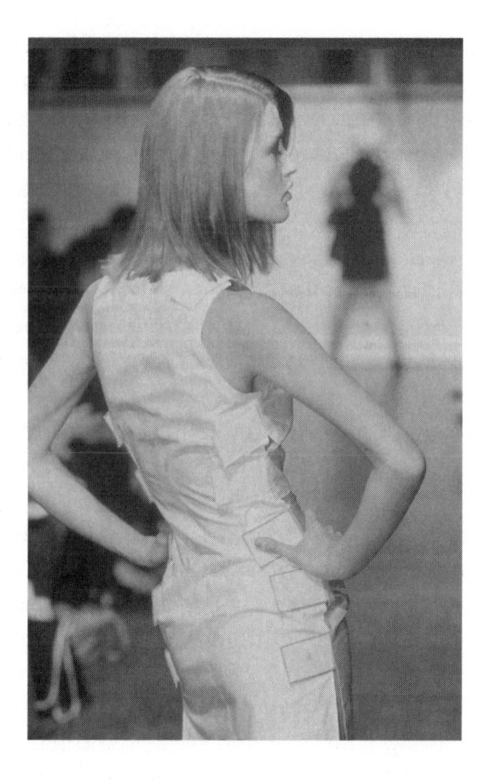

The theme of modularity is expressed in John Ribbe's 'Mummy Dress'. The entire dress can be dismantled to be worn as separates: a long skirt, a short skirt, a shirt and a bustier.

C P Company

Self-sufficiency, sanctuary, mobility: characteristics of the traditional pilgrim, or the modern nomad? The impact of fashion design on social and work environments has progressed into the urban realm with the arrival of transformable fashion, garments that embody the human fascination with extensions of themselves. As the car is an extension of our inherent mobility, and the telephone an extended mouthpiece, we become a society that depends on these technologies and others to create a sense of equilibrium.

Central to C P Company's philosophy is that we live in a world in transition. Living in an era characterized by unprecedented mobility impacts on our expectations and demands of clothing, which continue to evolve with our dual needs for independence and refuge. C P Company claim to have identified a new male consumer, the DUE (Dynamic, Urban, Educated) man, who likes the comfort of casual clothing, which he looks for in precisely tailored styles. The label splits its designs into four different collections: *Outerwear*, *Urban Protection*, *Transformables* and *C P Relax* (spring/summer 2001) to offer four distinct ranges that address the needs of navigating the urban sphere.

C P Company combines their simplified tailoring technique with advanced technological design and processes. Their streamlined tailoring eliminates the labels and exterior logos common to most high-performance clothing, retaining only a bright blue loop on the front seaming that identify it with C P Company. The unique performance of products like these makes the wearer distinctively individual through the innovations they are equipped with.

The spirit of the modern nomadic age, according to C P Company's designer Moreno Ferrari, comes from primal urges to build shelters and stake out our own territory. 'A man carries certain forms, colours and sensations deep inside himself,' said Ferrari.[6] Reportedly, these impulses are captured in the three unique inflatable items for the modern nomad, which C P Company attempt to imbue with these primal memories, and offer the wearer the means of expressing them through their clothing. Base instincts aside, the garments offer a distinctive urban utility and practicality that show they are also viable for use in the civilized world.

The *Transformables* range features three unique items: the 'Gilet', the 'Parka' and the 'Caban'. All three inflate, turning into a cushion, an armchair and an airbed, respectively. Their inflatable components are made from transparent blue polyurethane, or an opaque, earth-coloured PVC reinforced by a carbon coating. The outer layer is a thin nylon mesh that protects the items in a waterproof and tear-resistant tent-like covering. Each piece is made with magnetic buttons instead of snaps, and comes equipped with an air compressor to inflate them. They are laser cut and unlined, and made with simple detailing like Velcro tabs, expandable pockets, hoods and funnel necks.

The 'Parka' is made from an airtight polyurethane material that enables it to inflate into a one-person armchair when the wearer needs to recline. The compressor pumps up the shoulders and collar to form the chair's back, while the sleeves become armrests and the rear panel morphs into a seat cushion, allowing the wearer to stay comfortable while camping out in ticket lines, watching sports games, or take it to the beach. The 'Foldaway Hammock Jacket' from the *Urban Protection* range has a similar function. It stretches into a sleek hammock, comfortable enough to sleep in all night, or for children to take a nap in.

The 'Caban' is a long jacket with detachable layers that become both an inflated mattress and an aerodynamic one-man tent. The Caban comes complete with a torch, recalling camping equipment, should the wearer decide to take it on a trek into nature. In the urban realm, the Caban provides a perfect mini-environment for sleeping or privacy – a great solution for combating long plane delays and uncomfortable airport seating, or sleeping overnight at a friend's. The Caban can be supplemented with two other garments to maximize its performance. It could be packed away inside 'View' (from the *Urban Protection* range), which has interior carrying straps that support the back when carrying heavy loads. The 'Camelpack Jacket', as its name suggests, has watertight compartments for carrying rehydration liquids.

The 'Gilet' is a polyurethane waistcoat that becomes a cushion. Once inflated, the garment's back panel is strong enough to comfortably support full body weight, and

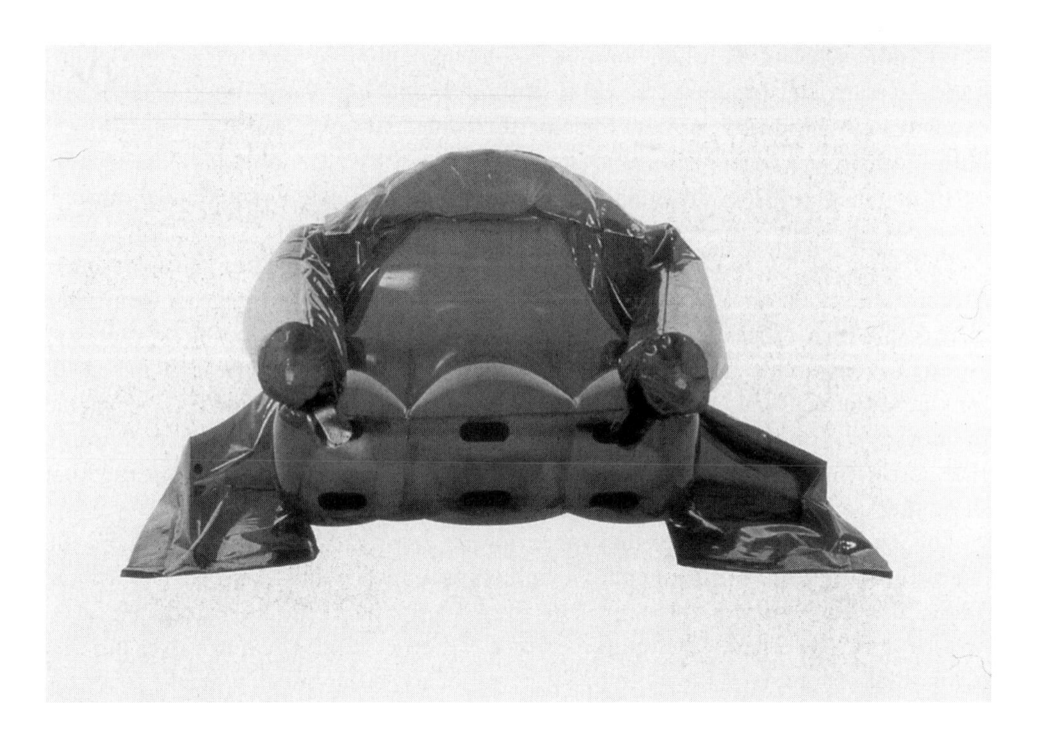

C P Company's 'Parka' inflates into an armchair when you need to recline. The shoulders and collar pump up to form the chair's back, while the sleeves become armrests as the rear panel morphs into a seat cushion.

durable enough to be placed on almost any surface. The waistcoat's front panels remain attached to the back, and can be inflated to flank either side of the main cushion to provide armrests. The 'Atlas', also from *Urban Protection*, is also inflatable. The collar serves as a cushion and headrest, designed to provide comfort and protect the traveller against whiplash.

The *Urban Protection* range also combines software technology developed by Sony to equip the wearer with functionality and comfort that extends beyond clothing. As communication tools have slimmed down and become easier to use, the amount of information transmitted electronically has dramatically increased. Being 'out of the loop' could result in a loss of vital information. Ferrari's team have adapted pre-existing communication technology with newly developed fabric technologies to create new information interfaces in clothing. The range's adjustable-length jacket, the 'REM', includes a Sony Dictaphone for dictating notes and instructions that can be listened to or transcribed back at the office.

The Sony sound technology converts two other models into mini music environments. 'Yo' is a long parka equipped with an integrated Sony Discman. 'Life' includes detachable headphones to give the wearer respite from city noises or create a relaxation

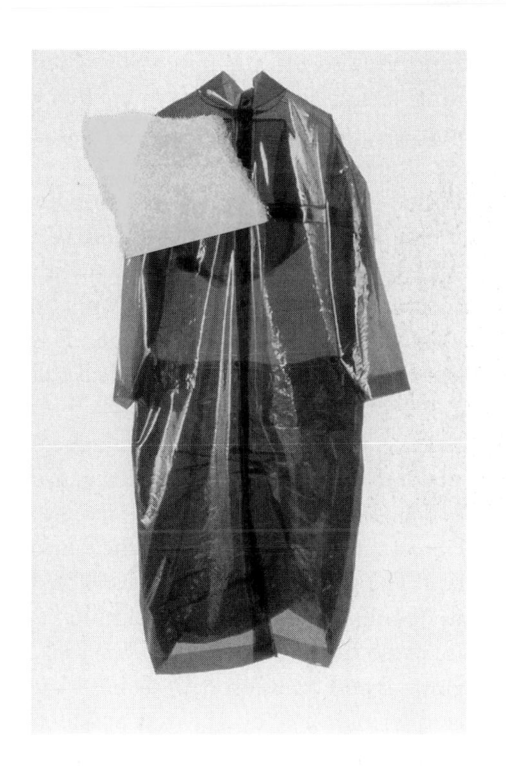

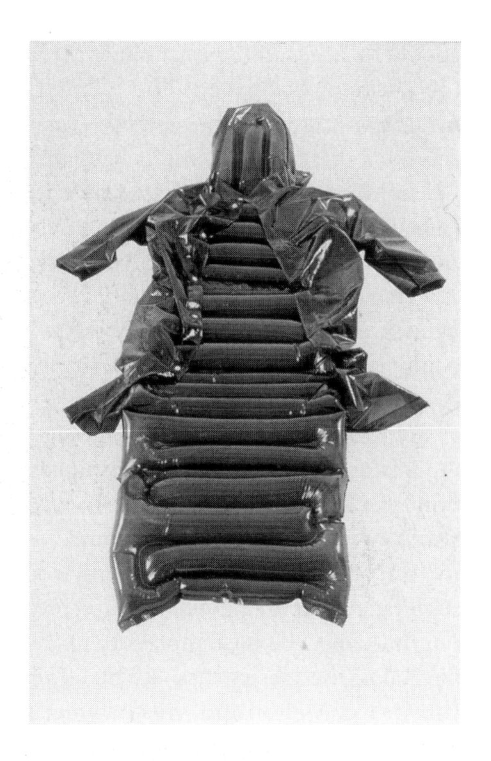

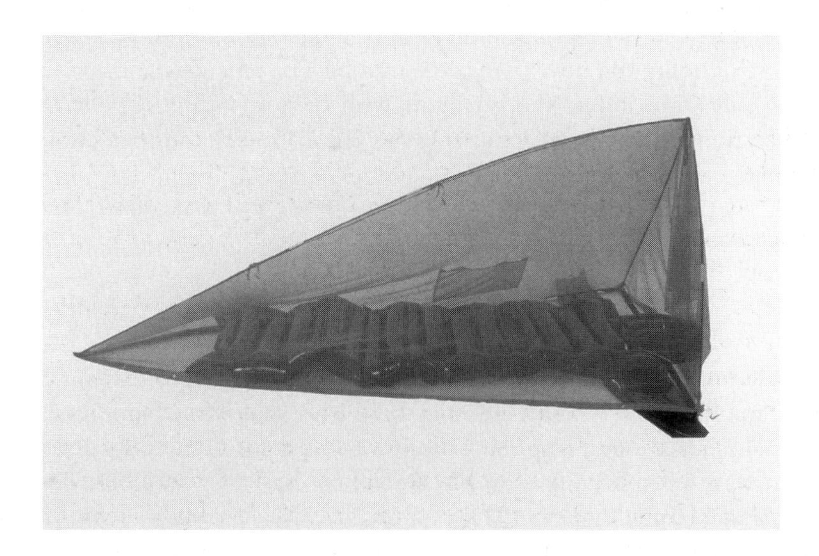

C P Company design for the modern nomad, creating overcoats that transform into inflatable mattresses and aerodynamic one-person tents. The inflatable components are made from polyurethane with an outer layer of thin nylon mesh, and come with an air compressor to inflate them.

zone. The interfaces they provide through clothing are discreet, and removable when the garment is cleaned. The 'Global Positioning Jacket' interfaces with an Etrex navigation system that enables the wearer to communicate with a ground control that can track their movements by satellite and advise alternative travel routes.

Health and personal safety concerns are addressed in the 'Munch' and 'Metropolis Jackets'. The Metropolis features an anti-smog mask that can be worn by pedestrians and cyclists. As technology moves on a new model is being developed that is fitted with a device that monitors air quality and warns against urban smog and air pollution. The Munch Jacket contains a safety feature to attract help if the wearer is in danger. It is equipped with a personal alarm that can be triggered to send out a high-pitched call to attract attention.

C P Company use fabric technology as the starting point of their designs, engineering textiles strong enough to be weatherproof and durable. Dynalfil, a high-performance polyester bonded to nylon mesh, was developed by C P Company to be rip- and abrasion-proof, oil-proof, wind- and waterproof. Steel threads are woven into the fabric to create a reinforced grid, making it tear-resistant. The garments are also constructed with taped seams to enhance waterproofing. After being cut and sewn, the clothing is put through a chemical process to re-dye them and wash them to simulate a worn look. Several of the fabrics they use blend organic materials and tradition with technology. Fabrics like Melton and worsted wool are rendered wrinkle-free by a process in which they are literally twisted to breaking point, giving them an elasticity that prevents creasing.

C P Company's *Transformables* range expresses mobility and multi-functionalism at their best, clothes that can enhance individuality and provide comfort – sentiments that bring a sense of utility and novelty to the wardrobe. The precise details and functionalism of the collection imbue the garments with design features that drive clothing beyond function, providing effective tools in combating the imperfections of their surroundings.

Kosuke Tsumura/Final Home

Most people just pass by the cardboard boxes and blanketed figures without a second glance, but not Kosuke Tsumura. Reflecting on the homeless, who brave harsh elements in their makeshift abodes, inspired Tsumura to start his own collection. Tsumura decided to leave his job with Issey Miyake, where he had worked for ten years, to launch his 'Final Home' label in 1993, a comprehensive shoes-to-coats-to-accessories collection to meet the needs of an itinerant society. Today, he is a highly respected designer whose collections have been shown in Paris for several seasons. Before that, he showed outstanding collections at London Fashion Week in 1997 and 1998.

The down-and-out might be the last people you would imagine high fashion would take inspiration from, but Tsumura is not the only designer to have referenced the plight of the homeless. John Galliano caused a stir when one of his autumn/winter collections for Christian Dior featured evening gowns of printed newspaper fabric, and tops and sweaters that appeared to be falling apart at the seams. Rather than see his own work characterized as a political comment on urban problems such as housing, homelessness and pollution, Tsumura was careful to articulate that he was not producing a fashion label geared towards reducing homelessness. His mandate was to create a shift in the concept of clothing, without implying that life on the streets or a decline into poverty could be solved by fashion alone.

Tsumura sees apparel as transformable environments, clothing that becomes intimate homes for the individual and a basis from which to find personal solutions for modern life. When Final Home was launched in 1994 it aimed to create a new wardrobe that incorporated the principles of survival and protection. Tsumura's message seems to be that, as urban nomads, we should be fully equipped with clothing that can transform into a protective shell equipped with extra warmth, objects that are important to us and enough supplies to enable us to spend a night away from home.

Kosuke's signature garment, the 'Final Home Jacket', is a multipocketed transparent nylon sheath. The jacket could function as Final Home's mission statement. Armed with forty-four multi-functional zipped pockets, the jacket is designed to maximize its storage ability, giving the wearer plenty of space to store belongings. The transparent outer pockets can be filled with pictures, postcards or artwork to customize its shell. The hidden pockets inside the jacket can be lined with warm materials for extra insulations, or cushions for comfort when you sit.

All the jackets and coats in the Final Home collection contain somewhere between forty-eight and twenty-four pockets fastened by zips or Velcro tabs, taking the practical functionalism of pockets to their very limit. Tsumura includes a range of Final Home accessories to bring a sense of cosy security to its wearers: pillows, teddy bears, terrycloth towels and sealant guns. A label is sewn on the outside of each garment requiring the wearer to write in their vital statistics, like 'Blood Type' (in case of emergency) or 'Airstream Trailers' (one coat comes with instructions on how to stuff its pockets with newspapers to keep warm at outdoor sporting events.)

Transformability is a key consideration in each design. Many of the jackets in the collection can be formal or casual, depending on how they are worn. A corporate-looking black wool buttoned blazer, for instance, reverses to become a sporty, water-repellent nylon jacket, complete with zips and snaps.

Tsumura's links with the worlds of art and design are numerous. His inspiration derives from architecture, crafts, textile production and technology. He has exhibited his designs at most of the major galleries in Japan. His Final Home collection was exhibited in the Japanese pavilion at the Seventh Venice Architectural Biennale. His project 'Mother', from the Final Home collection, was well suited to the theme of the exhibition: *City of Girls*. Mother is a cocoon-like range of suits and jackets designed to be made without any distinct form or shape of their own. Its stretchable, expandable dimensions can be worn by one person or two, because it was made to encompass a mother carrying her child. Tsumura's inspiration behind Mother was to create a single garment as an intimate clothing structure for mother and child, muting the distinction of clothing and shelter by assuming both roles. With a hood and belly that can be completely zipped up and closed, Tsumura's message is clear: protect the young from noise and pollution.

Tsumura's clothes are cut from high-tech fabrics, paper and recycled materials. Most of his designs are produced in high-performance textiles to maximize durability, while others, like his covered 'Camouflage T-shirt', have a top layer of polyester gauze that will slowly disappear as they are washed and worn. The 'Peel Out T-shirt' features a Plastisol layer that can be peeled away to transform the appearance of the graphic print to customize it.

Tsumura is interested in transforming waste into high-end products. His studio and workshop participate in a Japanese system of recycling called the 'waste business' where floss is made from scraps or is re-spun to be made into mops or work gloves. Tsumura is committed to sending surplus stock and former display garments to disaster areas through international aid organizations, a pledge he encourages other fashion designers to make.

In many ways, the designs of Final Home seem like practical clothing appropriate for an urban apocalypse, or survival in a world where Mother Nature and human disaster collide, but in Tsumura's designs, you will still look fabulous even amidst the ruins.

Jeff Griffin

While the rest of these fashion designers are busy making furniture, preparing for an urban apocalypse, or out flying kites, London design label Griffin are focused on getting back to nature. 'It's a lot easier than you think,' Jeff Griffin tells us – 'You just need the right clothing.'[7] The Griffin label produces clothing that provides warmth and protection for the wearer, equipping them to brave the great outdoors with little more than the coat on their back. Griffin makes a range of clothing with unexpected twists for design-conscious urbanites: coats that transform into sleeping bags, jackets that become ponchos or bedding. Whether the garments are worn on hiking trips, at outdoor festivals or to football matches, the wearer can withdraw into their own cosy environment and keep out the elements.

Jeff Griffin, the man behind the Griffin label, graduated from the MA degree programme at St Martin's, and headed straight to Italy. Griffin spent several years working for Valentino, Ferre and Fiorucci, also setting up and launching the successful Voyage design label. He returned to London to establish his own label, Griffin Laundry, in 1993, then set up the Griffin Studio the following year. Griffin Studio has evolved into an international forum for fashion design, where a team of fine artists, textile designers, graphic artists and sculptors work together to express conceptual themes and develop cutting-edge design. Griffin's own talent has spread far and wide; in addition to his own label he designs for a further six international labels, including Kenzo and Mandarina Duck. He famously turned down the offer to design Prada's sportswear line to focus on his own label – giving him a reputation for being a designer with talent and street cred rather than hype. In one of the collections he designed for Kenzo, Griffin used origami to create folds and geometry that questioned body shapes and fabric cuts. He went on to develop their skiwear collection, and even designed a boat interior for one of Kenzo's corporate clients.

'Transformability is important to the way I design, but I don't make things transformable just to make them more practical. The way I regard clothing is to try and put something more original into it, to bring something interesting to menswear,' Griffin explained. The Griffin label has injected originality and radical tailoring into menswear at a time when it was characterized by sportswear, street style or classic cuts, with little else in between. This is especially clear when you come across Griffin in retail environments typically known for their affinity with couture designers: Barneys and Fred Segal in Los Angeles, Harvey Nichols in London and Barneys in New York. In Japan, where there is a mania for all things British, his label ranks among the top Western brands – Griffin has even been mobbed in Tokyo for his autograph. That is not to say his ambitions mirror those of mainstream labels: 'To most people fashion means supermodels and mad clothes, but there are people nowadays who are aware of the real design that goes into it,' he said. 'Fashion has a need to make completely new clothes every season to keep moving. We keep doing the core pieces again and again, copying them from one season to the next, just changing the fabrics or a few details so that they grow and evolve over the seasons.'

The 'Pod Coat' is now one of Griffin's signature garments. It first came into the collection in autumn/winter 2000, designed with the international traveller in mind. The 'Pod' is a coat/sleeping bag hybrid with bottom seams that fasten together, then continue to zip straight up the front and over the head, enveloping the wearer from feet to face. 'It comes from the idea of containing rather than wearing, hence its name 'Pod'. The Pod was inspired by the principles behind flat-pack packaging, which Griffin applied to his fashion designs to develop a whole new way of pattern cutting. By spreading the human figure out and tracing around its outline three-dimensionally, Griffin gets a finished pattern that looks similar in shape to a gingerbread man, which he tailors and fits with zips to create a garment that looks like a long hooded overcoat. 'The Pod coat is also about travelling and moving and resisting a regimented lifestyle rather than having everyday clothes for an ordinary life,' Griffin said.

Once the transformation is complete, the wearer can pull their arms inside, and still look out through the opening in the hood. As a sleeping bag, it looks similar to most others, except that it zips down the front rather than on a side seam. For the first season it was constructed from what Griffin refers to as 'technologized nylon', but the following season it was made using breathable, natural fabrics. 'It will change each

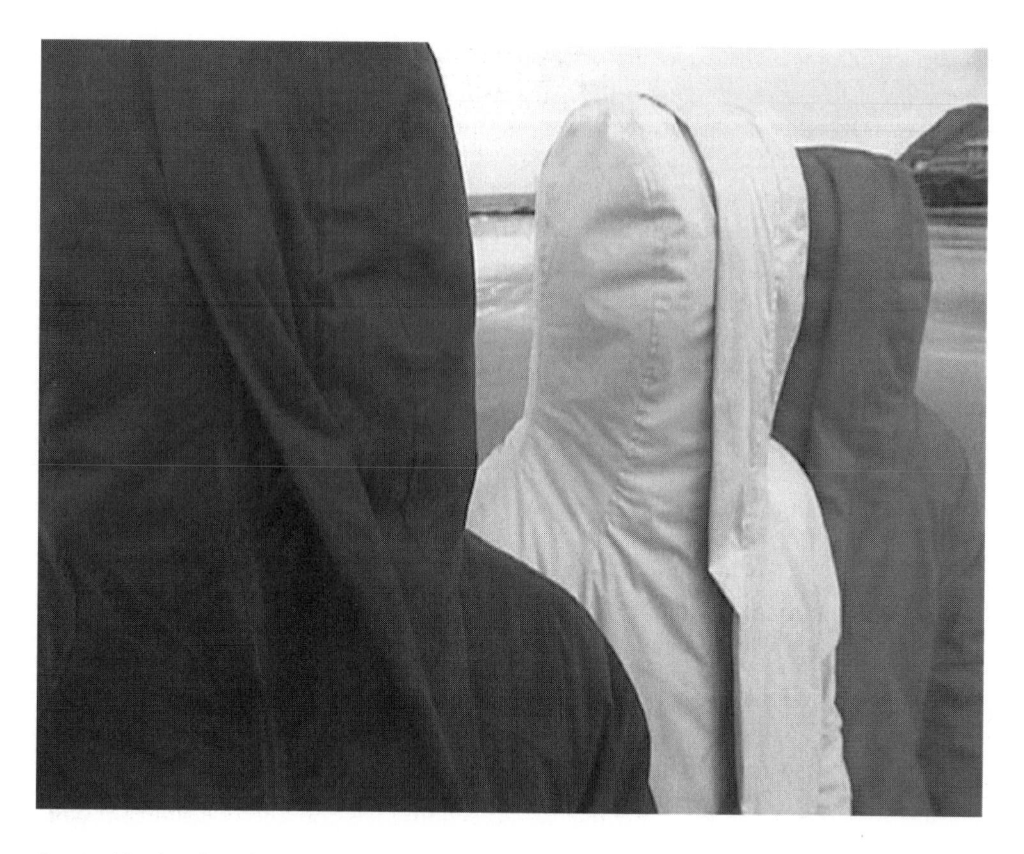

Inspired by the idea of containing rather than wearing, Griffin's 'Pod Coat' is an overcoat/sleeping bag hybrid that zips to envelop the wearer from head to toe.

season to grow and evolve with the rest of the collection. Maybe the design will stay the same but we'll try different fabrics. The natural fabrics don't have the waterproofing of the others, but they have a nicer feel to them which makes up for it,' he said. The coat comes in three different lengths and sizes to offer choices to the wearer. The small size is an adult-sized coat but transforms into a child-sized sleeping bag. 'The designs can sometimes be about creating a story. The Pod coat told a story of a mummy bear, a daddy bear and little baby bear through its large, medium and small sizing,' Griffin explained.

Griffin's 'Bare Skin Rug' is also a transformable jacket that provides warmth and comfort in three designs. Unzipping the sleeve seams turns it into a poncho – the unzipped version recalls raglan sleeves that allow the arms to extend from underneath the shoulder panels. Fully unzipped along each seam it opens completely – laid flat it resembles the shape of a bearskin rug. The jacket is padded enough to lie comfortably on top of, and warm enough to use as a quilted blanket.

Griffin's 'Bare Skin Rug' is a transformable jacket with unzipping sleeve seams that turn it into a poncho. When fully unzipped each seam opens completely, allowing the jacket to assume the shape of a bearskin rug for use as a blanket.

Jeff Griffin lives in the wilds of the countryside near Salisbury Plain in southwest England. His love for the outdoors is reflected in each piece he designs, from the themes of nature and survival in the outdoors to the distinctive checked fabrics characteristic of shooting parties and equestrian sports. He uses a palette of earth tones, khaki colours, or pinks, purples, lilacs and reds, often featuring leaves and grasses as motifs. Even so, the clothes are distinctively urban and modern. The collections can take the outdoor theme a bit too far: one collection was designed to tell the story of a kind-hearted moose – not exactly what you would expect to find roaming Salisbury Plain, but then neither is Jeff Griffin.

seven

Japanese Innovation

Provocative, radical, unwearable, incomprehensible: descriptions like these often reference the work of Japanese designers. Finding words to describe their approach is difficult because the conceptual nature of their clothes often defies the standard fashion vocabulary. Critics sometimes apply the terminology of art and architecture, but to interpret garments like these in terms of structure or function would be wrong – these are clothes made to be worn by the mind as well as the body. Their approach usually deconstructs the principles of classical tailoring, taking apart traditional methods and construction techniques, often ignoring the contours of the body to rethink the shape and design of clothing.

The process of designing and making clothes is often articulated as a feature of the finished garment, reflecting the importance Japanese designers place on experimentation and technique. Their interests in process and technology are often realized in fashions that reveal the experimentation behind their work or transforms one object into another. Japanese designers have been able to prove that shapes once considered unwearable can be fitted to the body, which they present in catwalk shows so extraordinary that they are more akin to performance art or installations.

Japanese fashion first gained attention in the West when Kenzo Takada arrived in Paris in 1965, followed by Issey Miyake and Hanae Mori. These three designers had a revolutionary impact on Paris fashion, breathing new life into a patient who may not actually have been dying, but was in urgent need of resuscitation. The next wave was led by Rei Kawakubo and Yohji Yamamoto, who also took their collections to Paris, proclaiming what European journalists xenophobically referred to as the Japanese invasion. In the 1990s, Junya Watanabe, Michiko Koshino, Yoshiki Hishinuma and Koji Hamai became the acknowledged leaders of the new wave, showing in London and New York as well as Paris. Although all of these designers are Japanese, they dislike any joint categorization due to their shared ethnicity, preferring to stand independently on fashion's international platform. But even in an industry that transcends national boundaries, there are still threads that bind them together by virtue of their aesthetics, concepts and reverence for the application of technology.

Rei Kawakubo, Issey Miyake and Yohji Yamamoto came at a time when Japan was emerging from the ranks of the developing world, where the policies and projects of post-war Japan established a new lifestyle for their generation. The rise of Western fashion symbolized modernity and progress, but in times of conflict with the West it was condemned as evidence of a hegemonic invasion. The designers worked within these opposing poles, moving towards fashion for its own sake, but starting at a point where they could appreciate influences from the ancient Nara and Edo periods, including the kimono, the quilted silk kosode and Noh costumes. At the same time, they also embraced principles of architecture in their garment construction (architects Tadao Ando, Toyo Ito and Arata Isozaki also evolved during this generation) to communicate very contemporary, forward-thinking attitudes. Kawakubo, Miyake and Yamamoto have been especially instrumental in pushing the boundaries of fashion in terms of fabrication, silhouette, function, concealment and colour.

The economic boom which allowed Japan to develop so quickly into a modern state enabled it to look towards the West in unequivocal terms and begin exporting creativity and innovation along with manufacturing and industry. As part of post-war regeneration, Japan revamped its industrial base and is now a world leader in the technological development of textiles. Japanese designers have played a key role in the progression of fashion technology, being the first to work alongside specialist technicians and fabric laboratories, looking to technology to find new materials to work with, which ultimately resulted in new design possibilities. They pioneered synthetic textiles that surpassed the labour-intensive production associated with organic fabrics, and developed new fibres, weaving techniques and methods of dyeing.

Kenzo's break away from traditional materials resulted in his distinctive use of colour, using bold primary pigments to define the form and motifs of his garments. This made Kenzo a revolutionary force in Europe, where his presence in Paris is said to have been an influence on Yves Saint Laurent, and the inspiration behind the colour gradations used by Benetton and Fiorucci. Kenzo also used a broad range of cultural influences, extending from Asia to Africa and Native America, and referenced Eastern and Western historical dress. Kenzo's fashion baton was picked up by Hishinuma, who also fused colour with ethnic influences, often combining the organic with the synthetic. Shown in Tokyo, Hishinuma's *Tribal* collection (spring/summer 1997) epitomized his interest in using technological advances to turn synthetics into body-clinging pleats, which he covered in vibrant prints. Hishinuma used only black models, painting their faces with primitive tribal markings and giving them exaggerated, almost architectural, hairstyles.

Perhaps more than any other Japanese designers, the work of Rei Kawakubo, Issey Miyake, Yohji Yamamoto, Junya Watanabe and Michiko Koshino is characterized by a shared compulsion to experiment, question and move forward. In the high-tech designs of Yohji Yamamoto are elements of construction that make them more like architecture than garments. Issey Miyake is also driven to simplify, minimalize and condense, resulting in clothes that are inherently functional and refreshingly non-elitist. Rei Kawakubo, on the other hand, treats fashion as an explosive medium with which to challenge issues concerning body shape, body image, gender and sexuality.

Michiko Koshino's garments shape and are shaped by modern life; bringing lived experience and an urban edge to her collections to reflect cultural diversity. Junya Watanabe shares Michiko's enthusiasm for urban culture and cyber styles. He describes his own design aesthetic as 'techno couture', because of his attention to technological innovations that pioneer new directions in clothing and fabric. As this chapter continues, the individual oeuvres of Kawakubo, Miyake, Yamamoto, Watanabe and Michiko Koshino will each be examined in turn, exploring how their search for new paradigms has had a resounding impact on the world of fashion.

Rei Kawakubo

'Body becomes dress becomes body,' proclaimed Rei Kawakubo, as she tried to sum up her radical perception of clothes and their function.[1] Blurring the boundaries between dress and the body itself is typical for her; it has been central to her work for three decades. Ever since she made her debut in Paris her enigmatic and provocative collections have sent shock waves resonating throughout the fashion world, and Kawakubo is still going strong.

Making such a bold statement about body and dress was not intended to signal her departure from conventional fashion, but to define her own boundaries. In Paris, Kawakubo operates in a milieu where most of her contemporaries can be categorized according to their respective interests in retro styles, traditional classicism, couture or *prêt-a-porter*. Kawakubo wants to open a new dialogue rather than pay lip service to a pre-existing one. 'I want to create something new,' she said in an interview with Susannah Frankel. 'I want to suggest to people different aesthetics and values. I want to question their being.'[2]

Kawakubo is one of the few designers capable of making the jaded, jet-lagged, seen-it-all fashion pack leave her fashion shows feeling totally amazed and uplifted. Her *Lumps* collection (spring/summer 1997) for Commes des Garçons was one of her most extreme, and is in many respects a seminal work that outlined her interpretation of the body. *Lumps* was lampooned by the Press, who wrote derisory comments like 'Lumps – The name says it all' and 'Does She Mean Tumours?'

The show charted Kawakubo's move away from conventional fashion shows to 'presentations' of her work. Kawakubo felt strongly that the official Paris Fashion Week schedule had become a circus-like parade, and decided it was time to move on to more sombre venues – a move that several other designers have followed. *Lumps* was presented at the momentous Musée d'Art d'Afrique et d'Oceanie without a catwalk or music. Three hundred spectators were positioned around a large square which the models used as an arena.

A streamlined, ankle-length dress made in white stretch organza with delicate caped shoulders was the first garment to come into view. As the model turned, two horn-like projections set on the shoulder blades vaguely implied wings, but suggested far more extreme things to come. As the show progressed, each model seemed to come out with increasingly larger swellings underneath semi-sheer gingham dresses. Most of the models had bumps on their sides, humps on their backs, or long sausage shapes wrapped around their torsos. Some had their shoulders padded to the extent that their necks disappeared. Each piece in the collection represented an abstract distortion of normal patterns. Rather than presenting designs cut in flattering silhouettes, Kawakubo used padded foam inserts and inflatable panels to distort the model's figures to absurd degrees.[3]

Radical contrast emerged in the form of balloon-like skirts constructed in waxed paper, reminiscent of Christo's *Wedding Dress* (1967), and gossamer-like tops, intricately pleated at the waist or gathered in undulating folds that suggested organic shapes. While the audience were mesmerized by the poetic movement of the paper skirts, the more radical designs caused them to voice disbelief. Those in tune with Kawakubo's sensibilities regarded the presentation as her most powerful collection in years.

While contemporary fashion is usually tailored in the front and back and follows the contours of the body, Kawakubo wrapped lengthy swathes of fabric around the body to obscure its margins. Other designs barely touched the body at all – she created monstrously oversized garments that moved with the body, but were constructed in a rigid shape that could stand independently of the body. This was Kawakubo's poetic expression of the uncelebrated void between body and fabric, an area she explores with surreal fascination.

A graduate of philosophy, Rei Kawakubo specialized in Eastern and Western aesthetics at Keio University in Japan. Kawakubo was born in Tokyo in 1942, and grew up in Japan during the period when it was still occupied by the US Army. Kawakubo is a self-taught designer. Her first engagement with fashion was working in the advertising department for a Japanese textiles company and later as a photographic stylist.

She established her own label in 1969, choosing the name 'Commes des Garçons' (meaning 'like the boys') arbitrarily, because she liked the way it sounded. During the early years of her career, the spirit of her sculptural fashions referenced innovations in architecture and philosophy in a way not previously seen in the West. Acutely aware of fashion's significance as a construct of identity, time and space, Kawakubo began using her clothes as a vehicle for exploring themes not commonly addressed by fashion. It was during this period that she established her formula for fashion: nothing seen before, nothing repeated, never uniform, never repetitive. 'I try to make clothes that are new, that didn't exist before, and hope that people get energy and feel positive when they wear them,' she told Tasmin Blanchard of *The Observer*. 'I believe that creativity is an essential part of life.'[4]

When Kawakubo and Yohji Yamamoto were invited to show at Paris Fashion Week in 1981, they made fashion history – they were the first foreign designers accepted on the official schedule. Paris, with its strict couture tradition and bourgeois heritage, was shaken by the austere vision of Kawakubo's work – one they regarded as resolutely minimal and nihilistic. In contrast with the opulent gowns, tailored suits, gentle colours and floral motifs of the houses of Saint Laurent and Dior, Kawakubo showed trousers with sweater cuffs around the ankles, tunics that transformed into shawls, oversized overcoats and shapeless boiled knitwear constructed with holes.

Even so, over the years she has attracted a strong following and established a healthy business; today she operates in thirty-three countries, generating a wholesale turnover reportedly worth $125 million a year. It is a measure of her own talent that designers as diverse as Jil Sander, Donna Karan and Alexander McQueen cite her as the world's most talented and inspirational designer, despite the fact that she regularly speaks out against the rest of the fashion industry.

Kawakubo seems to regard the conventions of fashion as a necessary evil. Her commitment to form over function and her esoteric approach to clothing construction echoes the abstractions of a visual artist more than a fashion designer. She cemented her alliance with the art world by opening a shop in the Chelsea 'gallery district' of New York. The white minimalism of the retail space and its location implied that it was an art gallery rather than a shopping destination. A cynical interpretation of this move dismisses it as a marketing ploy to cement her affinity with art patrons, whom she targeted as potential consumers of wearable art. In fact, Kawakubo often attempts to translate art styles – minimalism, abstraction, Postmodernism and Deconstruction – into wearable forms. In some ways she is in the league of painters, like Jackson Pollock, who pioneered abstract expressionism – Kawakubo is both praised and maligned by her contemporaries for pushing fashion forward.

Famous for declaring that she designed in many shades of black rather than black alone, Kawakubo announced in autumn 1988 that 'Red is Black', injecting a burst of colour into her sombre palate. In more recent collections she has continued to move away from her signature black, stating that its popularity among other designers had diluted its power. 'Black is no longer strong and has become harder to use,' Kawakubo said in an interview with Susannah Frankel.[5]

Kawakubo's work has both deconstructed and reconstructed the vernacular of Western tailoring. Often she deconstructs clothing by disregarding its function – she once made a dress that had no openings, making it impossible to put on. But it can be worn, she insisted, and decreed that it could be used as an apron. She focused on taking the lapel apart – she used jacket lapels to design halter-neck jackets and make scarves. Her menswear suits combined cropped trouser with double-breasted sports jackets, featured shawl collars and juxtaposed blown up and 'bleached' classic checked fabrics.

Many of her designs are multipurpose, designed to be worn in variety of unconventional ways, encouraging the boundaries between occasion-specific wear and everyday wear to collapse. Kawakubo carefully calculates exact proportions so that she can invert

Rei Kawakubo radically inverts proportions as she recalculates the distances between neckline, waistline and hemline, then projects them back onto the body in asymmetrical cuts. The patterns she uses here confuse the gaze by creating an optical illusion of false proportions.

them to radically rethink the distances between neckline, waistline and hemline, but rarely places them in the usual areas. Worn on the body, the garments are often draped or looped around the models rather than dressing them in them. Collars, fastenings and sleeves move around the garment with equal precision.

Kawakubo even deconstructs her models: their hair is often unkempt or brushed into straw-like configurations. Make-up is applied to look like bruises or blistering, highlighting the face with bold colours or erasing the mouth and eyebrows altogether. Kawakubo's juxtaposition of decay with elitism and luxury is shockingly effective – 'decay becomes luxury becomes decay' seems to summarize her move forward; a declaration Kawakubo would accept as the compliment it is intended.

Yohji Yamamoto

Yohji Yamamoto remains an enigma to most of those who have met him or worked for him. Not because he is reserved or reclusive, but because he is boundless. The artistic expression evident in his clothing has been labelled as poetry; his clothes, as sculpture. Yamamoto works within a poetic, associative and metaphorical sphere, where fashion principles are applied but not adhered to. He creates visually striking yet simple clothes, which often have more in common with architecture than traditional clothing construction. Yamamoto knows how to conquer space.

Understanding his highly aestheticized clothing is to position modern minimalism against an urban dreamscape. As much as he is pioneering a new direction for clothing, Yamamoto is creating a new environment for them. Whether it is virtual or tangible makes little difference to him – he imbues form and shape with emotions and ideas and releases them to metamorphose on the wearer. The garments themselves are designed to hang unambiguously or drape romantically around the body. Precise seams intersect the planes of fabric fitted against the body or extending from it, like joins between walls that tell the story of how the building is constructed. Every cut he makes is an act of defining space.

Yamamoto's world is famously closed and inaccessible. He is not a designer given in to the cult of the celebrity, or interested in expressing his personality through his work. In an effort to demystify him, German film director Wim Wenders made him the subject of an eighty-minute documentary, *Notebook on Cities and Clothes* (1989/90), which attempted to offer insight into Yamamoto's life and work. This undertaking was too mammoth even for a director of Wenders's experience. He succeeded in bringing Yamamoto into the public gaze – something Yamamoto notoriously avoids – but did not manage to reveal what lies behind the mystery behind the man behind the clothes.

As a child, Yohji Yamamoto helped his mother in her dressmaking business. He describes himself as a natural feminist, believing his design talent evolved as a result of learning about the world through women's eyes. He studied law at Keio University, then went on to study fashion at Bunka College of Fashion in Tokyo. He returned to work for his mother, then set up his own label around 1970. His father had been drafted into the Japanese army during World War II and was killed. 'He went against his will,' Yamamoto said in Wender's film, 'When I think of my father I realise that the war is still raging inside me.'

Yamamoto's work is invariably discussed in relation to that of Rei Kawakubo. Like Kawakubo, he has a reverence for the impractical and the imperfect, enabling him to push beyond the type of constraints that most designers hold on to. While Kawakubo avoids the influence of the external world, Yamamoto's outlook embraces history, culture and tradition, acknowledging that fashion is shaped by each. Like Kawakubo, he pioneered profoundly austere collections that espoused modern textiles, multi-functionality and radical shapes, and is considered one of the greatest living fashion designers in the world.

When he began showing his work internationally, Yamamoto brought the colour black to Paris at a time when it was not even recognized as a colour; he then abandoned black and opted for stark white. His white garments tend to have a future-orientated feel; light and air are represented in smooth open surfaces and beautifully curved shapes. To Yamamoto, white is the most contemporary colour of them all.

The expressiveness of his work is reinforced by stressing the presence of the materials he works with, and the volume he investigates around the body. Yamamoto layers opaque fabrics over transparent ones to balance the shape and texture of the textiles and reveal the body as the essence of the garment. He is a superb tailor, crafting subtle, soft silhouettes and sharply defined suits. He introduced the black suit to the white T-shirt in his menswear collection, which subsequently became the standard uniform for men working in the arts.

Yamamoto has designed many crinoline styles as a process of probing and observing space. Perhaps the most outstanding of these was the bridal dress and wedding hat ensemble shown on the model Jodie Kidd in his autumn/winter 1998 collection. The dress was monstrously oversized – Kidd wore a simple, streamlined bodice that dipped into a skirt some twelve metres in circumference. The hat mirrored the breadth and proportions of the skirt – it was so hugely oversized that four poles carried by attendants were required to support it. Yamamoto claimed he was caricaturing mainstream perceptions that fashion was excessive and extravagant.

As Kidd moved forward in the dress, its weight and bulk inexplicably turned into lightness, as if the laws of gravity had temporarily been suspended. Cocooned in the dress and hat and flanked by the attendants, the outfit brought strictly guarded borders to mind: not to lock anybody in but, rather, to keep them out. It is the viewers who are imprisoned, gazing covetously at the liberty beckoning behind the folds of the skirt. Yamamoto created a powerful relationship between the vast surface of the dress and the five humans around it. Everything connected to the dress is intended to be a part of it: the four attendants and the space between them, the dress and the model; the space between the poles and beneath the hat; the space beneath crinoline hidden by the surface of the dress. This work connects bodies and buildings, cities and cells, monuments and hidden intimacies – all within the realm of the individual. Yet, its mass does not obliterate the wearer, it strengthens her. Yamamoto understands the need for clothes to be interconnecting, yet become a fortress and a bunker at times.

Yamamoto later referenced the hidden intimacies of the fashioned body in a subsequent wedding dress (spring/summer 1999), when he used its volume to create zipped compartments. When opened on the catwalk, they disclosed a pair of high-heeled shoes, a wide-brimmed hat and a calico bouquet. The spirit of this approach suggested the practicalities of compartmentalizing the dress rather than accessorizing it, which Yamamoto defines by reapportioning the space around the body. Other versions of the dress were removed on the catwalk to reveal slimmer knee-length versions underneath.

The crinoline seems to be a recurring favourite, but Yamamoto signals other historical references too. He is fond of Gothic ornamentation, rustic medieval shapes and elaborate jet beading. A foray into the Belle Époque period inspired evening gowns attached to the body by knotted silk. His acclaimed spring/summer 1997 collection paid homage to early Parisian couturiers – including Chanel's signature black. Ethnic references are more international than tribal, collected on recent travels rather than used to evoke the past. African nomads inspired him to show oriental prints and kimono silks for his spring/summer 1982 collection. For autumn/winter 1991 he dressed women in layers like Russian dolls, and the autumn/winter 2001 collection included fur-lined coats inspired by the Inuit.

In addition to his couture collections, Yamamoto produces more affordable clothing lines, accessories and a fragrance. He started a youth-orientated collection which his daughter Limi is in charge of. Yamamoto has his own chain of retail shops, which are minimal to the extreme. They are often described as 'industrial', but the aesthetic is too austere to be adequately described by that look. The boutiques echo the art-gallery aesthetic pioneered by Kawakubo, with just a select few designs hung or folded at discreet intervals around the space.

During the late 1980s Yamamoto worked with photographer Nick Knight, stylist Marc Ascoli and graphic artist Peter Saville to produce biannual catalogues that survey his work over the two-year period. Within the pages of the catalogues lies the vernacular behind his vision – somehow made more comprehensible in its two-dimensionality. Nick Knight's photographs of Yamamoto's autumn/winter 1986 collection feature black dresses embellished with lengths of red tulle contorted into a form evocative of a late-nineteenth-century bustle. One image depicts a woman in profile, posed as if she has been captured in a moment of reverence. She stands upright, head bowed forward, the peak of her cap pitched directly towards the ground. The front of the garment's silhouette forms a single line running from collar to hem, broken only by the incline of her neck tilting out of the collar. The hemline appears to be squared off into a forty-five degree angle, which is mirrored in the inverted angle at the join of her 'bustle' to the back of the dress. The bustle explodes out of the dress, the fiery crimson of its fabric contrasting sharply with the otherwise monochrome dress and background. The bustle is swirling and unravelling – defying the control exerted over the wearer and the dress.

The image emphasizes form and texture – the sharp, precise lines of the silhouette highlight the rich texture of the bustle. Without the bustle in place, the dress is opened into a radically asymmetrical hemline, dropping precipitously from derrière to ankle. The dress is at once cumbersome yet curiously liberating. Though fashion projects the necessity of containing or being contained in garments, Yamamoto wants us to be free.

Issey Miyake

In his spring/summer and autumn/winter 1999 shows, Miyake dressed his assistants in black and sent them onto the catwalk with a model. The assistants produced a pattern, fabric and appropriate tools, then cut and constructed the garment while the audience watched. Once on the model it became a ground-breaking creation, marking the process of the garment's design and construction the focal point of the show, rather than the clothes themselves. Innovations like these have made Miyake a name in the fashion world.

Easy to make, easy to wear, fun to watch – Miyake's philosophy made simple. But simplicity is the result of a long and difficult process – a journey of exploration and experimentation that juxtaposes technology and aesthetics. While Miyake's works are renowned for their innovations, it is actually his quest to simplify, minimalize and condense that drives his practice. The functionality of Miyake's designs reflects his philosophy that clothes should reflect the specific needs of a people and their culture and not just espouse the whims of the fashion elite. He proved this point when he famously showed his clothes on women who were all in their eighties. The *Octogenarian* collection (autumn/winter 1995), as it became known, showed how wearable and how versatile his clothes could be.

Miyake's approach to form and construction have often been likened to fine-art methodology. Whether displayed in a gallery, or animated by the human body, they are often described in terms of spatial geometry or sculptural aesthetics – or simply as wearable art. Large-scale exhibitions of Miyake's clothes have been shown in prestigious galleries around the world. His first gallery exhibition was the 1963 *Ten Sen Men* exhibition at the Seibu Museum of Art in Tokyo, which explored his two-dimensional use of geometry. Many garments were shown flat to emphasize the graphic images he creates. In 1997, he showed *Arizona*, another major exhibition in Japan, at the Genichiro-Inokuma Museum in Marugame, this time suspending the garments on single wires to emphasize their sculptural abstraction.

European exhibitions included the *Bodyworks* show, held in London in 1985, in which Miyake suspended the garments on dress forms over pools of black dye. The *A-un* exhibition at the Musée des Arts Decoratifs in 1985 featured some of his most voluminous garments, fitted onto figures made out of wire intertwined into a human shape. More recently, Miyake presented his pleated clothing in his *Energieen* exhibition, held at the Stedelijk Museum in Amsterdam in 1990. This exhibition explored both the sculptural and three-dimensional characteristics of clothes. The garments were both exhibited on dress forms and laid flat to create a colourful geometric relationship between both shapes.

Miyake was born in Hiroshima in 1938. Seven years later he was cycling to school when the Americans dropped the atom bomb. Within a few months, more than 140,000 of the city's 350,000 population were dead, including most of Miyake's family. His mother, although severely burned, continued working as a schoolteacher for four years until she died. There was no medicine to give her; neighbours treated her burns with raw eggs. When Miyake was ten he developed bone-marrow disease as a result of the radiation, the effects of which he endures to this day.

Understandably, Miyake prefers to forget such things. Dwelling on the happy side of life is central to his philosophy that fashion should be imbued with a sense of fun, that clothing should be an expression of happiness. Miyake finds happiness in the celebration of nature – the wind, the sun, the seasons, the colours and forms of the earth, and injects these elements into clothes imbued with optimism for the future.

Miyake received a degree in Graphic Design from Tama Art University in Tokyo, then enrolled with the Chambre Syndicale de la Couture in Paris in 1965. He worked for Guy Laroche and Givenchy, then Geoffrey Beane in New York, before returning to Tokyo in 1970 to set up his own design studio. Although Miyake has shown his collections in New York and Paris and is now a well-established international designer, he continues to live and work in Tokyo. Despite his base in Japan, he resists being described as a Japanese designer because his inspiration is drawn from such a wide variety of sources. His clothes combine Japanese traditionalism with influences from France, the United States and England, eliminating the boundaries between East and West while retaining the essence of each culture.

Miyake's exploration of his own culture has rediscovered inspirations ranging from the kimono and the junihitoe, to the traditional blue and white Japanese workwear, to ultra-sophisticated high-performance clothing. His approach to fabric often echoes the precise cuts and folds of the kimono and its underlying principles of construction. Whereas Western clothing is cut and tailored, seamed and darted, classical Japanese dress tends to be shaped by the careful folding and wrapping of the fabric, binding it tightly on the torso. Miyake's signature layered look was inspired by the many layers found in the kimono – his 'Prism' dress (autumn/winter 1998) was made from a single piece of fabric wound around the body, mimicking the kimono's wrapped, cross-vented construction.

Miyake employs a team of designers and scientists in Tokyo to research fabric technology and construction techniques. Known as the Issey Miyake Design Studio, they experiment with a wide range of synthetic and organic materials, computer processes and production methods. Miyake and his team are driven by a mission to invent another fabric as revolutionary as polyester. In the meantime they create extreme designs from fabrics like neoprene, make bodices using natural materials like bamboo and rattan, and craft jackets and hats from waxed paper. Throughout the 1990s they worked with thermoplastic synthetics, crushing, twisting, creasing and folding them, and eventually pleating them. With the collaboration of Makiko Mingawa, they developed a holographic fabric and turned inflatable plastics into clothing. But Miyake's interests, as indicated in the developments he made in pleat technology, lie more in transformation and manipulation than creation.

The *Pleats Please* collection embodies Miyake's design philosophy, revealing the extent of his ability to innovate with new materials and technology. They are also a practical easy-to-wear solution to everyday dress, which is why Miyake refers to them as the jeans and T-shirts of the twenty-first century. Miyake has pointed out that pleats can be traced back to the ancient Egyptians and, by adapting this technique for the modern era, he is continuing an archaic tradition.

Miyake began working with pleats in his spring/summer 1989 collection, but started the *Pleats Please* line four years later, after refining the process. The fabric he uses is 100 per cent polyester jersey and can be pleated horizontally, vertically and diagonally. Miyake's approach, which is more typical of an architect or an engineer, is to cut and sew oversize garments, which then 'shrink' down to the right size in the pleating process. The fabric is fluid, lightweight and versatile, containing composite properties that retain pleating permanently after completing the production process. The polyester's elasticity allows enough stretch to pull it on and off comfortably, then mould to the body when worn. While thicker fabrics are less elastic and require the use of zips, the elasticity of thinner fabrics eliminates the need for fastenings.

The basic design of a *Pleats Please* garment starts with a simple tunic shape, cut close to the body. Sleeves are designed so that the garment resembles a simple T-shape or has added volume echoing Elizabethan puffed sleeves. The fabrics are produced in a wide range of colours and motifs, ranging from a rainbow-like pattern to bold, two-tone designs. The *Guest Artist* series (autumn/winter 1997 collection) was a collaboration with internationally acclaimed artists that featured prints taken from their artwork. Yasumasa Morimura, legendary for his dotted and spotted canvases and installations, was Miyake's first collaborator, followed by Nobuyoshi Araki, who designed optical illusions to appear and disappear with the movement of the pleats. Subsequent series had photographic images printed on limited-edition pleated garments, using them as blank canvases.

Miyake created the *A Piece of Cloth* concept with Dai Fujiwara, a textile engineer and designer at the Issey Miyake Design Studio. Dubbed *A-POC*, the line is constructed from Raschel knit tubes produced by computer-programmed industrial knitting machines. As the machine knits tubes of fabric they are pressed flat so that the shapes of garments can be woven into them. Each garment is made distinct by the ribbed outline demarcating its shape. After the patterns have been knitted into the tube it comes out in a roll; once unfurled, an entire wardrobe is revealed. Dresses, skirts, jumpers, socks, underwear and even bags are stitched into the tube. Once the garments are cut free with a pair of scissors, they are ready to be worn.

The *A-POC* garments could be produced without machine-sewn seams; a development that could revolutionize the ready-to-wear fashion industry. The possibilities presented by this type of clothing are endless. Imagine a vending machine programmed to knit a range of clothing according to an individual's selection of garment, colours, pattern and size. An entire customized wardrobe could be ready in minutes.

A-POC was engineered with environmental considerations in mind. To devote himself fully to *A-POC*, Miyake handed over design of his mainline collection to his creative director, Noaki Takizawa, in 1999. Like Miyake, Takizawa resists conventions of clothing. Takizawa's spring/summer 2001 collection for Miyake was well structured and characteristically innovative. Rejecting traditional circular hemlines, he designed full-length dresses with square hemlines. Inflatable tubes were inserted into the hems to give them their square shapes.

Despite the square hems and the pre-programmed knitwear patterns, Miyake is still committed to pioneering shapeless designs. His 'Wind Coats' for example, are described as being a 'free' style. The coats can be wrapped around the body like a duvet, billow with the blowing wind and fall back into shape. That makes the wearers the creators by allowing them, not the designer, to expand or compress the coats as they like. True to Miyake's philosophy, the coats are easy to make, easy to wear and fun to watch. For Miyake, this is modernism in clothing and, for him, *that* characterizes freedom.

Michiko Koshino

Michiko Koshino is a Japanese designer who lives and works in the West, but the clothing she creates belongs to neither culture. Her Japanese influences mean something to the West; her Anglo references are one of her hallmarks in Japan. Michiko can be claimed as a visionary, but one who is entirely practical and who accepts fashion as a hybrid of commerce and innovation. She has followed her own path, never allowing herself to be seduced by outright commercialism, yet not failing to accept the imperative that she must make a profit to survive. Michiko maintains a loyal following of British pop stars, celebrities and cult personalities, because she speaks the same language. But Michiko's work is not just a commentary on youth culture: it is a part of it.

While Watanabe, Kawakubo, Miyake and Yamamoto are keen to call themselves international designers, they are all based permanently in Japan, so their experiences

Michiko Koshino uses pleating to create the illusion of two surfaces. The top surface is coated in rubber but the folds retain the fabric's natural knitted finish. The natural fabric is soft against the skin, while the rubber coating protects it and renders a lustrous finish.

of Western culture are restricted. 'I've never thought of myself as a Japanese designer. I've been in London such a long time I see myself as a British designer now,' Michiko said. 'My work is much more connected to the London scene than any other place.' Unlike many of her Japanese contemporaries, Michiko understands the different attitudes to clothing found in the West, perhaps because she has been based there for more than twenty years. 'I just returned from Japan, and it feels so good to be back. In Tokyo everything is too hectic, too confusing. I feel able to connect to everything going on here in a way that I can take it all in and make sense of it,' she said.

Michiko cuts a distinctive figure on the London scene: cruising around her Notting Hill neighbourhood in her Mercedes coupé, shopping and lunching in Soho, drinking and dancing with her friends at hip nightspots and regularly attending services at a Christian church. Her experience of many different parts of the city and different types of people channels into her work, where she designs a specific look that appeals to a wide range of diverse personalities. 'My concept for clothing has always been to be casual, comfortable, really practical. When I first came to London I could see that people on the club scene really wanted these types of clothes to get dressed in and wear out to nightclubs. There was nothing like that in Tokyo then, or even Paris. Everything in Japan was really formal – too serious I thought,' she said.

Michiko has been showing at London Fashion Week for nearly twenty consecutive seasons. Under the umbrella of her Michiko Koshino label, she shows her Motorking collection and Yen Jeans denim range. Motorking became the signature club wear of the 1990s, making Michiko the undisputed icon of the hipster scene. It would be impossible to dismiss the strength of her vision and her impact on urban fashion at that time; Michiko was the first to show the 'cyber' look in the early 1990s, and coined the term 'techno couture' before it was appropriated by Watanabe. 'Cyber style relates to the music scene of the late 1980s/early 1990s,' Michiko explained. 'Techno music was big on the club scene and I decided to express the feeling of the music in my clothing. It was something new, there was a lot of energy in it, then my Motorking label launched cyber style. What the cyber look said was that fashion should always be something new.'

Michiko pushes forward with every new idea and innovation she can think of, never finding inspiration in bygone eras and never looking back. As well as staging fashion shows in Japan, Hong Kong, Taiwan and Korea, where she has a chain of boutiques, she has had shows in São Paulo, New York and Belgrade. 'Now I'm launching my collection in Italy. I can see that they are really ready for youth culture styles now, after a long tradition of dressing very formally and wearing conservative styles,' she said. Among the Japanese designers, Michiko is the designer most closely associated with youth culture; though she has had a major influence on younger fashion designers, her expressions of music, motor sports, and nightclubbing have distanced her from her peers.

But fashion is legendary for its elitism, and Michiko has undeservedly been the brunt of criticism from some of her high-minded contemporaries. Fashion, for Michiko, is a medium through which she reflects her personal interests rather than a vehicle to express profound concepts. Michiko approaches her craft with the same reverence and spirituality characteristic of Kawakubo, Miyake and Yamamoto, but takes her inspiration from the lived experience of people around her. Michiko's creations often result from the cultural diversity she has observed in cities around the world; influences she fuses into clothing and rebounds back onto the scene so that others can share in the experience. As subculture, nightlife and music merge through her designs, she creates garments influenced by modern life.

Fashion runs in the Koshino family. Hiroko Koshino, Michiko's mother, is a prominent Japanese couturier, while her sisters Ayoko and Junko also have their own labels. The four women have succeeded in putting the Koshino family name on just about every fabric surface in Japan, sometimes being referred to as Japan's first family of fashion. Part of Michiko's Western identity has been inspired by her wish to express herself individually, apart from the traditions that inspire the rest of the family. 'I'm so different from my mother and sisters it's unbelievable,' she said. 'I grew up with all these classical styles being made and remade around me, chiffon this, silk that, and it was too much. I had to break away and do my own thing. I even thought about being a tennis pro for a while – anything to not have to make the same dresses over and over!'

Her label offers a credible alternative to couture labels; rather than conferring status, she projects a young, cool, urban lifestyle that other designers find impossible to emulate. 'My concept actually links casual to functional, because it expresses what's going on in youth culture, and not the formality and aloofness of the fashion world. People can actually relate easier to new fabrics than old ones that have a traditional history. That's one of the reasons I started using industrial fabrics and materials like wadding, netting and padding. After having a background so full of expensive silk I don't have any desire to work in silk and chiffon, I got sick of looking at it.'

Michiko is one of a handful of designers in Britain pioneering the use of high-tech fabrics and new cutting techniques. Always one step ahead, her London shows were the first at Fashion Week to include inflatable clothing, transparent fabrics, reflective fabrics, PVC and metallic fabrics. In her *Soft Cyber* collection (autumn/winter 1997) she worked with thick bonded fabrics, cut at the joints and combined with knitted sections to aid mobility. Michiko took inspiration from flickering television screens for her *TV Couture* collection, creating a 'TV interference' pattern on a Lycra blend and combining layers of fabric printed with optical illusions. Michiko recently developed a range of fabrics and futuristic garments for the textile manufacturer Mitsubishi Rayon, who launched the range in Japan.

Michiko is focusing on techno fibres for her sportswear collection to give it a progressive edge that will not look like conventional sports clothing. In the short term, she is basing her M Jeans and mainline collections on natural fabrics that she treats and processes with synthetic materials. Her spring/summer 2002 collection included dresses and skirts made of natural fabrics that were moulded or coated to hold asymmetrical silhouettes. 'These dresses describe where the future of fabric is going,' she explained. 'They're pleated, so there is an outside surface and a hidden, inner surface between the

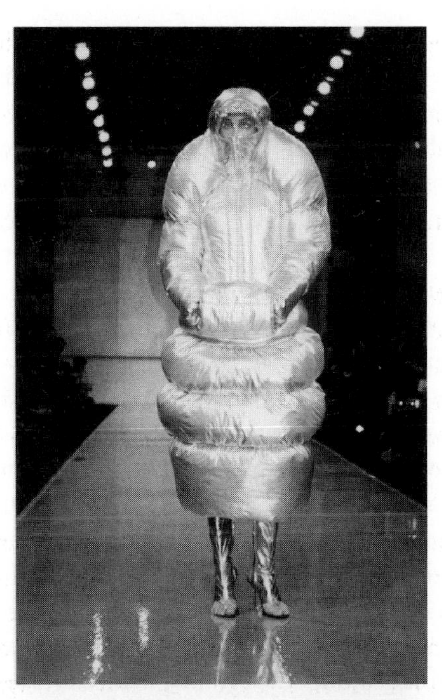

According to Michiko Koshino, new materials like wadding, netting and metallic fabrics are identified with futuristic ideals, which makes them more dynamic than textiles that have a traditional history.

folds. The top surface is coated in rubber, while the folds keep its natural knitted finish. The natural fabric gives them a nice feel, while the coating gives them protection and a modern look.'

For spring 2001, Michiko brought the audience to her homeland, showing Japanese influences on the clothes and the accessories for both the men's and womenswear collections. The Yen Jeans collection drew inspiration from legendary warriors. Michiko uses vintage denim and PVC to create a variety of shapes not typically seen in a jeans range. The Kendo Warrior jeans are low-cut baggy trousers, and the Arab jeans are a unisex hybrid of skirt and trousers. The kimono-style 'Torso Wrap' features a traditional dragon motif and is bound tightly at the waist.

Michiko stages many fashion events all over the world, which, because of her pop star patrons, verge on being underground music events. Her catwalk music might be a special commission from a leading band or artist, or a live mix by a leading club DJ. With clients like The Prodigy, All Saints, David Bowie, Sonique, Moby, Spice Girls, Placebo, Talvin Singh and Natalie Imbruglia, Michiko gets her share of fashion editorial in *Vogue* and *The Times*, but is a favourite of youth-orientated magazines like *The Face*, *i-D*, *Dazed & Confused*, *Arena*, *Ministry of Sound* and *Mixmag*.

Motorking and Yen Jeans include limited-edition pieces – many of them are already collector items – as signifiers of their design originality. The commercial success of her labels gave Michiko the capital to launch what she describes as 'lifestyle' collections, which include cosmetics, underwear, sunglasses and watches. Michiko was the first designer to market condoms under her own name and has been involved in such diverse projects as designing a Barbie Doll outfit entitled 'Millennium Barbie', and team uniforms for the Hashin Tigers, Japan's most famous baseball team. Michiko has also had success with her accessories range of hoods, visors, batons, facemasks and dagger-heeled shoes that explore themes of urban danger and protection. In 1999, Honda commissioned her to customize their new environmentally friendly scooter; on a whim she jumped on and roared out onto the catwalk at the close of her London Fashion Week show, sending models, journalists and photographers running for their lives.

Junya Watanabe

Watanabe describes his design aesthetic as 'techno couture', because of his emphasis on the technological construction of fabrics and individual garments. Watanabe explores the realm of fashion through the science of fabric, placing emphasis on the technological innovations that make new directions in clothing and fabric possible. He is driven to take fashion forward by whatever means possible, which has earned him the reputation of one of contemporary fashion's greatest visionaries. Watanabe achieved cult status in the world of avant-garde fashion after celebrities like Björk were photographed in his clothes.[6]

ent in his work is a complete disregard for trends. In fact, Watanabe seems ined to work in opposition to them. At the height of Paris' foray into lism, he created an autumn/winter 1996 collection characterized by an e fusion of fluorescent fabrics and acid-coloured PVC garments. Entitled *Mutants*, the collection rebelled against the streamlined silhouettes dominating the season by presenting a range of complex and intricate designs that inverted classical construction. The technology behind the collection was light years ahead of anything shown in Paris before, with garments made in neoprene, glass fibres, plastics and industrial fibres intended to insulate computer wiring and make chemical filters. Watanabe has printed motifs onto a fabric developed from computer film and the laminated paper textile Tyvek. His *Digital Modern Lighting for the Future* collection (spring/summer 2001) – chosen to launch the Paris collections that season – featured tops and dresses constructed from glossy coloured discs and rectangles, and semi-transparent jackets constructed from glow-in-the-dark textiles.

Having established a reputation for pioneering techno fabrics, he began working with organic materials like cotton and wool. For autumn/winter 1999 he introduced his 'unconstruction' look – sheets of Melton wool, wrapped around the body in an echo of pleated skirts or kilts and suspended from the body by coils of wire. These were shown with oversized men's cotton shirts that mimicked full-length dresses. His inspiration often comes from the London street scene, especially the second-hand shops and markets of Camden and Portobello. One season he presented a collection with a Gothic feel – pale, heavily tattooed models wore black leather clothes and black boiled wool knitwear – all with zips in unexpected places.

Other collections have been a *tour de force* of high-performance textiles acclaimed for their advances in fabric technology. Watanabe's autumn/winter 1996 collection was inspired by Fritz Lang's visionary film *Metropolis*, made in 1927. Some of the high-tech fabrics he used were dense and unyielding, requiring industrial cutting and contour seaming to fit them close to the body, and fixing flexible joints at the elbow, shoulder and knee to make them wearable. In his summer 1996 collection he used knitted polyamide laminated with polyurethane, inspired by the cellophane gels used to create coloured light effects in theatres. Cellophane-like fabrics were used to highlight technical details normally hidden in the garments. Simple, minimal tunic dresses were worn over stovepipe trousers in transparent materials and polyesters. Watanabe's *Function and Practicality* collection (spring/summer 2000) was entirely waterproof – even the evening gowns. Watanabe's fabric 'performed' on stage for the benefit of the audience – he demonstrated his advances in waterproof-fabric technology by splashing models with water from above as they walked down the catwalk.

Watanabe's designs are characterized by their innovative construction. He uses complex seaming and darting to rework and redefine classic shapes, or morph them into new silhouettes. He creates rich textures and exaggerated forms by using intricate origami folding, honeycomb weaves and ruffles that resemble flower petals. Origami has almost become his signature, because he uses it to construct whole garments and

Junya Watanabe's designs are characterized by complex seaming and darting, rich textures and exaggerated forms created by using delicate origami folding and honeycomb weaves.

embellish others. For his highly acclaimed autumn/winter 2001 collection, Watanabe stitched hundreds of layers of nylon organza together to create a complicated origami dress. The collection also features ruffled coats and dresses embellished with papery frills that had the childish beauty of flower costumes made for a school play. Underneath the extravagant garments were simple tweed shifts.

For autumn/winter 2000 Watanabe produced a romantic, upbeat collection presented like an intimate couture show. The models floated across a mosaic floor to a soundtrack of Viennese waltzes. Perhaps Watanabe's most nostalgic and whimsical collection, the full silhouettes of the origami dresses recalled the billowing sweep of nineteenth-century ball gowns. Especially striking were the chiffon dresses, richly textured, soft woollen jackets and capes all referencing decadent eras. Watanabe dabbled with a rich colour palette of bright yellow, fuchsia, rose-petal pinks, azure blue and crimson, and used bold prints ranging from non-traditional tartan to vivid chintz flowers. From beginning to end the show articulated a poetic investigation of femininity.

Watanabe attended the Bunka College of Fashion in Tokyo and worked for ten years as a pattern-cutter in Kawakubo's atelier. Promoted to designer, he worked a further seven years for the Comme des Garçons Tricot line, living in Tokyo and, like Kawakubo, going to Paris only for the collections. Watanabe struck out on his own in 1994, launching his first collection under Kawakubo's aegis. He is still described as Kawakubo's protégé today, because his label – which includes nineteen retail outlets in Japan and thirty in the United States and Europe – receives financial backing from Commes des Garçons. A less-confident designer may have felt threatened by Watanabe's talent, but Kawakubo encouraged it, although from another perspective, her sponsorship could serve to control and regulate Watanabe's expansion. With his incredible talent, he is virtually the only designer around who could directly compete in Kawakubo's unique arena.

In interviews Watanabe says he is indebted to Kawakubo, and even goes so far as to say that everything he knows was learned at Comme des Garçons.[7] Watanabe's conceptual clothing has its roots firmly planted in the signature Comme des Garçons aesthetic, mirrored in his mixes of bright and dark colours, upside-down pockets, extra-long sleeves and unconventional silhouettes. But Watanabe's use of layering, texture and historical resonance are his alone. Though his collections are considered cutting-edge, there is nothing sharp or aggressive about them. They imbibe a softness that makes them distinct from Kawakubo – much more 'Filles' than 'Garçons'.

With one foot in the past and one in the future, Watanabe's techno couture opens up a new dialogue with fashions from a bygone era through his innovative use of technique and materials. Following in the footsteps of Kawakubo and Yamamoto, he is the latest Japanese designer to base work on esoteric concepts and explore new directions in fabric cut and styling. Watanabe is not in a hurry either, because he 'creates clothes for women who take the time to understand them.'[8]

eight

Electric Textiles

The worlds of fashion and textile design are merging. As new materials and innovative techniques evolve in textile manufacturing, so does the synergy between fashion designers and textile designers. This crossover marks a specific moment in British fashion, where designers are excited by the possibilities of techno textiles, but wary that their widespread availability may create a uniform look that dominates the retail market. As a result, many labels are returning to traditional processes, couture principles and craft techniques to distinguish their garments from mass-produced fashion brands, drawing on both new and traditional textile methodology to create an aesthetic for the future.

Textile designers like Nigel Atkinson work to achieve a considered balance between techno processes and hand finishing, combining futuristic processes with traditional techniques. Shelley Fox rejects technology completely, using couture and craft traditions to make her garments distinctive, and impossible to copy. Like Fox, Daniel Herman designs his collections according to couture principles, but applies technology to broaden the range of practices and materials typically associated with couture.

While new raw materials are used to create ranges of high-tech fabrics, new technologized processes make it possible to adapt industrial materials for use as garments. Lightweight metals, reinforced plastics, glass fibres and industrial mesh are crafted into shapes more characteristic of architecture than clothing – in fact, techno fashions often contain a vocabulary of forms and materials more common to a building site than a design studio. Moulded shapes, transparent materials and waterproof fabrics all mirror materials used to construct the built environment, while details like invisible zips, transparent ties and exposed elastic cords reveal the garment's construction process without adopting the ruptured look characteristic of fashions inspired by Deconstruction architecture. The work of fashion designer Kei Kagami, for example, collapses the boundary between textiles and building materials by creating garments made from moulded glass. Textile designer Sophie Roet makes dresses out of metal sandwiched between fabric sheaths, while the fashion and textile designer Shelley Fox's designs take inspiration from the twisted buildings of Karel Jan Vollers's architecture.

New technologies free textile designers from many of the physical demands of production, allowing them to focus on the creative aspects of translating their ideas into tangible materials. Even maquettes can be created more quickly now, enabling designers to fine-tune ideas before executing the final piece. Weaving technologies and laser cutting create innovative textures and mesh-like structures, while chemical dyes and new printing methods produce digital prints, reflective prints and unusual reliefs. Industrial processes are being explored for their potential to create sophisticated fabrics for everyday use. The adaptation of alloys like Nitinol for fashion fabrics will enable garments to automatically lengthen and shorten with fluctuations in temperature, as shown in the 'Shape-shifting Dress' that IFM are developing.

Environmental issues have had a strong impact on the types of textiles being developed today. Because it can take synthetic materials hundreds of years to biodegrade, manufacturers are producing fabrics from recycled materials found outside the fabric industry. Non-woven fabrics, though completely inorganic, are among the most environmentally friendly because the processes used to make them are low in toxicity. The focus on environmental issues means that now the entire life cycle of the fabric must be accounted for, from the raw material through to each stage of textile development and its disposal.[1] Some of the manufacturing by-products are being explored to make new textiles, while salvaged textiles are produced from fabric scraps, rags and vintage clothing. Recycled glass is used to manufacture lightweight, breathable fabrics like Polartec, which is completely biodegradable, while discarded plastic bottles can be used to synthesize microfleece.

It is a surprising fact that synthetic and regenerated fibres create fewer toxic by-products than organic materials. Most of the synthetic textiles are actually more environmentally friendly than some natural fibres, because the pesticides, fertilizers and fungicides used to grow them kill other plants and insects, and the chemical processes used to bleach and dye them cause pollution. Synthetic materials do not rely on agricultural markets and crop availability, and can be modified during their production to control density, texture and cross-section, and developed in a particular staple or filament. This means there is generally no need for additional finishing treatments, which is sometimes the most intensely chemical process in textile production. The American textile company Natural Cotton Colors Inc. is using technology to engineer cotton that grows with its own naturally produced colour to make dyeing unnecessary.

The Japanese textile manufacturer Kanebo predict that their 'Corn Fiber'[2] will be the ultimate environmentally friendly material of the twenty-first century. It is made from a polylactic acid fibre prepared from the lactic acid obtained through the fermentation of corn starch. Derived from a plant and not petroleum, Corn Fiber is an entirely new type of synthetic that biodegrades safely into carbon dioxide, hydrogen and oxygen when buried in soil. Kanebo plan to market Corn Fiber as a futuristic material that has potential in a wide range of clothing, as well as non-apparel applications.

A growth area for fashion textiles is the integration of materials developed by the cosmetic and health care industries. Antibacterial substances and cosmetic products can be spun into fibres to give clothing medicinal properties. Kanebo, for example, have developed textiles that deodorize the wearer, while Elisabeth de Senneville's clothes can coat the wearer with sunscreen. Innovations like these are found in the 'smart fabrics' made possible by processes that coat polymers and monofilaments with silver ions and produce microcapsules made from ceramics, polymers, or gelatine films.

Kanebo are also developing 'Biosafe', a nylon filament yarn embedded with microscopic ceramic spheres (chemically bound to the fibres) that release a constant stream of silver ions, which has a powerful antibacterial effect. The fabric is ideal for sportswear, high-performance gear, underwear and hospital gowns. Since the anti-microbial deodorant in Biosafe is kneaded into the fibre itself, its properties are highly durable and withstand repeated washing. Tests have shown the fabric will destroy some harmful bacteria and inhibit the growth of others, making the fabric ideal for hospitals or clinical environments.[3]

The Japanese textile industry seems to be leading the world in its revolutionary approach to materials and weaving. Textile artists and designers are combining traditional techniques with modern industrial methods to create new expressions and increased functionality in interior textiles as well as fashion. A ground-breaking process known as triaxial weaving produces textiles of unprecedented strength and flexibility. The triaxial process interlaces three yarns at sixty to seventy degree angles, creating material versatile enough to function as solar panels and furniture.

A new crop of metallic yarns has resulted from weaving metals with synthetic fibres. 'Polyester slit-film', for example, is made by vacuum-sealing a layer of aluminium, titanium or chrome to a polyester/nylon base fabric which is then slit into fine threads. When woven polyester and aluminium fabric is treated with a 'melt-off' technique, the metallic threads are dissolved completely to leave behind a transparent fabric especially well-suited to heat-transfer printing. Polyester textiles also react well to coatings of powdered metals, taking on a lustrous stainless steel finish when spatter-plated with components of stainless steel, chrome, iron or nickel.

Japanese designers are also acclaimed for their ability to combine different materials to create richly-coloured sculpted surfaces. Highly articulated landscapes are formed by manipulating the plasticity of the yarns as they are stretched, layered or compressed into pleats. The needle-punching method fuses layers of fabrics together by overlaying them and striking needles through them to intertwine the collage elements. The finished result renders a painted appearance – the surface is textured with layers of colour that can be blended together or isolated as separate blocks, producing a unique, one-of-a-kind textile.

In the sections that follow, the work of Daniel Herman, Shelley Fox, Elisabeth de Senneville and Kei Kagami provides a survey of the innovations resulting from fashion designers' engagement with techno textiles and new processes. The designs of Nigel Atkinson, Sophie Roet, Rebecca Earley and Savithri Bartlett reveals that advanced techniques enable textile designers to enhance and refine their creative processes in ways not previously possible. The work of these fashion and textile designers charts the future axis of the two disciplines, giving an overview of the growing relationship between them.

Daniel Herman

To Daniel Herman, light is magic. He takes inspiration from times of day when the quality of light is changing; the dawn and twilight are times imbued with illusions and fantasy. The play of light over the body is the essence of his laser-cut designs, where space, shadow and movement are considerations factored into his visionary fashions. Herman's collections do not follow current fashion trends *per se*, but succeed in capturing the spirit of contemporary fashion as it moves in a new direction.

It is difficult to pigeonhole or specifically attribute Herman's work to one particular genre. Though he likes raw, unfinished edges and slashed fabrics, his refined cuts recall Fontana canvases more than deconstructed clothing. His shapes are streamlined and simple, but too rich to be strictly minimal. His motifs can be both flowery and geometric; though they are carefully raised over the surface of the fabric they are not embroidery, because they constitute a part of the fabric itself. Visionary and futuristic, yes – but mingled with handcrafted elements that recall traditional techniques. His clothes are based on ideas, but are not always specifically conceptual.

Herman is based in Zurich but studied at St Martin's in London. He graduated with a first-class BA degree and went on to show his autumn/winter 2002 collection on the London Fashion Week schedule in February 2001. While still at St Martin's he briefly assisted John Galliano, working alongside a designer and cutting technician to develop new draping and folding techniques. After graduation, he returned to his native Switzerland where he freelanced in the textile industries and secured sponsorship from the Swiss Textile Association.

Herman's *Branded Beauties* collection (spring/summer 2002) included a range of simple, monochromatic shapes cut with lasers. Almost all his work pioneers the use of lasers in fashion design, redefining the relationship of light to fabric, taking both methodology and aesthetics forward. To create a pattern, the lasers slowly burn away 'cut-out' shapes in the design, creating a motif based on the positive image. Herman cuts his fabrics with lasers to create precise geometric detailing; he cuts patterns that create provocative see-through looks, but that also cast ephemeral shadows over the surface of the female body. The shadowing renders a *trompe l'oeil* effect of layering or textured surfaces.

The *Branded Beauties* collection focused on the changing shadows and patterns that his laser cuts project onto the body, making the garments appear to be worn over reactive body suits or revealing skin marked with tattoos underneath. Herman also highlights areas like the breast or the bottom – designing the structure of the garment

Daniel Herman's Branded Beauties *collection (spring/summer 2002) featured latex bikinis laser-cut with a traditional lace pattern. Rather than creating the white triangles on the breasts typical of a conventional bikini, the latex bikini left a lacy suntan pattern on the skin underneath. The bikini top is shown here with a hand-pleated skirt also sculpted by lasers.*

to partially conceal them, but creating a risqué feeling by bathing them in alternating light and shadow. 'The reason I gave the collection this name is because the "lace" patterns I make lets sunlight touch the skin,' Herman explained. 'I used latex to make bikinis but created a special atmosphere by cutting a lace pattern into it like you would find in traditional underwear. Wearing a normal bikini leaves a white triangle on the breasts, but women wearing my latex bikini would get a nice lacy suntan pattern on their breasts instead.'[4]

Herman leaves his mark on the body like a henna tattoo – temporary, but lasting long enough to become a feature revealed by skimpy dresses or plunging necklines. Herman even views the suntan as a stage in the design process, because it marks the body's encounter with fashion and leaves it branded within a system of designs, indicating the wearer's affinity for the aesthetic of the image. 'Taking this idea further, the pattern is being softly burned into the skin in the way that the laser is burning away the shapes cut out of the cloth,' he said. Explained this way, the suntan represents the negative spaces cut out of the pattern into the fabric; the pattern on the skin is a reconstruction of the pieces of fabric originally excised from the latex.

Laser cuts can be concentrated in certain areas to break down the fabric's taut surface and make it more flexible. 'I started working with lasers because I was thinking in a functional way. I wanted to make dresses without side seams or darts in a way that the fabric would still shift and move with the body,' Herman said. Controlled cuts are the key to his process; these cuts follow the curves of the body, resulting in streamlined, body-hugging silhouettes. Cuts under the arm and beneath the bust line eliminate the need for darts but do not flatten the bosom. Series of diagonal cuts down either side of the dress allow it to cinch the waistline, yet stretch over the hips and buttocks. Herman uses only single linear cuts in the body of the fabric, only taking pieces away when he is creating a specific motif or detail like his lace pattern.

Herman's technique achieves what many other designers have not been able to do: unite the principles of concealing and revealing. Lying the dress flat makes the cuts visible only as fine lines; once on the body, the wearer's own contours will push the cut edges away from each other, opening up a space between them. This creates a patterned effect but also displays the flesh around the breasts and hips. Herman usually keeps necklines near the throat and hemlines low around the knee, which gives his subtle method of revealing the body added impact.

One of Herman's seminal pieces is the 'Suzanna Dress', which fuses his expressions of light and shadow, layering and utilitarian construction. The Suzanna Dress was designed with the fastenings fitted into the back of the dress, and without seams on either side. Short seams on each shoulder join the front and back of the dress together, and from that point the fabric follows the line of the body from shoulder to thigh. Herman explained: 'Obviously the dress needs to move and expand with the body, so laser cuts in the fabric allow movement. A close concentration of laser cuts creates more "give" in the fabric, allowing it to stretch. Areas without laser cuts keep the fabric tight over the body and hold the shape of the garment perfectly.' Some of these dresses come with the option of having a simple silk chiffon dress underneath to line them. Herman thinks the simplicity of the dress and its utilitarian construction signal the stopping point in the design process, and he resists the temptation to ornament the dress any further, or even accessorize it.

Many leading designers are experimenting with new soft lining materials that react against other fabrics when worn underneath them; Hussein Chalayan and Issey Miyake have superimposed sheer tops over glow-in-the-dark linings. This is not a direction Herman wishes to explore. He said: 'I'm not into multi-functionality at all, you know. I like to use very modern technology but in combination with traditional elements.'

That said, all Herman's designs are engineered through the combination of technological processes and high-tech industrial production, which normally work best with high-tech fabrics or textiles made specifically to be processed and finished. Organic fibres rarely have the strength and durability to withstand technologized processes, or are too inherently volatile to retain their finishing for very long. 'Polyester

Herman uses laser cuts instead of darts to allow his seamless fabric to follow the curves of the body, resulting in streamlined, body-hugging silhouettes, or daring pattern effects that dramatically display the flesh around the breasts and hips.

This cape is created by a series of symmetrical laser cuts that reveal a vertebrae of interconnecting shapes as it drapes around the body. Lasers can work at great speed, taking only minutes to transform a single length of fabric into a web-like sheath.

is good to work with since the edges melt as the fabric is cut by the laser, which gives it a clean cutting edge that doesn't fray like natural fabrics,' he said. Polyester has a smooth, contemporary look and feel, it is lightweight, elastic and bonds well with other materials to create finishes and patterns. It is being engineered to blend with fibres like polyamide and ultimately developed into a microfibre refined enough to be bonded with regenerated silks and cottons.

Herman is not a textile designer, but thinks in terms of how he can expand their uses to innovate further in his own work. Being based in Zurich gives him convenient access to progressive textile designers and the chance to collaborate with international designers like Jakob Schlaepfer. 'I rediscovered the textile industry in Switzerland when I returned from London after college,' he said. 'There are many interesting and original textiles here, but they are very expensive to produce because of the high cost of manufacturing in Switzerland. But this means that they have to justify their high prices by being very unique.'

The durability and expandability of latex make it one of the most versatile textiles available, and its reflective qualities can be manipulated to create a range of surfaces. Herman is experimenting with latex now by using a Computer Assisted Design (CAD) cutting machine, which can work like a drill or jigsaw and cut the structures necessary to create a mould for the latex. Herman sees latex as the quintessential technologized fabric, one which holds great potential for future fashions.

Tantamount to his fascination with the use of industrial applications is Herman's regard for hand-finishing techniques. In his own work, he uses individual craftsmanship to compliment technologized garments. Herman said, 'Combining crafts and technology is very important to me. My fabrics are laser cut, then pleated by hand, so that human imperfection makes them less cold.' This *modus operandi* mirrors the process of many other designers interested in technology today. The return to couture principles evolved as the Belgian designers became well known internationally; by the late 1990s it almost characterized the work of conceptual designers, or designers who worked within a Deconstructivist or Reconstructivist genre.

The pleating Herman refers to is his technique of folding and processing polyester fabric for his skirt designs. Placed between two sheets of thick paper, the fabric is folded according to predetermined measurements, then rolled through an industrial steaming process. The fabric is passed through edged rollers afterwards and heated, then allowed to cool and unfold. Lasers cut out a pattern in accordance with Herman's designs, so that the fabric will have the look of intricately woven textile or lace. The fabric is then refolded by hand into the same folds created by the machine, and finally hand sewn into a skirt. When completed, the finished skirt combines the laser precision apparent in the pattern with the machined pleats, and the random stitching of a hand-tailored garment.

Though Herman considers the development and technologization of textiles to herald a revolution, he is not convinced that technology is the future for fashion. 'Developments in technology interest me very much, but I am always using technology in combination with the body, and not trying to push the body into technology. But I like the fragile body of a woman that is the opposite of everything you see that is technology.'

Shelley Fox

Shelley Fox does not reflect on preconceived ideas about dress to find inspiration, she uses fashion to reflect her thinking and the topics she finds interesting. Fox is one of the most original designers on the London scene today. Her work articulates a moment in British fashion resulting from experimentation with new materials and technologies, and a revived interest in craft and couture traditions. Fox trained first in fashion and later in textile design, and her work emphasizes craft traditions as the focus of her collection. Since establishing her label in 1995, her collections reveal acute sensitivity to ideas and forms; she is committed to expressing ideas and concepts rather than specific styles or trends. 'The research, ideas and concepts behind the collections come first,' she explained, 'designing the actual clothes comes fairly late in the process.'[5]

While most designers describe their workspace as a studio, Fox regards hers as a laboratory, because in many ways she is a technician. 'New technology is something I'm trying to stay away from,' she said. 'I have a fundamental need to be as self-sufficient as possible in terms of what I can make myself. Staying away from technology and sticking to traditional methods helps me keep things under my own control.' Fox's use of natural fibres has universal appeal because they have a long-established tradition associated with them that microfibres and techno textiles do not. 'The most technologized I got was when I had someone collaborating with me to cut fabric and bond layers together. She used lasers to cut the fabric and ultrasound technology to bond the fabric,' she said. Instead of using a regular fusing press, ultrasound technology gauged the density and movement of the fabric by scanning it as it moved through the heat-bonding process.

Her contemporaries describe Fox as a 'master of fabric techniques', and her 'lab' is a place where fabrics can be manipulated, tested, enhanced and even destroyed; some of her favourite creations are the results of lucky accidents. Manipulating and transforming fabrics enables her to work with materials not commonly used for fashion garments, or create her own evocative textiles. 'I think being in touch with fabric development has been really important,' she said. 'I've never been satisfied with buying fabrics. There is so much of the same around that it is difficult to keep an identity as a designer if you stick to mainstream fabrics.'

Not only is Fox creating a signature aesthetic, she is taking deliberate steps to create a look that cannot easily be imitated by other designers. 'At the moment a lot of smaller designers complain that as soon as they show their work on the Fashion Week catwalk, their ideas have been taken by big fashion companies that can get them into the high street shops in a matter of weeks. That is where technology catches them out – they

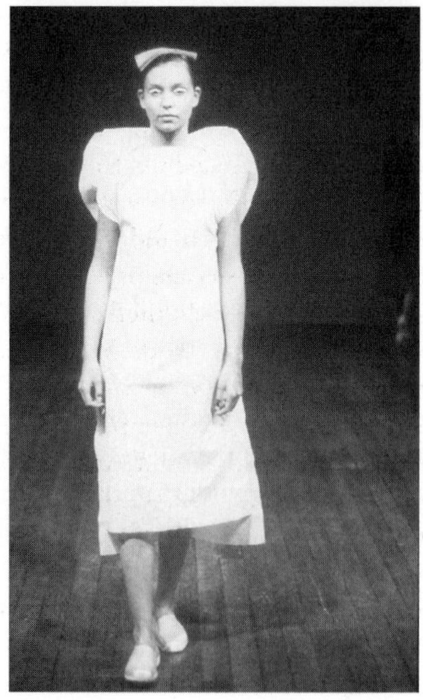

Self-confessed technophobe Shelley Fox uses handcrafted techniques and labour-intensive constructions that cannot be duplicated industrially. 'I make my cutting more difficult than anyone can interpret easily, and develop my own fabrics so that what I make is really unique,' Fox explained.

use the same materials that high street labels can get hold of, who then use the same industrial processes to turn them out quickly,' she said. Fox's handcrafted techniques are labour intensive processes that can not be duplicated industrially. 'I make my cutting more difficult than anyone can interpret easily, and develop my own fabrics so that what I make is really unique,' she explained.

'Recently an established fashion label hired a friend of mine as a consultant designer, and told him to that they'd like to have some garments covered with burned sequins, just like the ones Shelley Fox is doing. He told them "I can't do that, she's a friend of mine". I couldn't believe that a famous label wanted to use something I did so literally,' she said. Fox's discovery of burned sequins resulted from a commission she accepted from *The Independent* newspaper. The fashion editor, Susannah Frankel, asked Fox to make a dress for a millennium fashion feature that would show what looks were taking fashion into the twenty-first century and beyond. 'Immediately all the glittering, sparkling things that the other designers would probably do, came to mind, so I said, '"Susannah, why are you asking me?" and she said it was because she knew that I wouldn't make a sparkling silver dress,' Fox said. The dress that resulted did feature sequins, which Fox burned to change their shape and texture. 'The project gave me some ideas about working with materials associated with glamour, and how I could use them in my own aesthetic. I decided to blow-torch the sequins to destroy the idea of superficial glamour, and it turned them into something more beautiful,' she said.

The felted wool Fox produces is a signature feature of her work; its density and weight impact on the design of the garment, since both are progressed at the same time. Felt easily accumulates burn marks from overcooking; when this happens Fox just shrugs them off as a natural pattern, or embosses the felt with a pattern of her own design. Its inherent strength renders Fox with a versatile material that can withstand the wear-and-tear of being moulded, layered and stitched during the manufacturing process. 'Felt has poor associations. Poor people used to make blankets out of it or it was underlining for old carpets. When I exhibited some felt clothes in Poland they thought it was weird to see couture dresses made in felt, because they had used it to insulate the walls with,' she said.

Each garment presents a challenge to conventional fashion thinking. Fox is not tyrannized by conventional cutting and simplified lines, but applies mathematical principles to the garments themselves, balancing their construction against the geometry of the body. 'It's a bit like being an architect – I look at the minimum requirements. In the case of an architect it's to construct a building. With a garment, it has to go over the head or round the head; the arms have to come through and be able to move, same with the legs. In a way those are my only constraints. There's going to be other limitations later on, so I try and get rid of them in the beginning. Like a house needs a door, you need to get in and out, and after that it is how it's achieved that is open to interpretation,' she explained.

Geometry is echoed in Fox's shapes and silhouettes more than in her patterns. Many of Fox's tops and dresses create a circular silhouette; the fabric is rounded from the collar into the shoulders, arcing around the elbows to meet the forearms or wrists. The look is raglan in shape, but the sleeves create wing-like half circles hovering over the arms and shoulders or behind them. The 'Circle Skirt' is actually a circle of fabric with a discreet slit cut directly into it; the waist is the opening in the centre of the material. 'We kept working with that idea,' Fox said, 'until we did a version of the skirt with two or three waists in them. It can be worn like a regular skirt by stepping into the waist in the very centre, because the fabric will hang symmetrically. Wearing one of the waists closer to the edge makes it hang asymmetrically for something more unusual.' Rather than fitting the skirt with zips or buttons, each waist was made hip-width so that the wearer could slide into it easily, adjusting the fit with a metal bar that fastened like a cuff link. Fox concealed the other waist openings by positioning them so that they would be hidden in the folds of the fabric.

Layering fabrics gives her work a rich, textured look that counters the extreme sculptural forms of the garments. Typically, Fox would superimpose a graph design printed on gossamer muslin over a woven cotton tapestry fabric, then use another translucent fabric as a top layer over both. Garments may also be cut in simple shapes to give prominence to the fabric itself. Some of Fox's favourite textiles are the Elastoplast fabrics that originated in the medical industry, because they can withstand the stretching and burning necessary to create a pattern of scorch marks on the surface.

Fox's layering and generous proportions de-emphasize the conventional fashion approach to femininity. She does not support the view that the female body's sex appeal should be maximized by garments that put it on display. 'I'm not putting breasts on a plate,' laughed Fox. 'There are many more levels of female sexuality than people realise, much more beneath the surface than people let themselves imagine. I see sexuality as coming from something more complex.' This may be the reason that Fox is one of the few designers whose clothes appeal to all age groups. 'I don't design with a particular type of woman in mind, but with a look that is just human, that can appeal to any woman. Walking down Bond Street the other day I was approached three different times by women saying they liked what I was wearing.' Fox was wearing garments of her own design. 'One was a film producer, another was a business woman – they were all very different in age group and dress sense,' she said.

Fox interprets clothing as a signifier that says something about the personality of its wearer. Her collections draw on fashion's capacity to be a communicative medium, and the patterns she designed in Braille and Morse code combined her interest in concepts with her liking for minimal graphics. 'On a visit to the RNIB[6] I went into the Braille shop and saw the things they sell to help blind people in everyday life. Stuff that I never thought about, like choosing clothes and getting dressed can obviously be really difficult for the blind. There were special buttons that could be sewn inside garments to say "front", "back", "red", or "yellow",' she said. Staying true to the medium, Fox printed Braille patterns in relief on the fabrics rather than as two-dimensional markings. The patterns said, 'This is a dress.', 'This is a skirt.', 'This is the front.' and 'This is the back.'

Morse code appeared as a graph pattern on garments; in one dress Fox transferred it onto muslin by using a pearl powder printing process, in another it was printed on soft jersey and brushed to distress the pattern. 'Morse Code is very basic, but I find the hidden ideas in code really fascinating. Those ideas aren't taken literally into the clothing but they are a spark that sets me off on a pathway. They're starting points to the collection,' she explained.

The Morse code theme resulted from listening to a radio interview with a wartime SOE agent who headed an operation of civilian code-breakers. The agent talked about establishing the Bletchley Park compound, where thousands of people worked in round-the-clock shifts to decode German military transmissions and pass vital information on to military intelligence centres. 'None of the code breakers were allowed to talk about what they were doing, because they had signed an agreement under the Official Secrets Act that prevented them discussing it,' she said. Fox drove to Bletchley Park to visit the former wartime centre, which she described as a surreal experience: 'Going there had a lot of impact, seeing this big mansion and a lot of wooden barracks and thinking about the lives of the eight thousand people that were there. A lot of the ideas that I've used – whether it's Braille or Morse Code or burning fabrics – come from a feeling. I felt something at Bletchley Park that I wanted to put across in the catwalk presentation.'

Wartime Bletchley Park sparked off Fox's military collection (spring/summer 2001), which included military hats, wartime styles, and a colour palette of drab olive green, earthy browns and khaki. Held at the National Army Museum in London, the show unfolded against a background of military tanks and munitions, where Fox's own messages were decoded to acclaim from the audience and Press.

Elisabeth de Senneville

For twenty-five years Elisabeth de Senneville has been an innovator of prints, textiles and materials that she designs and uses. She was one of the first fashion designers to use computer-generated prints, aluminium-treated wool and microfibres, and was an early devotee of Velcro. It comes as no surprise that de Senneville is changing the French fashion landscape through the use of new, high-tech fabrics. De Senneville was reportedly the first designer to create a jacket that featured built-in protection against mobile telephone radiation, and one of the first to produce clothes that change colour in response to changes in temperature.

Her Paris boutique sells a range of clothing that changes colour in response to fluctuations in temperature. The fibres contain microcapsules loaded with pigments containing heat-sensitive dyes that change colour according to body temperature. 'I was also thinking one day, why not come up with clothes that are useful as well as being fashionable? So in October 1999, I created clothes that tell you what the weather is like,' de Senneville explained in an interview with CNN.[7] The microcapsules are micrometre-sized and made from polymers, ceramics or gelatine films. The capsules can be filled with dyes, drugs or cosmetic substances like sunscreen. When mixed with polyurethane or silicone binders they can be sprayed on textiles to coat them.

In recent years, Elisabeth de Senneville has focused her design on the development of new materials, while continuing to use traditional fabrics. 'I like the idea of transferring existing technology into a new medium. The idea for me is to adapt that technology to everyday needs. It's very difficult to continuously create new ideas and stay ahead of the game, because you're followed very quickly by other people,' she said.[8] De Senneville was one of the first French designers to use high-tech materials, featuring them in her line of accessories, her prints for her interior range and her *prêt-a-porter* line. Her household range 'Senneville-Casa', launched in September 2000, features window blinds that turn grey when it rains and blue when the sun shines. 'For the spring/summer collection I worked with microcapsules, which are tiny balls that are invisible to the naked eye,' de Senneville explained. 'You can put anything inside the microcapsules, from pigments to scents. The problem with working with new fabrics like microcapsules is that they're very expensive. I have to get the microcapsules from Japan and 1 kilo currently costs about £3,000.'[9]

De Senneville began her own label in 1977, which was characterized by futuristic shapes, prints and innovative textiles, including the use of holograms in clothing. Throughout the 1980s she worked with prints of video screen stills and created jackets made from the NASA materials developed for spacesuits. For her prints, de Senneville found inspiration in the work of artists like Andy Warhol and Roy Lichenstein.

De Senneville also designs garments with fibre-optic trim that glows in the dark. The optical fibres form a network resting underneath a fine mesh covering, and light up at the switch of a battery-powered circuit in the garment. De Senneville regards this type of fibre-optic motif as a new type of embroidery, which will eventually feature in more of her garments. 'For me, working with new fabrics is a way of advancing in fashion . . . of not looking back or becoming too retro. There's a lot of excitement in new textiles. After working twelve hours a day, exploring new textiles gives you a reason and motivation to continue working in fashion, because every day is a new discovery and challenge,' she said.[10]

Kei Kagami

Glass really is the cutting edge of fashion. No one knows that better than Japanese designer Kei Kagami, whose skirts and bustiers in toughened glass are clear indications of its potential for fashion. Few fashion designers have worked in solid glass, much less create a wearable glass garment. Some, like Junya Watanabe, have used fabrics woven from glass fibres, but glass is more typically used industrially to reinforce synthetic

Transparency was a theme that Kei Kagami explored in his spring/summer 2002 collection, culminating in a glass skirt. The glass exposes the inner layers of the garment and presents a contemporary view of the body; it is exposed, but protected.

materials, or manufacture protective clothing for welders and firemen.

Uninspired by what most of his contemporaries were doing and determined to challenge convention, Kagami started exploring the possibilities of moulding glass into garments. 'I wanted to move away from current trends, to escape from the real world to a place of transparent beauty,' he said. 'I think the present fashion scene has become too casual, sporty and girlish. I really wanted to think of the intrinsic meaning of high fashion. Therefore, I included something both sophisticated and symbolic,' he explained.[11]

Kagami presented a glass skirt and a glass bustier for his spring/summer 2002 collection during London Fashion Week. Working with such fragile and inflexible material involved researching production methods and glass types, as well as a certain amount of trial and error. But Kagami devised a method to fashion it into clothing by hand. 'First I think of how I want the garment to look, then make a pattern, and get the glass cut in the shape of the pattern,' he explained. 'Then I drive it to a factory that makes glass strong enough for car window screens, who use a special toughening process that heats the glass on a hotplate for four hours. I pick it up and coat both sides in bond film, then smash it, because it's the tiny fissures that make it flexible. I then curve it into shape and use leather laces to secure the seam.'

Transparency was a theme that Kagami gave full reign on the catwalk, manifesting as elaborate dresses constructed from strands of translucent thread, sophisticated skirts and tops cut in beautiful diaphanous fabrics, and futuristic garments made from transparent zips. Some of the garments recalled the architecture of modern Japan, as seen in the Crystal Light Building of Masaharu Takasaki, and the nebulous structures of Tadao Ando. 'I tried to depict a being of the future seeking and chasing light as hope. In the collection I used a lot of bias-cutting to achieve an organic image of life and suspension constructions to create a space for light,' he said. Because the glass exposes the inner layers of the garment, there is no real front or back, inside or outside. It presents a modern view of the body – exposed, but protected. The look is very in tune with our age, a step away from the 'underwear as outerwear' theme that became a fashion standard at the end of the 1990s.

The glass garments were shown individually on different models. The skirt was worn with a simplistic top constructed in several abstract panels; a disjointed section folding over one arm in place of a sleeve. While the top confined the torso in an opaque sheath, the skirt revealed the experiences of the fabric's inner surface, by showing how a fitted skirt presses into the folds of the skin, and creates tension against the body as the it moves with the wearer, bringing the intimacies of clothing into public view. 'I am interested in exploring this space between body and material,' Kagami explained. 'This space is like a house built for the body, and maybe the glass around the body is a window into the space. I enjoy the construction of clothing rather than just making a surface.'

Kagami is a graduate of architecture who worked with Kenzo Tange in Tokyo before pursuing a career in fashion. Kagami trained with Junko Koshino in Japan before coming to London in 1989 to work with John Galliano. After completing his MA at St Martin's, Kagami started his own label in London, where he lives and works today. 'My architectural skills naturally come out when I design clothes,' he explained. 'I map out plans for clothes two-dimensionally, like for a building. When the clothes are made they become like three-dimensional models, like buildings designed and then built.'

In 1999, Kagami exhibited alongside Kenzo, Tadao Ando and Masaru Amano in the 'Mohri Colour and Space' show in Japan. His architecturally inspired garment took the shape of a ballerina's tutu, constructed around the concept of a living environment. Kagami explained: 'I set up three elements in and on the tutu; a habitation, a natural environment and a living being. On the body of the tutu I created a habitation, which is made of zips. On the skirt I grew moss to express a natural environment – during the exhibition you could see cress growing as well. The space inside the tutu was then ready for a living being.'

'It is important to experiment with these materials and progress them more and more. Glass is being developed all the time, so there is the potential to make an evening dress once glass becomes sophisticated enough to mould into bigger shapes.' Kagami's architectural influences seem to be what pushes him forward, away from trends, and to make symbolic comments on beauty and processes.

Nigel Atkinson

The British textile designer Nigel Atkinson creates a range of luxurious fashion fabrics, as well as his own range of fashion accessories. He also creates textiles for some of the world's top designers: Azeddine Alaïa has featured Atkinson's fabrics in three collections, Romeo Gigli used his designs for five, and John Rocha, Alberta Ferretti and Cerutti number among his clients.

Atkinson's work is distinctive in its combination of different technologized processes and craft techniques. The fabrics range from being richly textured and densely embroidered to hauntingly spare and transparent. He also uses the latest innovations in fabric dyeing and pigment-printing processes to create unconventional patterns and textures. 'I look at traditional designs and give them my own interpretation by using processes that don't make it look like a reproduction of a historical pattern,' Atkinson explained.[12]

One of Atkinson's signature designs is a material resulting from his layering technique. By combining up to six lengths of different fabric and cutting it on the bias, an organic, sensuous look is created that highlights the rich textures and opposing shapes formed by the colours and densities of the fabrics. For this layering technique, Atkinson chose fabrics that have markedly different properties, combining them in a measure that contrasts the malleable fabrics with the stiff ones, the transparents alongside the opaques.

Atkinson has pioneered a printing technique that applies heat-reactive chemicals to the reverse of textiles. The effect is a strikingly contoured surface that renders a complex, but subtle, relief. Atkinson uses a textile blend of silk and rayon, which he hand prints using heat-reactive dyes to alter the structure of the textile, giving it the look of embossed fabric. The result is 'Sea Anemone', a soft, silky reversible fabric that has the colours and relief patterns of delicate plants. Atkinson gave considerable thought to the benefits of using a technologized process before he started exploring the technique: 'I had a clear vision that I wanted to change this textile to get an embossed look. New techniques and processes can be a gimmick or a just a thing of the moment if you don't use them to achieve something lasting.'

The embroidery techniques Atkinson uses range from a pseudo-embroidery created by printing motifs onto the garment in Spandex, to a labour-intensive traditional process used to make his 'Rice Flower' knotting relief. Both look very contemporary but suggest traditional methodology. 'It's not just the process itself that makes something appear modern, it's how that it is used with the design itself,' he said. The most modern textile Atkinson does is actually engineered to look very old.

'It has been described as something you find in a very old chateau when you remove the false panels and look at the old embossed leather behind it. It's actually a silk combined with polyurethane and Spandex. I don't think in terms of it being futuristic or modern but think of how much easier it can be to use Spandex for detailing the fabric rather than traditional embroidery. The end result is something that's modern, but not necessarily futuristic,' he said.

Atkinson has been exploring the uses of Spandex since he was at college, using it to mimic fine embroidery. 'Spandex was around in the 1970s, used mostly for making logos on T-shirts and sweatshirts. When I was at college in the late eighties the technicians said it wasn't possible to use Spandex like this, but I tried and it worked,' he said. Atkinson also uses Spandex with rich materials like velvets and silks, by printing motifs with it on their reverse side. This process makes the fabric contract, creating a raised relief on its surface. Because Spandex changes the structure and the weight of the material, it changes the way it hangs on the body itself.

'When I work with embroidery techniques they change the structure and weight just like Spandex does,' Atkinson said. Using labour-intensive hand-finishing techniques is one of his distinctive hallmarks, because of the luxurious feel they give the fabric. He recently employed Bengali craftsmen to hand-embroider and bead his designs in a way that combines elements from their own craft traditions. 'Putting tiny mirrors on fabrics may seem like something modern but it is an old tradition. I have a lightweight cashmere that has tiny mirrors embroidered in it to create weight so that it falls in a certain way,' he said.

As textile design slowly merges the traditional with the technological, designers like Atkinson are finding inspiration in the latest innovations while remaining true to craft traditions. Atkinson supports new technologized processes and the innovations they can create, but feels that these must always remain linked to tradition. 'However contemporary a textile is, whether it is fashion or upholstery, it has to be connected to traditions and history,' he said, 'because that's what people respond to most.'

Rebecca Earley

Known for her prints depicting everyday objects like pins, herbs, lace, knitwear weaves and flowers, Rebecca Earley uses classical cuts and simple shapes as a background for her whimsical motifs. Earley prints on fabrics, ranging from shiny synthetics to light-absorbing fleece made from recycled plastic bottles, using a special technique she developed for transferring detailed images of objects onto the textiles. The images that result are so life-like that they create *trompe l'oeil* effects.

Earley initially experimented with the heat photogram method of printing while studying for her MA in Fashion Textiles at St Martin's, and has since pioneered using new types of ink. Earley was one of the first to use 'retroflective' ink, which reflects light back to its source using a principle similar to the reflectors embedded in roads and motorways. Retroflective ink is able to mirror flashes of light via the microscopic aluminium-coated glass orbs suspended in it. The ink can be either oil-based or water-based, which enables it to adhere to a wide range of fabrics, or be used in screen-printing pigments.

Earley produces a line of womenswear, a collection of scarves and specially commissioned textile artworks. In 1999, she was commissioned to make gowns for cancer patients undergoing treatment at the Queen Elizabeth Centre for the Treatment of Cancer in Birmingham. Earley designed the gowns to be easy to put on and take off, but wanted them to look more shapely than normal hospital gowns. Homeopathy was the inspiration behind the printed designs she made, and each design was based on a plant recognized for its healing properties. Garlic, echinacea, green tea and beetroot have anti-carcinogenic properties, which she hoped would provide a boost to the immune system and the wearer's spirits.

Earley's work has been exhibited in London at the Crafts Council, the Victoria & Albert Museum, the Barbican Centre and the Ruskin Gallery. She has also made printed designs for Karl Lagerfeld and Donna Karan.

Sophie Roet

Sophie Roet combines traditional craftsmanship with the latest industrial processes to create textiles that appear both traditional and contemporary, a look that her peers have described as 'transcending time'. Over the years Roet's textiles have featured in the collections of fashion designers like John Galliano, Romeo Gigli and Alexander McQueen. One of her first clients was Hussein Chalayan, who used one of her Japanese-inspired gossamer fabrics. Chalayan sewed the textile into an overdress, revealing flashes of light underneath when the glow-in-the-dark underdress was shown on a dimly lit catwalk.

Roet is Australian, and settled in Britain when she came to study at the University of Brighton. She went on to complete her MA at the Royal College of Art, then worked in Paris as a trend forecaster with Li Edelkoort, where she developed new fabrics. After returning to England, Roet started working as a freelance consultant to fashion designers and developed her own range of fabrics. Recently Roet joined Nino Cerruti as a consultant to forecast and develop new fabrics for future seasons. She also works with the London label Eskandar as a trend consultant and textile-production organizer. One of the fabrics she produced is the 'Oyster Shell' textile that transforms its shape and texture. 'The fabric is made from a highly-twisted yarn that that crinkles into a crepe texture when it is immersed in hot water. It has a "memory", which enables it to alter shape,' she said.

Sophie Roet's 'Oyster Shell' textile transforms its shape and texture. Made from a highly-twisted yarn that that crinkles into a crepe texture, the fabric has a 'memory', which enables it to change shape.

Roet visited Japan to study both contemporary and traditional textile-manufacturing methods, citing their simplicity and use of traditional forms and fibres as a source of inspiration. 'A lot of the Japanese traditional techniques and textiles have influenced my work. I like to analyse the traditional techniques and then develop my own work using contemporary techniques and processes,' she said.[13] Roet derived one of her fabrics from a hemp kimono fabric known as 'water silk', which is created by manipulating the weft fibres by hand or by reeds. Some Japanese weavers even notch the edges of their fingernails to beat the silk weft with their fingers. 'The technique for making water silk cloth is one I found interesting. It's an old technique for weaving silk for kimonos without beating the cloth down. In my method I manipulate the yarn and burn out fibres with acid,' she explained. Roet's adaptation of this technique creates a devoré finish to give a similar effect, by weaving the fabric from polyamide monofilament fibres and cotton. The devoré technique removes the cotton to render a delicate spider's-web finish.

Roet produced a new series of high-tech fabrics in collaboration with British textile manufacturer C S Interglas.[14] By using industrial processes normally used for high-performance applications, Roet fused a layer of fine aluminium with lightweight cotton fabric. She bonded the three layers together using a heat-bonding process to seal them as one piece of fabric, then hand-printed it. The fabric looked like it would have a normal density, but the metal layer made it incredibly mouldable. Another of Roet's heat-bonded fabrics won her the Textprint's Weave Prize in 1995, awarded by the International Wool Secretariat. Her winning fabric is made of a polyamide monofilament and polypropylene yarn woven together and than deliberately shrunk in the heat-bonding process. This makes the synthetic fibre shrink to become a new material with an irregular blistered surface or rippled texture.

For the *Hitec-Lotec* show (2000-2001), a touring exhibition of British design, Roet used the same heat-bonding process to fuse lengths of cotton, silk and jersey fabrics with sheets of aluminium. 'I wanted to combine a hand woven textile length together with delicate, simple, feminine fashion textiles and give them a hidden ability to change shape. I imagined crumpling a soft satin textile and finding that it holds a scrunched shape on its own, and that's the effect I wanted,' she explained. Roet showed two simple dresses in the exhibition – one was lightly scrunched to show how the technique could create texture, the other was radically creased to demonstrate the effect of the technique on changing shape.

Roet continues to work closely with textile manufacturers in England, Scotland and France to source the newest developments. In Italy she recently discovered new fibres she is interested in exploring. 'There is an Italian yarn made out of paper for interiors, which I may be able to use in fashion textiles,' she said. 'There are also yarns that have been created using milk protein that I like. And there is a new stainless steel and silk mix that creates a fabric as fine as hair.'

Roet's skilful mix of different processes, traditions and materials creates a unique aesthetic that has a growing influence on the work of some of the fashion industry's leading designers.

Savithri Bartlett

Savithri Bartlett is a textile designer interested in new technologies, exploring non-woven fabrics and laser-etching techniques. Bartlett studied architecture before specializing in textiles, then began experimenting with printed imagery and woven textiles before investigating the possibilities rendered by non-woven fabrics. Her work challenges assumptions about non-wovens textiles, particularly their potential to be fashion garments rather than their conventional use as industrial workwear.

Bartlett's work centres around the properties of thermoplastic fabrics, which she tests with a variety of techniques to extend their range of use. Thermoplasticity is a characteristic of most synthetic fabrics, which means they can be heat-set to render a wide variety of textured and relief surfaces. They can also be moulded into new forms altogether through a heat process. As they are heated, the molecular structure of the fibre breaks down and assumes the new shape, which it maintains permanently on cooling. Bartlett has pioneered the application of heat-pressed and cold-pressed techniques to measure the limitations and variations they produce in the materials, creating fabrics that are mouldable and dyeable. Bartlett developed a technique to create seamless, moulded textiles for Chanel's hat line, in collaboration with the mould-maker Keese van der Graaf.

Bartlett has worked closely with the design label Boudicca to create fabrics for two of their collections. For their *Immortality* collection, she created laser-cut textiles that were inscribed with text. Bartlett's control over lasers results partly from her use of the electron microscope to examine the reaction that individual fibres have when they come in contact with the laser beam.

Shape-shifting Textiles

Though the designers detailed in this chapter have produced extraordinary textures and innovations, none have yet created a garment that can change shape of its own volition. IFM are making a dress that does just this, based on fabric woven from fibres of the shape-memory alloy Nitinol, interspersed with nylon. The alloy is highly elastic and capable of changing shape when temperatures rise and fall, then returning to its original shape when temperatures stabilize. It is this shape-memory property that enables the fabric to shorten and lengthen, which is how the dress will perform when temperatures fluctuate. By fashioning the material into a 'Shape Shifting Dress', IFM plan to develop a versatile garment that will help the wearer maintain a comfortable temperature despite environmental changes. 'The sleeves and hemlines could be programmed to shorten as soon as the room temperature becomes a few degrees hotter,' said Joanna Berzowska of IFM.[15]

Nitinol, an acronym for Nickel Titanium Naval Ordinance Laboratory, is a family of intermetallic materials that contain a mixture of nickel and titanium. Other materials can be added to enhance or adjust the material's properties. Nitinol's unique properties are termed Superelasticity and Shape Memory. Because the fabric's weave has five nylon fibres to every Nitinol fibre, the clothing made from it will be high performance, washable and comfortable.

The fabric is also a traveller's dream. 'Even if the fabric is screwed up into a ball, pleated and creased, a blast from a hairdryer pops it back to its former shape,' explained Susan Clowes, a spokeswoman for the Italian fashion company Corpo Nove, who are developing a shirt from the material.[16] This means the shirt will smooth itself as it is put on, making ironing unnecessary. Like the dress IFM are researching, the sleeves and length will contract as it gets warmer, giving the shirt the ability to roll up its own sleeves. Do not expect to be able to buy either of these on your next shopping trip – the projects have a long way to go before the garments are ready.

nine

Sportswear

As we slide deeper into a high-tech lifestyle of hours spent motionless in front of computer screens, the more sports and active leisure appeal. Until recently, sport and fashion have been at opposite extremes of the style spectrum. Fashion placed emphasis on looks and trends, mostly targeted at female consumers, while sport delivered performance and functionality to a predominately male audience. The sports industry has always been a market leader in developing fabric technology and high-performance designs; strategies currently explored in fashion through utilitarian styles, multipurpose garments and functional details. Sportswear also encouraged the movement of materials and technologies across disciplines, moving high-performance fabrics into the collections of forward-thinking fashion designers.

The combination of sportswear and urban fashion is something of a contemporary phenomenon, which many city dwellers now view as a necessity. Lifestyle sports like roller-blading, cycling and scootering increase the demand for durable urban clothing that keep the wearer perspiration-free and looking cool, while the rise of gym culture creates a demand for body-conscious sportswear. As men and women mould their bodies into silhouettes once created with the use of corsetry and shoulder pads they spend more time transforming their physiques into slimmer or fashionably muscular shapes. Even beyond the exercise routine, sportswear gets a workout on the dance floor, in shopping mall marathons, on the golf course and on the commute in to work.

The label-conscious youth of today are as likely to wear sports brands like Nike, Puma and Adidas as they are designer logos, or accessorize fashion looks with trainers and sports bags. As fashion designers became more sensitized to the new trends generated by the sports industry, they incorporate vestiges of sportswear into their own collections. The appeal is modern and dynamic; the utilitarian features of sportswear have influenced both avant-garde and mainstream fashions. Hoods, zip-fronted shirts, windproof jackets, pouch pockets, Velcro and magnetic fastenings have now become part of the everyday fashion vocabulary, while drawstrings at the neck, sleeve and waist make zips and buttons redundant.

With the sports industry at the forefront of advanced textile developments, the new generation of sportswear includes fabric with antibacterial and deodorizing agents, screens against ultraviolet rays and the self-medicating components described in previous chapters. Textile manufacturers continue to research technologized fabrics for all areas of sportswear, including outdoor and adventure gear, high-performance sports and Olympic uniforms – even exploring materials developed for space and military applications. Phase Change technology is one such material, ideal for warming athletes on long-range winter sport competitions without causing them to overheat. Adapted for the fashion market, Phase Change technology appeals to individuals moving between climate-controlled environments.

Temperature regulation is one of the many fabric technologies Nike has pioneered, along with waterproof, anti-moisture and aerodynamic systems of clothing. Nike revolutionized sportswear, changing both fabric performance and the expectations of the consumer. When designers like Prada launched their own sportswear lines, they were faced with designing sports clothing for a new type of consumer who, largely due to Nike's innovations, expected sports products to be manufactured in performance materials that were easy to care for, stretchable and comfortable. As Prada began incorporating these principles into their sportswear, they created performance garments with a classical clothing aesthetic, and began using techno textiles in their underwear, swimwear and causal wear collections.

Labels like Fashion Active Laboratory and Nova USA also took the same approach, designing sportswear so chic it is virtually indistinguishable from casual wear. The shoes that Nike, Puma and Adidas develop can run cross-country marathons, but are designed to look compatible with even the most avant-garde wardrobe. As sportswear and fashion slowly fuse together, the work of these and other designers reveals a complex relationship between them. While we question where the boundaries between them now lie, the axis between the two reveals a mutual concern for aesthetics and performance, and an appreciation for new design methods.

Technology in Motion

For more than a decade, Nike led the industry in both technological innovation and style. The tailored details of Nike sportswear influenced the sportswear collections of established fashion labels and cutting edge designers. Nike pioneered a streamlined, modern look usually associated with minimal fashion, that appealed to fashion-conscious urban dwellers whether they were gym devotees or not. Advanced technology gives Nike garments and shoes ventilation, water repellency and stretchability, making them a practical choice for professional athletes, as well as fitness pros and amateur sports players.

The comfortable, relaxed look that Nike engineered gradually moved beyond gyms and sports grounds into urban streets and city parks. The range appealed to cyclists, scooter-fanatics and roller-bladers looking for practical, modern clothing that moved easily and kept the wearer from getting too sweaty. Nike's signature Lycra and fleece silhouettes leapt into mainstream casual wear, creating a look that went beyond sporty associations to identify the wearer as an active, trendy, health-conscious individual. Nike's body-hugging designs were produced in vibrant colours or basic black – creating shapes and tones that mirrored those worn on the nightclub scene. Nike's vests for men and bra tops for women were popularized by youth culture around the world, spreading to nightclub dance floors and rave parties.

From the 1990s onward, Nike concentrated on combining technological knowledge with new developments in textiles and design systems, launching a series of initiatives to research and enhance athletic performance. 'Project Swift',[1] was established in 1997 to identify, analyse and overcome problems faced by athletes during competition. Their initial research identified the key factors that affect competitive performance as physiology, training methods, racing strategy, biomechanics, aerodynamics, altitude and weather. Project Swift combined these and other findings with independent research to produce running apparel that would maximize performance.

Project Swift signalled a new direction for Nike. According to Eddie Harber, Nike's Senior Designer, 'Innovation is accomplished by a process of elimination. Only by testing ideas can we find out what really works.'[2] Harber broadened the range of research traditionally conducted on sportswear to include three more topics: the possibility of integrating mechanical devices into clothing, the possibility of reshaping the body to configure a more aerodynamic silhouette and consideration of psychological factors that garments could have on performance. Colour psychology, for example, was researched, but no conclusive results were found to link the use of colour to physical performance, or even to mood. Several of the other ideas eventually proved futile as well, enabling Nike effectively to rule out several misconceptions being explored generally in the sports industry. Nike was then able to move on and focus on more progressive ideas.

One of the project's goals was to create a 'Swift Suit' that would give the body an aerodynamic capacity exceeding that of the human skin. Forty fabrics were tested in wind tunnels in California and Canada, but only five were identified as aerodynamic enough to improve performance significantly. The natural shape of the body was adjusted to enhance its aerodynamic potential with the use of fairings – small, contoured foam blocks – placed inside the Swift Suit on either side of the neck and along other strategic points. The fairings did reduce drag, but the ergonomic cost of running with them outweighed their benefit.

Another design experimented with the possibility of using mechanical devices in the suit. Garments were equipped with springs, shocks and compressors to increase flexibility and tension control, giving the athlete an added performance boost. Harber's

Nike's 'Swift Suit' gives the body an aerodynamic capacity exceeding that of human skin. Its high-performance characteristics combine technological breakthroughs with new developments in textiles and design systems.

team decided that mechanical assistance would not be appropriate on ethical grounds, so the idea was abandoned.

The use of compression in the Swift Suit's shorts was explored in sprint activities, through tests conducted with the United Stated Army and the Louisiana State University sprint team. Laser timing was used over a set distance during several days of testing, but no significant performance benefit was found in using compression during sprint activities.

Project Swift also designed a temperature-regulating top that has as much appeal in the fashion world as it does in the sports world. The 'Stand-Off Distance Singlet', a running top, is mainly constructed from recycled material and keeps the body cool in hot temperatures. The singlet is constructed to maximize the body's own cooling methods; evaporation, convection and radiant heat reduction are all factored into the design. The combined effects of the fabric's properties and the garment's construction helps keep an athlete cooler in hot weather, but can also equip an urban dweller or a traveller for the summer heat. Small 'nodes' on the back panel of the fabric allow air to flow freely over the body, enhancing both convection and evaporation. The

Nike's 'Dri-Fit' system combines hydrophobic and hydrophilic layers to move moisture away from the body, yet remains breathable, with stretch and flexibility that do not impede movement.

perforations in the mesh fabric are sized to allow for maximum air entry and exit from the fabric. The fabric absorbs almost no moisture, allowing perspiration to evaporate directly from the skin.[3]

The Stand-Off singlet is also one of the most environmentally friendly pieces of athletic apparel available, which Nike refer to as their 'Eco-Friendly Techno-Vest'. The fibre in the singlet is made from 75 per cent recycled polyester, the majority of which is derived from recycled plastic bottles. The fabric is the colour of the fibre – white in this case – and does not undergo the dyeing and finishing treatments that are among the most toxic processes in fabric manufacturing.

Nike's moisture management fabric system, 'Dri-Fit' (also written as DRI F. I. T.), is a system that combines hydrophobic (water-repellent) and hydrophilic (water-attracting) layers to move moisture away from the body. The underlayer is hydrophobic, neither absorbing nor withholding the moisture; instead it functions as a pump or siphon, forcing the moisture to the hydrophilic layer. The hydrophilic layer forms the garment's surface, dispersing the moisture by spreading it over a large area, where body heat makes it evaporate quickly. In addition to breaking down moisture, the layers also

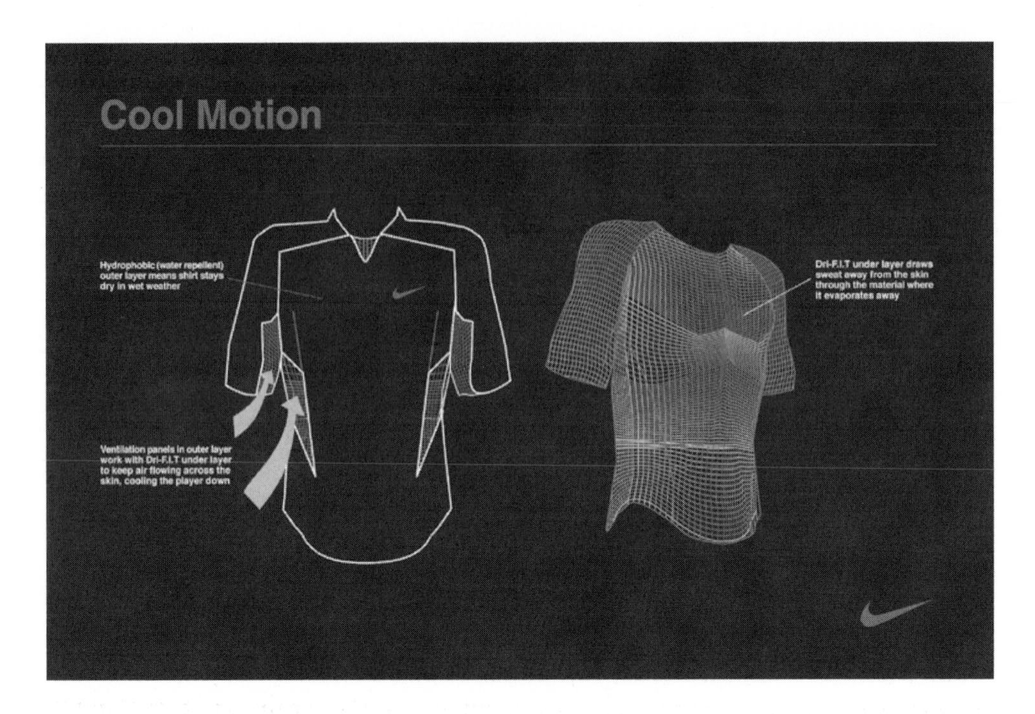

The technology behind Nike's 'Cool Motion' allows athletes to reduce their body temperature through natural convection, dispersing body heat and moisture through fabric panels that ventilate them over the torso.

provide an effective wind barrier. Dri-Fit is distinctive among other moisture-control systems because it is 100 per cent breathable, and has stretch and flexibility that do not impede movement.

'Cool Motion'[4] is a revolutionary technology based on a two-layer concept. The shirt consists of one Dri-Fit inner layer and one fabric outer layer with mesh ventilation panels that regulate body heat through the movement of the athlete. The hydrophobic properties of the shirt's outer layer enable it to remain dry despite the moisture generated during an aerobic workout. The venting panels sewn into the shirt's sides maximize the airflow to the body as it moves during exercise or a sport event. This allows the athletes to reduce their body heat through natural convection, enabling body heat and moisture to be ventilated away from the body more effectively. As the athlete runs, air is channelled in through the lower ventilation panels and then distributed over the torso, before leaving through the upper vents. This helps lower body temperature and disperse moisture.[5]

Starlab also researched technology that regulated temperature and configured data on heartbeat, perspiration, blood pressure and sugar levels as the wearer ran. One of their i-Wear prototypes was a tracksuit that functioned like a second skin, with interfaces on the outside and sensors on the inside. The tracksuit was programmed to detect when the wearer was losing momentum and encourage them to speed up by playing music and adapting its rhythm to push them harder or slow them down. The suit was designed to immediately adapt the training routine for the next session by using its mobile telephone function to email the data to the sports club. Outside, the tracksuit would monitor the weather and the characteristics of the terrain (e.g. hilly or flat) the wearer was running on. The suit could then plot the best course, and give suggestions on the duration and intensity of the exercise.

Sensatex picked up where Starlab left off, also preparing to inject technology into exercise clothing. Sensatex's research team is incorporating a computer motherboard into a workout top that can monitor the wearer's vital signs. The top is aimed at a potential sports market ranging from ordinary fitness enthusiasts to triathletes. 'You basically throw on a shirt and your EKG is monitored,' said Sensatex's co-founder, Jeff Wolf.[6] The 'intelligent' sports top uses fabric woven with optical fibres to send and receive electrical impulses. Sensatex have licensed the technology from the Georgia Institute of Technology, where the researchers developed it through funding from DARPA.[7] Like the Starlab tracksuit, the garment is still on the drawing board, and researchers estimate it will be several years before the designs are ready to be sold on the shelves of sportswear shops. Sensatex continues to pioneer the latest revolutions in the garment industry and apply them to health care as well as sport.

The Reima-Tutta Company, a Finnish sportswear manufacturer, is working with Clothing+, a research centre partly funded by the Finnish government, to integrate communication technology into a line of clothing designed especially for winter sports.[8] Like the research projects led by Nike, Starlab and Sensatex, Clothing+ draws on the expertise of scientists from several fields, including industrial design, clothing design, software and engineering.

One of Clothing+'s first commercial ventures was the 'Smart Shout' body belt, a wearable communication device compatible with GSM mobile-phone networks. Smart Shout was developed with skiers and snowboarders in mind, to create a communication platform that enables them to maintain constant contact on long-distance excursions. Conventional mobile phones can be problematic for winter-sports enthusiasts, whose thick gloves, mufflers, hoods and hats make it difficult to operate them. Even with the use of earphones, mobile devices have tiny buttons and small displays that are not easy to negotiate on the ski slope.

Clothing+ took the principles behind a conference call and redesigned it to suit the needs of a group of people snow-boarding down a mountain. The Smart Shout system contains a short-wave radio transmitter/receiver, a microphone and a loud-speaker, volume control, an embedded battery, a central processing unit, memory, a messaging pull tag and a grouping tag. To initiate or link into a group call, Smart Shout users simply pull a tag on the belt and start talking. The system can also digitize and save voicemail messages, then call the other group members and forward the message to them. The data connector for the GSM mobile phone is sealed in a waterproof pocket.

To activate the system, the users must first plug their personal GSM phone into a data connector embedded inside the Smart Shout bandolier. The group of users – now defined as a 'tribe' – then activates a grouping tag attached to each bandolier. By using a short-range radio that operates at 433 MHz, a licence-free frequency in Europe and the United States, the group can then send and receive messages over any distance just by talking aloud – the sensitive microphones in the bandolier can relay their voice without needing a mouthpiece.

Clothing+ are also developing an emergency-equipped snowsuit, 'Cyberia', that monitors the wearer's vital signs and transmits an emergency signal to the nearest rescue patrol through a GSM network. The researchers are also designing T-shirts with integral cooling systems or adjustable thermal insulation for winter clothes. They plan to continue developing wearable user interfaces for GSM phones and GPS receivers for other types of sportswear, and investigate the practicalities of washing and drying technologized clothing.

Bridging the Gap

The combination of a waterproof jacket and a cashmere scarf worn with a denim skirt, Lycra top, a pair of trainers and an ergonomic backpack may appear to be just another winter look, but it could also relay mixed messages about the wearer. The Lycra, trainers and backpack suggests a sportswear aesthetic, while the denim and cashmere could point to a love of natural materials. Mixing street clothes with sports gear is nothing new, but it does signal a regard for performance garments that extends beyond sportswear and blend into the urban wardrobe. As consumers look for street clothes that have the feel and flexibility of sportswear, they often have to combine the two to blend the sportswear into an office or a professional look.

Prada launched their ground-breaking *Prada Sport* collection to bridge the gap between sportswear and casuals, creating clothes that have durability and performance, without looking like sportswear at all. What Nike did for sports technology, Prada did for the sports aesthetic by bringing a high-performance look to the fashion world that actually was high-performance. Nike's scientific innovations showed us what fabric technology should *feel* like; Prada showed what it should *look* like. In fact, most of the sportswear looks so sophisticated that the gym is probably the last place you would expect to see it.

Prada proved that size really does matter, at least when it comes to sportswear. One of the most significant contributions Prada made was refuting the institutionalized sportswear sizing of S, M and L, and the ubiquitous 'all-in-one', in favour of European

Prada's designers worked in tandem with professional athletes and sports technicians to launch Prada Sport. *Bridging the gap between sportswear and casuals, the line has durability and performance, without looking like typical sportswear.*

clothing sizes. The designers radically contoured each piece to fit the body like a glove, streamlining sportswear beyond recognition, eliminating excess bulk and tailoring it to emphasize a sleek physique. Prada paired down the tracksuit by cutting away big pockets and hefty fastenings, getting rid of baggy seams and updating it with stretchable collars and cuffs rather than elasticized arm bands and rounded necks.

While Nike marries their brand to competitiveness and team sports, Prada allies itself to the idea of 'high challenge', 'personal achievement' and a 'wide range of thrilling sports' rather than teams and players.[9] Prada's designs are for luxury sports – sailing, skiing and motor racing – far away from the urban context and budget of the average sports enthusiast. Prada has launched several sports publicity initiatives and sponsorship programmes. Prada is also a patron of yachting competitions, including the Prada Challenge for Classic Yachts, a series of regattas coordinated by the Yacht Club de Monaco, and the International Twelve Metre Class World Championship in Cowes during the America's Cup 2001.

Prada's designers and stylists worked in tandem with professional athletes and sports technicians to research and develop each item in the collection. Though their sportswear rates highly among the garments worn by professionals, Prada's price range and design aesthetic articulates an exclusive urban lifestyle that extends to the mountains, sea and golf course more than the competition arena. The collection even features golf bags and Dynastar skis among the cycling shorts, tracksuits and skiwear. But who wants to buy a golf bag in a fashion boutique? If it has a Prada label, everyone does.

Fashion Active Lab

Jeffrey Grübb, the New York-based creator of Fashion Active Laboratory, nicknamed F A L, predicts that technology will bring the biggest innovations fashion has ever seen. 'Because sooner or later,' he said, 'fashion will run out of retro and have to find new ideas.'[10] With this in mind, Grübb creates a collection of forward-thinking designs that have the ability to 'multi-task' throughout the day, by moving with the wearer throughout their office routine, gym classes and nightlife. The result is a collection of easy-to-wear clothing that looks and feels amazing. 'I think what we're doing compliments what's going on in couture, because I design with that in mind. A woman could buy our pants to wear with her couture clothes, and not necessarily realise they were sweatpants,' he said.

Though F A L clearly have a couture aesthetic, the label differs from Prada by deliberately maintaining a low profile; a position Grübb is happy to keep. 'I feel strongly that my clothes don't dictate a brand to show status, they are aimed at people who just want to live better and treat themselves better,' he explained. Grübb also punctuates the clothes with innovations that give the collection a progressive feel. 'I've included a radiation resistant lining in one of our sports jackets. The jacket is made from techno suede sourced from Italy, inside, the lining is nickel-plated to protect whoever wears it from cell phone radiation,' he said, 'giving it one more functional quality.'

That is not to say that the collection is without luxury – a surprising twist is finding garments made in fabrics like cashmere and pima cotton alongside sports fabrics like nylon Lycra. Grübb reasons that something very soft, comfortable and warming should be worn on the post-workout cool-down, so he designed the 'Cashmere Hoodie', a cashmere cardigan cut like a hooded tracksuit jacket. The cashmere is blended with a high-denier nylon Lycra fibre spun so that the cashmere is wrapped completely around each individual nylon fibre, giving it the look of 100 per cent cashmere but with added flexibility. The Lycra that F A L use was sourced from Kanebo; finely coated with silver ions, it has outstanding antibacterial properties.

What makes F A L unique is that they bridge the gap between sportswear and designer clothing. Their collections bring a new reality to versatile wardrobes, because their clothing really can perform in the gym and be worn out on the town. 'The sort of person I design for is the one who wants to get the most out of what they wear,' Grübb explained. 'So someone could put on our T-shirt and our pants, do what they had to do in the office all day, run around, go to yoga, stretch, then out to dinner, to a bar and keep going. What they would have, in their messenger bag, would be an amazing McQueen shirt or top to just put on and wear and go out, and the whole thing would be great.'

Grübb's vision is to merge sportswear with casual wear to promote a comfortable, functional, modern way of dressing that stretches to all occasions. The collection dictates a lifestyle that is efficient, maximizing the multipurpose potential of each item, and using fewer garments because each one performs a multitude of tasks throughout a single day or over a weekend. 'Successful modern people today lead busy lives and don't want to think too hard when it comes to putting together a look. Most of us travel often, work out and go to yoga, and cram our schedules full every day. So we need clothes on a day-to-day basis that work efficiently and with style and ease,' Grübb said. His idea of efficiency excludes accessories like belts and scarves, keeping the look as streamlined as possible.

The collections are conspicuously non-sporty in appearance, sitting on the threshold of ease and elegance. The garments all feature exceptional elasticity and stretch recovery that define the body without looking skin-tight. Each piece is crease free, giving it the ability to remain folded in a sports bag all day and then worn out in the evening.

F A L's 'Perfect Pants' are flared hipster trousers that perform like tracksuit bottoms. They have the cut of dress trousers but the feel and flexibility of Lycra leggings. F A L's double-thickness reversible T-shirt is thick enough to have thermal properties and yet lightweight enough to be worn underneath a cardigan or jumper. The collection also includes a tunic dress; shapely and elastic, it can be worn while roller-blading or riding a scooter and stay fitted to the body, without being blown around in the breeze. Previously F A L have designed for women only, but Grübb has plans to launch a menswear line of twenty pieces.

Fashion Active Lab bridge the gap between sportswear and designer clothing. Their collections bring a new versatility to fashion in clothing that can perform in the gym and still be worn out on the town.

Nova USA, like FAL, also look to make sportswear more modern and versatile. Their philosophy is that sex appeal is the blatant truth behind all sportswear; we go to the gym to work towards a good physique and then want to show off the results. The label was started in 1998 by Tony Melillo, the former Style Director of *Esquire* magazine, and business partner Gregory Frehling. They identified a need for sleek and streamlined sports basics for men that had appeal outside the gym. Sexy sportswear for the modern lifestyle means clothes that are elastic and movable enough to perform in the gym, and form-fitting enough to emphasize the line of a well-developed physique. Like Prada and F A L, they abandon the principles of traditional sportswear to focus on creating a body conscious aesthetic. The stability and stretchability of nylon Lycras and Spandex-type fabrics creates garments that are revealing and provocative, without slipping out of place during exercise.

Sports Shoes

Few fashion items are as universal as sports shoes. They are complex constructions designed to be durable, comfortable and look good, with a wide appeal among fashion conscious individuals of almost all ages and cultures. Because the market for shoes is immense and highly competitive, sportswear companies have invested a tremendous amount of resources, research and investment into developing lightweight shoes that move faster, perform better and travel easily across a variety of terrains and surfaces.

High-performance shoes are made possible through the research of physiologists, sportswear designers and textiles technicians. New materials with shock absorbency are adapted for complex compression-moulded forms that interact with sprung technologies. The diversity of fabrics used for a single model of sports shoe is breathtaking; in addition to cushioning and supports, a trainer can contain a range of nylon, rubber, geomembranes, latex and neoprene, plus a number of coatings and finishes to waterproof it and enhance durability. Computer-aided design and production are enabling designers to create more aesthetic innovations that can still be mass-produced. The level of innovation and the pace of change in sports shoes remain higher than in any other field of fashion design.

As the most primary extension of our body into the landscape, footwear is an expression of speed, power, fitness and protection. Sports shoe designers express these characteristics in their task to encase and protect the foot, creating an aesthetic for the outer surface charged with speed, originality and physical power. This is where sport shoes meet fashion; they are no longer dismissed as purely functional, but now play an essential role in the fashion wardrobe.

The research conducted by Nike has led to technological breakthroughs that have revolutionized the supports and cushioning systems used in shoes. Their 'Nike Air' technology uses a blow-moulded urethane cushioning in the sole to reduce the shock of impact and provide the wearer with protection and comfort. The 'Nike Shox' model evolved over more than sixteen years of testing, developing technology built in the form of four spring-like columns in the heel of the shoe. Using high-specification materials similar to those used as shock absorbers in Formula One race cars, Nike Shox provides protection and reinforcement by absorbing the negative effects of impact into the sole of the shoe. The spring columns in the Nike Shox system are positioned between two Peebax plates that work in tandem with the columns as they are set in motion. The synergy between the wearer's movement, the plates and the columns produces a responsive cushioning system that compresses and then returns to its original height and shape after impact.

In recent years, firms such as Adidas have applied technological research to develop cushioning systems of their own. Most of their sports shoes are designed with cushioning systems that contain shock-absorbent moulds and reinforced membranes. Among the materials they have developed are 'adiPRENE-', placed in the heel to

'Nike Shox' provides protection and reinforcement by absorbing impact into the sole of the shoe, using high-specification materials similar to those used as shock absorbers in Formula One racing cars.

protect it from impact and stabilize its position within the shoe; 'adiPRENE+' which gives flexibility and efficient mobility in the forefoot of the foot; the 'Torsion' system, which encases the foot to create stability; a 'Traxion' layer to maximize the shoe's grip on impact; the 'adiDRY' waterproof membrane to keep moisture out; 'adiTUFF' to strengthen and reinforce the shoe's upper for added wearability; and the 'adiWEAR' layer to provide greater abrasion resistance and durability to the sole.

Puma, probably more than any other sports shoe brand, are directly engaging with a high-fashion aesthetic, rapidly making it their hallmark. Their *Platinum* collection takes the technological innovations of the athletic shoe industry to the realm of high fashion. The *Platinum* designs barely resemble sport shoes at all, but contain the shock absorbency, stability and flexibility of high-tech trainers. The exterior of the shoes has a futuristic, machine-like aesthetic, created through re-examination of the materials now typical of high-performance sports shoes, innovatively re-shaped and re-moulded into cutting-edge designs. Puma's 'Race Cat Hi J Shoe' is the result of Puma's collaboration with Jordan Grand Prix, which brought their sports performance and aesthetic sensibilities to the fashionable world of motor sports. The Race Cat Hi J features a low-profile, pedal-sensitive sole made of moulded non-slip rubber. The shoe's upper is fully fireproof, made of a soft nubuc material with both conventional shoelaces and Velcro closures.

Karim Rashid's vision of the trainer of the future leaves fashion far behind. Rashid's 'Shmoo Shoe', which automatically adjusts to fit the size, weight and gait of the wearer, is a running shoe with a digital camera built into its heel. Rashid plans to use the

Shmoo to record in real time exactly what the wearer cannot see happening behind them and then broadcast it over the Internet. 'What's interesting about this,' explained Rashid, 'is that first of all, the image is not as predictable and second of all, now anybody you know, wherever they are in the world, can see the vistas and the panoramas and the views behind you.'[11]

In the dynamic worlds of fashion and sport, there is no looking back. The growing synergy between them signifies one of first steps towards the technological innovations of tomorrow. Fashion designers are demonstrating a new understanding of the changing approach to the body, and the shifts in lifestyle resulting from the arrival of the Internet and new communication technology. It is now clear in fashion, as well as in sport, that designers are no longer simply working within the limits of human potential, but moving beyond them, and adapting clothing and footwear to facilitate this process.

In pioneering an alliance that could revolutionize clothing design, sports technicians and fashion designers are forging a new dialogue between them, forever disrupting the historical narrative of fashion, making it less apparent where the boundaries between fashion and sport now lie. From sportswear, fashion has learned to protect and equip the body, while from fashion, sportswear has learned to decorate the body and tailor clothing to follow its shape. By challenging assumptions about design and appropriateness of materials, fashion has understood that clothing and footwear can feel almost indistinguishable from the body itself. The combined sense of utility, functionality, performance and transformability inherent in sportswear is moving fashion forward.

Not only are some of the most powerful and influential designers producing sportswear lines, they are also applying sportswear principles to their main collections. This requires a re-examination of not only appearance and construction, but other issues too: individuality, functionality, health and performance. While sports companies were once more interested in function, their fashion awareness and sales ambitions could lead to casual or streetwear collections, blurring the boundaries even further.

The question asked by designers and trend experts alike is whether fashion's adherence to sportswear ethics and technological innovations will be its downfall. The acceptance of new functionality may not indicate fashion's ruin, but indicates that the traditional woman of fashion is disappearing. Her disappearance has been masterminded by changes in the lifestyles of urban women around the globe, and their increasing use of fashion to provide for their practical concerns. Sportswear provides many sensible solutions, and now offers a range of shapely clothing and cutting-edge designs that suit and adapt to a wider range of body shapes than most fashion designs do. With them comes the comfort, performance and durability necessary for the fast-paced, high-tech world we now live in.

While trends and styles will inevitably change, sportswear seems to have laid the strongest foundations for fashion's future in the short term, at least until intelligent designs are ready to launch the unwired world of the future. Compared to the innovations that sports designers developed in such a short time, techno fashions are not as radical as they seem. If anything, it is a surprise fashion took so long to embrace the sense of utility, functionality, performance and transformability inherent in sportswear. Ultimately, the exchanges between fashion and sport will simplify our wardrobes, but the route to simplicity may be long and complex.

Notes

Introduction

1. I.e. channel moisture away from the skin and disperse it across the fabric's surface to evaporate quickly.
2. Hussein Chalayan was interviewed by the author in London.
3. Quoted from panel discussion at 'The New Yorker Festival' (2001), 21 May 2001, *Fashion Wire Daily*, New York.
4. Tristan Webber was interviewed by the author in London.
5. *Vogue*, New York, 1 February 1939, pp. 71–3, 137–46.
6. Quoted in Valerie Steele (1998), *Paris Fashion*, Oxford: Berg, p. 279.
7. Angela Buttolph *et al* (1998), *The Fashion Book*, London: Phaidon.
8. Quoted in 'Plastics' essay by Peter Wollen (1997) in *The Warhol Look*, exhibition catalogue, New York: Little Brown and Company.
9. From 'Plastics' essay by Wollen in *The Warhol Look*.
10. Quoted in Steele, *Paris Fashion*, p. 282.

Chapter One Fashion and the Built Environment

1. At this time Bolton held the position of Joint Victoria & Albert Museum and London College of Fashion Research Fellow in Contemporary Fashion.
2. *The Supermodern Wardrobe* (2001) is published by V&A Publications, London.
3. Andrew Bolton was interviewed by the author in London. Part of this text is reprinted with the permission of *Merge* Magazine.
4. See Augé's text, *non-places* (1995), London: Verso.

5. Marshall McLuhan (1994), *Understanding Media*, Cambridge, MA: The MIT Press, pp. 119–20.
6. Note that this aesthetic came into fashion at the approach of the new millennium, a time when governments and industries voiced uncertainty about how computers would handle the rollover to the year 2000. Individuals were unnerved by the threat of Y2K system breakdowns, many describing feelings of paranoia and a growing sense of apprehension as 2000 drew nearer.
7. Augé, *non-places*, pp. 35–6.
8. Yeohlee was interviewed by the author in New York and in London. Part of this text is reprinted with the permission of *Merge* Magazine.
9. Susan Sidlauskas (1982), *Intimate Architecture: Contemporary Clothing Design*, Cambridge, MA: The MIT Committee on the Visual Arts.
10. Richard Martin (1998), 'Yeohlee: Energy and Economy, Measure and Magic', *Fashion Theory*, pp. 287–93.
11. Lucy Orta was interviewed by the author in London.
12. Though based in Paris, Lucy Orta holds the Rootstein Hopkins Chair in Fashion at the London College of Fashion. She was invested as a professor of The London Institute in 2002.
13. Paul Virilio (1996), *Refuge Wear*, Paris: Editions Jean Michel Place.
14. See www.studio-orta.com for more information.
15. Chalayan produced the *Temporary Interference* collection with British fashion label Jigsaw's sponsorship, designed knitwear collections for TSE in New York, created a capsule collection for the British retail chain Topshop, and became the creative director of fashion for British jewellery company Asprey & Garrard.
16. Hussein Chalayan was interviewed by the author in London.
17. Gaston Bachelard (1994 Edition), *The Poetics of Space*, Boston, MA: The Beacon Press, p. 107.

Chapter Two Twenty-first-century Bodies

1. Rebecca Arnold (2001), Fashion, Desire and Anxiety, London: I B Taurus & Co, p. 89.
2. See 'Cyborgology', *The Cyborg Handbook* (1995), ed. Chris Hables Gray, Steven Mentor & Heidi Figueroa-Sarriera, London: Routledge.
3. In the thinking of Michel Foucault.
4. Tristan Webber was interviewed by the author in London.
5. The feature was published in the September 1998 issue.
6. Quoted in Susannah Frankel's 'Body Beautiful' article in *The Guardian*, 9 September 1999.
7. Valerie Steele (1996), *Fetish: Fashion, Sex and Power*, Oxford: Oxford University Press, p. 27.

8. Valerie Steele (2001), *The Corset*, New Haven, CT: Yale University Press, p. 176.
9. Quoted in *The Standard Times*, 3 October 1998 ,www.s-t.com/daily. McQueen's interview with *Le Figaro* was published on 2 October 1998.
10. 'Poupée' translates as 'doll; figure; pretty empty-headed woman' in *The Concise Oxford French Dictionary* (1980). Oxford: Oxford University Press.
11. See Caroline Evans (2001), 'Desire and Dread', in Joanne Entwistle and Elizabeth Wilson ed. *Body Dressing*, Oxford: Berg.
12. *Dante* hallmarked death, but the morbid masks, hoods and corsets worn by the models were adorned with animal trophies and crucifixes; all of which referenced the rubric of fetishism.
13. Shaun Leane was interviewed by the author in London.
14. Susannah Frankel, 'The Real McQueen', *The Independent* Magazine, 8 September 1999.
15. Frankel, *The Independent* Magazine, 8 September 1999.
16. Frankel, *The Independent* Magazine, 8 September 1999.
17. See Caroline Evans, *Body Dressing*.
18. Quoted in Steele, *Fetish: Fashion, Sex and Power*, p. 38.
19. 'His jewellery' refers to the pieces Alexander McQueen commissions from Shaun Leane.
20. Gilles Deleuze (1991), *Coldness and Cruelty*, New York: Zone Books.
21. *The Shining* was based on a novel by Stephen King.
22. From 'The Pay List 2001', *The Sunday Times Magazine*, 4 November 2001.
23. Frankel, *The Independent* Magazine, 8 September 1999.
24. Hussein Chalayan was interviewed by the author in London.
25. The emphasis here is on fashion – although MIT's Media Lab developed wearable technology throughout the 1990s, none of them were presented in the context of the fashion industry.
26. The human cyborg is distinguished from the cyborgs of classical literature and mythology, and the animal cyborgs of experimental research.
27. Manfred E Clynes and Nathan S Kline (1960), 'Cyborgs and Space', *Astronautics*, September pp. 26–7, 75–6.
28. Donna Haraway (1999), 'A Manifesto for Cyborgs', *The Gendered Cyborg*, ed. Gill Kirkup *et al.*, New York: Routledge, pp. 50–7.
29. These areas were identified in 'Cyborgology', *The Cyborg Handbook* (1995).
30. See Foucault's texts *Discipline and Punish* and *Madness and Civilisation*.

Chapter Three Surveillance

1. Simon Thorogood was interviewed by the author in London.
2. The ICA is the Institute of Contemporary Arts.

3. Quoted from www.judithclarkcostume.org.
4. Adam Thorpe was interviewed by the author in London.
5. Joe Hunter was interviewed by the author in London.
6. Beyond Katrina Barillova's own accounts of her espionage experience, the author was unable to find further evidence to verify her claims. However, her knowledge of surveillance systems is considerable, and her descriptions of them is completely accurate.
7. Katrina Barillova was interviewed by the author in Los Angeles.
8. Barillova worked with Charmed Technology until May 2001, when she left to develop other projects.

Chapter Four Cybercouture

1. Anne Balsamo (1997), *Technologies of the Gendered Body*, Durham, NC: Duke University Press, p. 116.
2. Pia Myrvold was interviewed by the author in New York.
3. Julian Roberts was interviewed by the author in London.
4. London Fashion Week is held in the grounds of the Natural History Museum in South Kensington. Each season the British Fashion Council erect tents in front of the main museum building for 'on-schedule' designers to use.
5. Simon Thorogood was interviewed by the author in London.

Chapter Five Intelligent Fashion

1. The individuals and organizations pioneering intelligent clothing include a wide range of researchers, scientists and technicians – these terms are used loosely and interchangeably as a definitive professional title has not yet been established.
2. *The Daily Telegraph*, London, 21 October 1997.
3. The technical name for this product is the Xenium Global System for Mobile Communication.
4. These ICD+ jackets were no longer in production at time of publication.
5. www.levis-icd.com.
6. www.levis-icd.com.
7. The Media Lab is also known for its research on projects to develop motion-activated sensors, electronic hyper-instruments, facial recognition, imaging and three-dimensional holography.
8. The model was based on the AT-286 chip.
9. The first phase was led by Thad Starner, who had tried previous wearables based on a

TRS-80 model 100 and a SPARC Workstation, but they did not function reliably. The 'twiddler chording keyboard and a private eye display' model designed by DeVaul and Schwartz became the first wearable computer device (www.media.mit.edu/projects/wearables/lizzy).

10. As well as a project to develop 'intelligent clothing', Starlab conducted research on 'bits, atoms, neurons, and genes' (or 'BANG'), and explored 'growth areas of the future' such as nanotechnology, medicine, artificial intelligence, bio-informatics, quantum physics, time travel and consciousness.
11. www.charmed.com.
12. Van Beirendonck also designs the 'W.&L.T.', (or 'Wild and Lethal Trash') street fashion and techno/clubwear collection.
13. The research of John Seely Brown, chief scientist and director at Xerox PARC, is developing a digital technology that could turn almost any surface into a form of digital display.
14. In the way that SIM cards enable mobile telephones to work on a particular network, i-Wear's communication systems would be linked to one or several operational networks.
15. By the end of 2002, wireless communication was not evolved enough to facilitate the high-speed transmissions required to operate these systems. Wireless communications are only capable of sending and receiving data at speeds of up to 9.6 kb/s, while a standard dial-up modem sends data at the speed of 56 Bb/s. Homes equipped with broadband, ADSL and digital cable connections can transmit data at the speed of 576 kb/s, which is ten times faster. New technologies such as Bluetooth and GPRS will present opportunities for new applications, like a home network based around a central broadband server. Already advanced digital cable links are able to transmit high-speed (500 kb/s) data wirelessly to the home. The home networks will then be able to connect wirelessly to other devices.
16. Margaret Orth was interviewed by the author.
17. From Charmed Technology Press Release, 'From Science Fiction to Scent Fact', 23 May 2000.
18. Quoted in Charmed Technology Press Release, 23 May 2000.
19. Scott Lafee, 'Geek Chic', *The New Scientist*, Vol 169, Issue 2279, p. 33.
20. Lafee, *The New Scientist*, p. 33.
21. John Quain (2000), 'I am Cyborg', *Popular Science*, March 2000, pp. 56–60.
22. Sensatex/Lifelink reportedly have the exclusive worldwide rights to commercialize this research in other products they may develop.
23. Alan Goldstein, 'Addison Firm Puts 'Smart' in Sensor Shirt', www.sensatex.com.
24. See 'News Release', www.darpa.mil.
25. See 'News Release', www.darpa.mil.
26. DARPA also oversees the project developing Tactical Information Assistants (TIAs). For more information visit www.spectrum.ieee.org/publicaccess.
27. The author conducted a case study of Charmed's prototypes at their Los Angeles headquarters.

28. Context Aware, a system incorporated into Xybernaut's Mobile Assistant MA V platform, allows users to simultaneously display critical information and different data components on multiple display devices, such as Xybernaut's flat-panel displays (FPDs) and/or head-mount displays (HMDs).
29. Ramon G. McLeod, November 2001, 'Airport Security Adopts Wearable Computers', www.PCWorld.com.

Chapter Six Transformables

1. Joe Hunter was interviewed by the author in London.
2. Note that neither Cary-Williams's or Margiela's work can be categorized as transformable, since their garments remain static in the form they are constructed in.
3. The *Pieces* range is no longer in production.
4. Galya Rosenfeld was interviewed by the author.
5. Isabelle Peron was interviewed by the author.
6. Quoted in C P Company's spring/summer 2001 press release.
7. Jeff Griffin was interviewed by the author.

Chapter Seven Japanese Innovation

1. Rei Kawakubo was interviewed by Susannah Frankel in her book, *Fashion Visionaries* (2001), London:V&A Publications, p. 154.
2. Frankel, *Fashion Visionaries*, p. 158.
3. The designs from this collection were later used as costumes by the Merce Cunningham dance group.
4. Quoted in 'Radical Fashion', 7 October 2001, *The Observer.*
5. Frankel, *Fashion Visionaries*, p. 160.
6. Björk was photographed in one of Watanabe's dresses for a portrait in American *Vogue.*
7. Junya Watanabe was interviewed by Susannah Frankel in *Fashion Visionaries*, p. 186.
8. Quoted in *Vogue*, March 1996.

Chapter Eight Electric Textiles

1. New textiles are now tested and approved for their compliance with environmental standards. Manufacturers within the EEC are issued with an Environmental Certificate to certify their ecologically sound resources and production methods, and consumers are being encouraged to buy fashions made with ecological textiles.

2. 'Corn Fiber' is the trade name Kanebo have given to this particular Lactron textile.
3. According to Kanebo, these are colon bacillus, Staphylococcus aureus, Pseudomonas aeruginosa, Klebsiella pneumoniae and MRSA.
4. Daniel Herman was interviewed by the author in London.
5. Shelley Fox was interviewed by the author in London.
6. The Royal National Institute for the Blind, a London-based charitable organization.
7. unattributed author, 'Future Fabrics', www.cnn.com/2000/STYLE/ELLE, 8 September 2000.
8. www.cnn.com/2000/STYLE/ELLE, 8 September 2000.
9. www.cnn.com/2000/STYLE/ELLE, 8 September 2000.
10. www.cnn.com/2000/STYLE/ELLE, 8 September 2000.
11. Kei Kagami was interviewed by the author in London.
12. Nigel Atkinson was interviewed by the author in London.
13. Sophie Roet was interviewed by the author in London.
14. C S Interglas is a textile mill based in Dorset, England, which produces highly technologized textiles for commercial vehicles, sports equipment and the aircraft industry.
15. Joanna Berzowska was interviewed by the author.
16. Paul Marks, 'Shirt Rolls Up Its Own Sleeves', 25 July 2001, www.newscientist.com.

Chapter Nine Sportswear

1. The 'Project Swift' team was led by Senior Designer Eddie Harber and Innovation Director Rick MacDonald.
2. Quoted in Nike's 'Road Not Taken' publicity material, 30 November 2001.
3. The Stand-Off singlet has been designed exclusively for Nike's Olympic athletes and was not available in the shops at the time of publication.
4. Originally developed to design World Cup jerseys that would combat the extreme heat footballers face in Japan and Korea at World Cup 2002.
5. Cool Motion is the most extensively tested apparel technology from Nike, both in terms of field testing as well as lab testing. The Cool Motion technology was developed and tested at Nike's Research & Development Lab in the United States and at an independent lab in the Netherlands.
6. *Greg Dalton,* 'A Shirt That Thinks', *The Industry Standard Magazine*, 18 June 2001.
7. DARPA is the Defence Advanced Research Projects Agency, the central research and development unit of the US Department of Defense.
8. For more information visit www.reima.com.
9. Quoted from undated press release, obtained by the author in November 2002.
10. Jeffrey Grübb was interviewed by the author.
11. Jennifer Morrison, 'A Real Artist of Everyday Life', *Toronto Observer*, 22 January 2001.

List of Credits

The author and the publishers would like to thank the following sources for granting permission to reproduce their images in this book:

Front cover: With permission Chris Moore, © Chris Moore

Black and White Illustrations

Page 4: With permission NASA, © NASA

Page 5: With permission Royal College of Art, © Lucy Orta 1998

Page 7: With permission Yeohlee, © Dan Lecca 1999

Page 12: With permission Vexed Generation, © Jonny Thompson

Page 17: With permission Yeohlee, © Dan Lecca 1997

Page 18: With permission Yeohlee, © Dan Lecca 1999

Page 19: With permission Lucy Orta, © Lucy Orta 2000

Page 23: With permission Galerie Anne de Villepoix, © Lucy Orta 1992

Page 25: With permission Lucy Orta, © Lucy Orta 2000

Page 27: With permission Chris Moore, © Chris Moore

Page 31: With permission Chris Moore, © Chris Moore

Page 43: With permission Chris Moore, © Chris Moore

Page 44: With permission Chris Moore, © Chris Moore

Page 45: With permission Perles de Tahiti, © Perles de Tahiti. Credit: Feather and Tahitian Pearl headdress by Philip Treacy for Alexander McQueen in association with Perles de Tahiti. Photographer: Chris Moore

Page 49: With permission American Express, © American Express 2001

Page 51: With permission Chris Moore, © Chris Moore

Page 52: With permission Chris Moore, © Chris Moore

Page 59: With permission Simon Thorogood, © Tim Brett-Day (top); with permission Simon Thorogood, © Tim Brett-Day (bottom)

Page 65: With permission Vexed Generation, © Jonny Thompson

Page 66: With permission Vexed Generation, © Hannes

Page 67: With permission Vexed Generation, © Hannes

Page 71: With permission Vexed Generation, © Hannes

Page 74: With permission Charmed Technology, © Charmed Technology 2000 (top); with permission Charmed Technology, © Charmed Technology 2000 (bottom)

Page 80: With permission Pia Myrvold, © Pia Myrvold 1996

Page 82: With permission Pia Myrvold, © Ann Elin Wang 1997

Page 83: With permission Pia Myrvold, © Pia Myrvold 2001

Page 85: With permission Pia Myrvold, © Pia Myrvold 2002 (left); with permission Pia Myrvold, © Pia Myrvold 2002 (right)

Page 88: With permission Julian Roberts, © Ian Gillett

Page 90: With permission Julian Roberts, © Ian Gillett

Page 102: With permission Charmed Technology, © Charmed Technology 2000 (top); with permission Charmed Technology, © Charmed Technology 2000 (bottom)

Page 107: With permission International Fashion Machines, © International Fashion Machines 2001 (top); with permission International Fashion Machines, © International Fashion Machines 2001 (bottom)

Page 109: With permission Ranier/Eleksen, © Ranier/Eleksen 2001

Page 111: With permission Charmed Technology, © Charmed Technology 2000

Page 118: With permission Mandarina Duck, © Mandarina Duck

Page 122: With permission Chris Moore, © Chris Moore (top); with permission Chris Moore, © Chris Moore (bottom)

Page 124: With permission Patrick Cox, © Giovanna 1999 (top); with permission Patrick Cox, © Giovanna 1999 (bottom)

Page 126: With permission Galya Rosenfeld, © Galya Rosenfeld 2001

Page 128: With permission Ilana Rosenfeld, © Ilana Rosenfeld 2001

Page 130: With permission John Ribbe, © Gerard Cambon 2000

Page 132: With permission C P Company, © C P Company 2001

Page 133: With permission C P Company, © C P Company 2001 (top left); with permission C P Company, © C P Company 2001 (top right); with permission C P Company, © C P Company 2001 (bottom)

Page 138: With permission Jeff Griffin © Donald Christie 2001

Page 139: With permission Jeff Griffin © Donald Christie 2001

Page 146: With permission Comme des Garçons, © J Françoise Jose 2000 (top); with permission Comme des Garçons, © J Françoise Jose 2000 (bottom)

Page 154: With permission Michiko Koshino, © Michael Maier 2001

Page 157: With permission Chris Moore, © Chris Moore (top); with permission Chris Moore, © Chris Moore (bottom)

Page 160: With permission Comme des Garçons, © Comme des Garçons 2000

Page 167: With permission Daniel Herman, © Christian Wiggert 2001

Page 169: With permission Daniel Herman, © Christian Wiggert 2001 (top); with permission Daniel Herman, © Christian Wiggert 2001 (bottom)

Page 172: With permission Chris Moore, © Chris Moore (top); with permission Chris Moore, © Chris Moore (bottom)

Page 177: With permission Kei Kagami, © Yayoi

Page 182: With permission Sophie Roet, © Lon Van Keulen

Page 188: With permission Nike, © Nike 2001

Page 189: With permission Nike, © Nike 2001

Page 190: With permission Nike, © Nike 2001

Page 193: With permission Prada, © Prada (top); with permission Prada, © Prada (bottom)

Page 196: With permission Fashion Active Lab, © Edel Verzyl 2001
Page 198: With permission Nike, © Nike 2001

Colour Illustrations

Lucy Orta's *Modular Architecture*: with permission Lucy Orta, © John Akehurst 1996
Hussein Chalayan: with permission Chris Moore, © Chris Moore
Lucy Orta's *Refuge Wear*: with permission Lucy Orta, © Lucy Orta
Alexander McQueen's Red Glass-slide and Ostrich Feather Dress: with permission Chris Moore, © Chris Moore, from *Radical Fashion*, V&A 2001
Shaun Leane's Black Pearl Mantle: with permission Chris Moore, © Chris Moore
Shaun Leane's Rose Corset: with permission Chris Moore, © Chris Moore
Simon Thorogood's couture dress: with permission Simon Thorogood, © Tim Brett-Day
Pia Myrvold's *Clothes As Publishing* suit: with permission Pia Myrvold, © Robert Fairer 1995
Patrick Cox's Lightboot: with permission Patrick Cox, © Simon Bower 2001
Galya Rosenfeld's modular separates: with permission Yael Dahan, © Yael Dahan 2002
John Ribbe's Mummy Dress: with permission John Ribbe, © Patrice Sable 1999
Shelley Fox's Morse Code dress: with permission Chris Moore, © Chris Moore
Shelley Fox's geometric silhouettes: with permission Chris Moore, © Chris Moore

Index

NB: Where shown in bold, page numbers indicate images and illustrations rather than text references.